The American Assembly, *Columbia University*

ALCOHOLISM
AND
RELATED PROBLEMS:
ISSUES FOR THE
AMERICAN PUBLIC

Prentice-Hall, Inc., *Englewood Cliffs, New Jersey*

A SPECTRUM BOOK

Library of Congress Cataloging in Publication Data
Main entry under title:

Alcoholism and related problems.

  At head of title: The American Assembly, Columbia
University.
  "A Spectrum Book."
  Bibliography: p.
  Includes index.
  1. Alcoholism—United States—Addresses, essays,
lectures. 2. Alcohol—Physiological effect—Addresses,
essays, lectures. I. West, Louis Jolyon. II. American
Assembly.
HV5292.A388 1984   362.2′92′0973   84-13451
ISBN 0-13-021486-8
ISBN 0-13-021478-7 (pbk.)

This book is available at a special discount when ordered in bulk quantities. Contact Prentice-Hall, Inc., General Publishing Division, Special Sales, Englewood Cliffs, N. J. 07632.

Editorial/production supervision by Betty Neville
Cover design © 1984 by Jeannette Jacobs
Manufacturing buyers: Edward Ellis and Anne Armeny

Table 1 on page 70 is from Philip J. Cook, "The Effect of Liquor Taxes on Drinking, Cirrhosis, and Auto Fatalities," in *Alcohol and Public Policy: Beyond the Shadow of Prohibition,* eds. Mark H. Moore and Dean R. Gerstein (Washington, D.C.: National Academy Press, 1981). It is reprinted by permission of the publisher.

10 9 8 7 6 5 4 3 2 1

ISBN 0-13-021486-8

ISBN 0-13-021478-7 {PBK.}

Prentice-Hall International, Inc. (*London*)
Prentice-Hall of Australia Pty. Limited (*Sydney*)
Prentice-Hall of Canada, Inc. (*Toronto*)
Prentice-Hall of India Private Limited (*New Delhi*)
Prentice-Hall of Japan, Inc. (*Tokyo*)
Prentice-Hall of Southeast Asia Pte. Ltd. (*Singapore*)
Whitehall Books Limited (*Wellington, New Zealand*)
Editora Prentice-Hall do Brasil Ltda. (*Rio de Janeiro*)

Table of Contents

8   *Sheila B. Blume*
    Public Policy Issues:
    A Summary   176

Preface

Ever since the nation's disastrous experiment with prohibition, our political leaders have been understandably reluctant to address a comprehensive public policy with respect to alcohol problems in the United States. It has been our experience, nevertheless, that abuse of alcohol and alcoholism have led to extremely serious problems for the health, safety, and quality of life for all Americans.

In recent years, many initiatives from private groups, from local and state governments, and even a few from the federal government have been directed toward various aspects of the nation's concern with these alcohol problems. Some of these developments have resulted in conflicts, many have contended with each other for limited resources, but all have fallen considerably short of shaping an overall national policy. These circumstances have prompted the director of the National Institute on Alcohol Abuse and Alcoholism to say, "I wonder if, in our sincere and honest attempts to focus on trees in the forest, we're not losing sight of managing the forest."

Moreover, much of the public discussion of these problems has become acrimonious, with sharp differences between those who wish to control the use of alcoholic beverages and those who produce and sell them, between those who advocate a medical approach to the problems and those who prefer social and psychological efforts, and even between those who sponsor specific types of treatment within these broader categories.

In an effort to elevate the discussion of public policy above these conflicts and to seek some broader agreement on the scope of that policy, The American Assembly convened a meeting at Arden House, Harriman, New York, from April 26 to 29, 1984. Participants attended from the federal, state, and local governments; the medical profession; the universities; private associations; trade unions; the clergy; the legal profession; business; the alcoholic beverage industry; and the communications media. In preparation for that meeting, the Assembly retained Dr. Louis Jolyon West of the Neuropsychiatric Institute at the University of California at Los Angeles as editor and director of the undertaking. Under his editorial supervision, background papers on various aspects of alcohol problems were prepared and read by the participants in the Arden House discussions.

The participants, in the course of their deliberations, achieved a substantial consensus on recommendations for public policy. Their proposals, which call for actions with respect to prevention of alcohol abuse and alcoholism; the legal, economic, and political aspects of alcohol problems; as well as research, diagnosis, and treatment of those problems, are contained in a report entitled *Public Policy on Alcohol Problems*. Copies of the report can be obtained by writing directly to The American Assembly, Columbia University, New York, New York 10027. The text of the report appears at the end of this volume.

The background papers used by the participants have been compiled into the present volume, which is published as a stimulus to further thinking and discussion about this subject among informed and concerned citizens. We hope this book will serve to provoke a broader consensus for action to address a serious national problem of compelling dimensions.

Funding for this project was provided by the National Institute on Alcohol Abuse and Alcoholism; the J. M. Foundation; the Richard King Mellon Foundation; the Conrad N. Hilton Foundation; Humana, Inc.; and Mr. David A. Jones. The opinions expressed in this volume are those of the individual authors and not necessarily those of the sponsors nor of The American Assembly, which does not take stands on the issues it presents for public discussion.

William S. Sullivan
President
The American Assembly

Louis Jolyon West, M.D.

1

Alcoholism and Related Problems:

An Overview

Introduction

Alcoholism is an illness caused by the prolonged ingestion of ethyl alcohol (especially in biologically vulnerable people) and manifested by a variety of harmful physical, mental, behavioral, and social effects. Alcohol intoxication or abuse, even by people who are not—or not yet—suffering from alcoholism, may also produce undesirable or dangerous effects. Alcoholism, alcohol abuse, and related problems, taken as a whole, must be of profound concern to the American people and those responsible for public policy.

In 1974 (Keller) the National Institute on Alcohol Abuse and

LOUIS JOLYON WEST *is professor and chairman of the Department of Psychiatry and Biobehavioral Sciences at the UCLA School of Medicine, psychiatrist-in-chief of the UCLA Hospital and Clinics, and director of the Neuropsychiatric Institute, UCLA Center for the Health Sciences. Dr. West has established and directed alcohol research and treatment programs in the U.S. Air Force, at the University of Oklahoma (where the alcohol facility is now named for him), and at UCLA. Formerly a member of the National Advisory Committee on Alcoholism to the Secretary of Health, Education and Welfare and other national advisory bodies, Dr. West is the author of seven books and more than 150 scientific articles.*

Alcoholism (NIAAA) estimated that alcohol abuse and alcoholism cost the American people $25 billion. In 1983 the congressional Office of Technology Assessment estimated that cost to be $120 billion—nearly a 400 percent increase in nine years. A recent study conducted by the National Institute of Medicine (1980) documented a rise in alcohol consumption of more than 30 percent between 1960 and 1980.

Between 200,000 and 300,000 Americans died or were injured as a result of alcoholism or alcohol related episodes in 1977. One in every ten deaths annually is alcohol related. On any given day up to 33 percent of adult patients in U.S. hospitals are likely to have problems related to alcohol. For various reasons, only a fraction of these will be formally or correctly diagnosed. Nevertheless, it is estimated that 20 percent of the national expenditure for *hospital* care and 12 percent of the *total* national health expenditure on behalf of adults derive directly from alcohol abuse.

The most important substance-abuse problem in the Western or developed nations is that caused by alcohol. *Addiction* to alcohol is well known and includes the general characteristics of addiction: craving, tolerance, and withdrawal phenomena. However, *alcoholism* is variously defined to include more than just the classical addiction syndrome—the "physical dependence" of the gamma alcoholic in E. M. Jellinek's (1960) famous classification. A generally employed dictionary definition is broader and defines alcoholism as:

> A chronic behavioral disorder manifested by repeated drinking of alcoholic beverages in excess of the dietary and social uses of the community and to an extent that interferes with the drinker's health or his social or economic functioning; some degree of habituation, dependence, or addiction is implied (Dorland, 1981).

But health issues relating to the use of alcoholic beverages clearly extend beyond the diagnosable cases of alcholism. Even occasional or sporadic intoxication may have dire consequences.

It is commonly estimated that some 10 percent of the more than 100 million Americans who drink (similar percentages occur in Europe) have significant alcohol related problems affecting their work, family life, social adjustment, or health. Most either will not accept the need to stop drinking or fail to stop even though they try. Such people are generally called "alcoholics." They comprise approximately 7 or 8 percent of American adults. However, one way or another, the shadow of the bottle actually falls across approximately 20 percent of the American population, either as a consequence of their own abuse of alcohol or because of the impact upon them from the alcoholism of others.

The rise in drinking was a trend even before the 30 percent increase between 1960 and 1980. Since World War II, per capita consumption of alcoholic beverages has steadily increased in the United States, part of a roughly consistent international trend, despite differences in general economic development or specific cultural factors. (The per capita consumption of alcohol in most West European countries [other than Norway, Sweden, and the British Isles] is even higher than in the U.S.; France is twice as high.) Surprisingly, the social factors commonly advanced as explanations for drinking in general or problem drinking in particular—buying power, amount of leisure time, social misery, industrialization, urbanization, etc.—do not fully account for changes in alcohol consumption internationally and across time. The general trend toward increased aggregate per capita consumption apparently also reflects the advent of new demographic groups of drinkers, recent marketing practices, new socially acceptable drinking situations, changes in individual drinking patterns, and, perhaps, an increase in the proportion of people who possess a genetic predisposition toward alcoholism. Ironically, the last trend may be the result of advances in biomedical science and in the quality of medical care, which are enabling more alcoholics to survive longer while fit enough to reproduce.

During the 1960s and 1970s the rate of alcohol consumption (per capita sales) continued to rise in most Western countries, although its rate of increase presently appears to be slowing. Between 1960 and 1976 the apparent consumption of alcohol in the United States increased by 24 percent, to reach 10.7 liters of 100 percent ethanol per year per person aged fifteen years or older. Of this total, beer accounted for nearly half; distilled spirits, more than a third; and wine, the remainder. The rate of consumption is still rising.

In 1979 self-reported consumption in the U.S. showed no recent dramatic change—approximately 33 percent of the adult population reported abstention and 33 percent light, 25 percent moderate, and 9 percent heavy drinking. In the heavy drinking category, men continued to outnumber women by more than three to one; in the abstention category women outnumbered men by nearly two to one. Heavy drinking reached a peak at an earlier age for men (twenty-one to thirty-five) than for women (thirty-five to forty-nine), declining thereafter for both sexes. Continuing the trends noted in earlier surveys, moderate and heavy drinking among high school students increased with age to about seventeen and then leveled off, about 15 percent reporting heavy drinking. Although the drinking problems of youth tend to be acute rather than chronic, increasing evidence indicates that early drinking behavior generally predicts drinking habits later in life.

While only a fraction of all alcohol users—the alcoholics—have most of the alcohol related illness, there is a distinct correlation between the total consumption of alcohol by a society and the prevalence of all alcohol related problems and diseases including alcoholism per se. For example, in Finland from 1950 to 1965, the rate of alcohol consumption rose only slightly; during this period death rates from liver cirrhosis also rose only very slightly, and arrest rates for drunkenness remained about the same. However, from 1965 to 1975 the per capita consumption of alcohol in Finland increased dramatically—in fact, it tripled! During that decade, both the death rates from cirrhosis and the arrest rates for drunkenness doubled.

Between 1950 and 1960, France, with Europe's highest per capita consumption of alcohol, suffered from such high rates of alcohol problems that it became a national scandal. Over the protests of the beverage industries, President DeGaulle instituted a nationwide program of education toward moderation. As a result, between 1960 and 1976, per capita consumption in France, although still very high, fell by 12 percent (while rising in twenty-four other developed countries in Europe, North America, and the Pacific); a corresponding decrease in many alcohol related problems in France (including the death rate from cirrhosis) has followed.

These and many other observations make it clear that a major goal in the prevention or reduction of alcoholism, alcohol abuse, and alcohol related problems in America must be a reduction in total consumption of beverage alcohol. Furthermore, such a national public health strategy must take into account considerable variability among the states, even between neighbors. For example, per capita consumption of alcohol in hard-drinking Nevada is more than in abstemious Utah.

Reviewing recent studies, the U.S. Department of Health and Human Services (DHHS) in 1979 defined "drinking problems" in terms of (1) physical dependence, (2) adverse social or psychological effects of consumption, and (3) the amount and frequency of consumption. The DHHS noted that these "drinking problems," while not synonymous with "alcoholism" or even "problem drinking," are likely to correlate positively with them. Using these criteria, and considering only adults, 20 percent of all male drinkers and 10 percent of female drinkers reported at least one symptom of alcohol dependence and loss of control within the previous year. The symptoms include skipping meals when drinking, sneaking drinks, morning drinking, drinking before a party to be sure of getting enough, blackouts, gulping drinks, trembling hands after drinking, and morning drinking to alleviate hangover. Many experienced clinicians would diagnose such individuals as early-stage alcoholics and urge them to abstain from drinking alcoholic beverages.

Adverse social or psychological consequences—alcohol-specific relationship problems with spouse, family, or friends; police problems; automobile or other accidents involving injury or property damage; job problems—were reported by 9 percent of male and 5 percent of female drinkers. In terms of consumption, 28 percent of male and 8 percent of female drinkers reported 60 or more drinks per month; 15 percent of men and 3 percent of women consumed the equivalent of more than 120 drinks per month. Three or more symptoms of alcohol dependence were experienced by 5 percent of the men and 2 percent of the women.

Children from alcoholic families are twice as likely to develop alcohol problems as are those from nonalcoholic families. The divorce rate among alcoholic families is significantly higher than for the general population.

As noted previously, immoderate drinking and its consequences are not confined to adults. Of the entire national sample of adolescents (including nondrinkers), 31 percent were judged to be misusers of alcohol, that is, drunk at least six times per year or experiencing untoward consequences at least twice in at least three of five social areas. Among adolescents who drink, 15 percent reported drinking at least once a week *and* consuming five or more drinks per occasion.

In considering the significance of "drinks" as calculated in such studies, one should remember that a bottle or can of beer, a glass of wine, and a highball, shot of whiskey, or other distilled spirits are roughly equal in ethanol content. Beer or wine drinkers are risking alcoholism in proportion to their ingestion of ethanol just as much as are drinkers of vodka, brandy, bourbon, or scotch.

Based on several large-scale studies, it appears clear that the level of ethanol consumption is strongly related both to physical dependence and adverse effects. Heavy drinking on a regular basis is likely to result in both dependence and adverse effects; intermittent heavy drinking is also related to adverse effects but does not promote as great a likelihood of physical dependence. Because adverse effects, with or without physical dependence, fall largely within the domain of national health concerns, this volume generally includes them, regardless of whether or not an accompanying physiological dependence can be shown.

Pathogenesis or Causation

Discussion of biomedical data on pathogenesis and pathology of alcoholism can be found in chapter 2 and chapter 5. It is now generally accepted that three major factors enter into the development of alcoholism. In each individual case the relative weights of such factors may differ—sometimes markedly. These factors are genetic, developmental, and environmental.

GENETIC FACTORS

Studies of twins have confirmed the longstanding impression that there is an inherited vulnerability to alcoholism. While the nature of this vulnerability is not yet known, it is presently being investigated actively by multidisciplinary research teams in several countries. It seems most likely that genetically determined differences in alcohol metabolism at the biochemical-physiological level significantly influence the likelihood that alcohol ingestion will be progressively reinforced in some people more than in others. It has been accepted for centuries that alcoholism runs in families. Only in recent years, however, has it become clear that a genetic or hereditary factor plays a role.

DEVELOPMENTAL FACTORS

These factors may begin to exercise their influences in the womb. The fetus is subtly, if not grossly, affected by the alcohol consumed by its mother and may be more vulnerable to the effects of alcohol later in life than would otherwise have been the case. However, postpartum developmental factors are also very important. These include the presence of neurobehavioral developmental disorders. For example, hyperkinetic children—especially if untreated—are far more likely than controls to develop a number of later problems, including adult alcoholism. Certain types of personality disorders, most likely generated by faulty upbringing, are also likely to be accompanied by alcohol abuse. Examples of alcohol and drug use and abuse displayed in the family during a child's development will influence the child's behavior with regard to these substances. While some children who see and perhaps suffer from the effects of drunkenness in a parent may reject the use of alcohol as a reaction against it, the far more likely pattern is one of imitation and identification.

ENVIRONMENTAL FACTORS

Regardless of predispositional genetic and developmental factors, alcoholism can only develop if an individual drinks alcohol. If alcohol is not available or its use is successfully forbidden or prohibited, even the most vulnerable individual will never become alcoholic. Thus, the rates of alcoholism are very low not only in most Islamic countries, but anywhere among the devout whose religion prohibits alcohol's use. Attitudes and customs with regard to drinking also exert powerful influences upon alcohol use and abuse, and even upon comportment when intoxicated. In certain isolated cultures where alcoholism is common, violent behavior while intoxicated is not. The Tarahumara Indians of the Sierra Madre Occidental in north-central Mexico get drunk periodically on their native beer, *tesguino,* throughout their adult lives; but the circumstances of drinking in their culture are such that violence is extremely rare, and alcoholism as an illness does not develop (Paredes, West, and Snow, 1970) .

In our own culture, as in most developed nations of the world, several secular factors in the environment are known to affect the likelihood and pattern of an individual's drinking. These include the availability of alcoholic beverages; their cost relative to consumer resources; social circumstances of consumption; general acceptability of use in various settings; effectiveness of marketing practices such as advertising and packaging by purveyors; the modes and rigor of enforcement of the antidrinking or anti-drunkenness laws or rules in the community; cultural beliefs about drinking or intoxication in relationship to such issues as maturity and sexuality; social acceptability; healthiness; individual responsibility; and known or portrayed drinking practices of role models. The net effect of all these environmental influences on total ingestion of ethyl alcohol by individuals will influence their likelihood of remaining abstainers or becoming light, moderate, or heavy drinkers or alcoholics.

One particularly pervasive environmental force is television, since 98 percent of all U.S. households have at least one television set. According to Breed and DeFoe's study (1981B) of fifteen weekly situation comedies and one-hour dramas in the 1976–77 season, "Alcohol beverages easily outnumber other beverages (water, coffee, tea, and carbonated soft drinks) consumed on television. . . . The pattern of use . . . on television is virtually the inverse of the pattern in daily life"; the ratio of alcohol drinking acts on television to water drinking acts is 15.6 to 1. The authors suggest that television legitimizes the use of alcohol by showing (1) young characters eager to start drinking, (2) alcohol use as a way to face a crisis, (3) characters who rarely refuse a drink, (4) ineffective disapproval of drinking by other characters, and (5) drinking behavior with few serious consequences—particularly for series regulars or guest stars. This last finding may be particularly insidious because "studies in the related areas of aggressive behavior show that when people see violence, and a justification of the violence is implied, they themselves are more likely to engage in aggressive behavior." Armed with this information and in a rare example of "cooperative consultation" between science and business, Breed and DeFoe (1982) found that it is possible to work with writers, producers, and directors to portray a more accurate use of alcohol and its consequences in television entertainment programs.

Morbidity and Mortality

Ethyl alcohol is the most widely abused chemical in the Western world, implicated in far more deaths than any other substance. Its chronic use in large quantities usually leads to marked deteriorative changes in the consumer's health. In short, alcohol abuse results in both increased mortality (the actual number of deaths compared to the expected number of deaths) and increased morbidity (the proportion of sickness or of a specific disease within a given population). Mortality rates for alcoholics continue to be approximately 250 percent above those expected for nonalcoholics.

Slow alcohol ingestion generally leads to unconsciousness before the drinker consumes enough to reach a lethal blood level. Rapid alcohol ingestion *while sober* often causes vomiting. However, because intoxication depresses the brain's emetic mechanisms, rapid alcohol ingestion by a person *already intoxicated* can be fatal. Approximately 33 percent of all deaths attributed to the direct effect of alcohol result from rapid ingestion of lethal quantities, usually by individuals already intoxicated. Death caused by alcohol overdose is a result of respiratory paralysis, and typical autopsy findings show swelling at the base of the brain and congestion of the lining of the stomach. As a poison, second only to carbon monoxide, alcohol is the agent responsible for the most deaths in the U.S. Each year these two compounds cause more deaths than all other poisons combined.

In cases of severe and prolonged alcohol dependence and chronic abuse, abrupt withdrawal of alcohol from the body precipitates a well-known acute syndrome, often including delirium tremens. The alcohol withdrawal syndrome can be so traumatic that it results in death—even in healthy young adults.

MEDICAL CONSEQUENCES

Alcoholics need far more medical services than do nonalcoholics; one study reports two to three times as many illnesses and two to three times more expenses for health care. Alcohol abuse not only exerts direct toxic effects on the body, but it often leads to dietary deficiencies that result in more subtle biochemical imbalances.

The digestive system is a frequent victim of alcohol damage. This includes the gastrointestinal tract (alcohol contributes to gastritis, erosion of gastric mucosa, gastric and duodenal ulcers, bowel motility disorders, and malabsorption syndromes); the pancreas (alcohol is involved in acute and chronic pancreatitis); and the liver (alcohol causes cloudy swelling, alcoholic hepatitis, and cirrhosis in approximately 10 percent of all alcoholic patients). With regard to cirrhosis, it should be noted that U.S. rates are falling from their 1973 peak. This may be due to vitamin fortification of many food products or to changes in other variables. However, even with this decrease, cirrhosis remains the most common cause of death in alcoholics; up to 95 percent of cirrhosis cases—and 80 percent of deaths due to cirrhosis—are alcohol related. Unfortunately, the recent decline in cirrhosis deaths has been more than offset by increased alcohol related mortality from other causes, especially interpersonal violence and highway accidents.

In addition to its direct and indirect toxic effects, heavy alcohol consumption is also a risk factor for cancer of the mouth, pharynx, larynx, esophagus, and liver—a factor further increased in heavy drinkers who use tobacco. Alcoholic patients with cancer not only have poorer chances of survival, but they also have greater chances of developing another primary tumor than do nonalcoholic patients with the same type of cancer.

Alcohol is implicated in a variety of cardiovascular disorders that include phlebitis, varicose veins, and types of angina pectoris. Compared to infrequent drinkers, heavy drinkers suffer a 300 percent greater likelihood of mortality from strokes. Currently under debate is arguable evidence that small, regular doses of alcohol may help protect against coronary atherosclerosis. However, larger doses certainly correlate positively with elevations in blood pressure for both sexes and all races, and prolonged abuse of alcohol may damage the heart muscle permanently.

Heavy drinking by pregnant women is detrimental to the development of the fetus. Effects may range from mild physical and behavioral deficits to the tragic fetal alcohol syndrome (FAS), which is characterized by mental retardation, poor motor development, extreme growth deficiency, and facial malformations. FAS (see chapter 5) is a significant risk factor in children born to women who drink three or more ounces of ethanol per day during pregnancy. Other possible consequences of heavy drinking during pregnancy include decreased birth weight, an increased rate of spontaneous abortion, an increased perinatal mortality rate, and various behavioral and neurological defects. More subtle impairments of other offspring or of children whose mothers consume smaller amounts of alcohol may very well occur and are currently under investigation.

The nervous system can suffer *directly* from alcohol's effects on nerve cells (neurons) and also *indirectly* through failure of the alcohol damaged liver to detoxify the body (hepatic insufficiency); alcohol withdrawal syndromes, including delirium and convulsions; traumatic injury resulting from intoxication; and malnutrition, especially avitaminosis. Alcohol related damage to the nervous system can cause cerebral atrophy, degeneration of the corpus callosum and cerebellum, central pontine myelinolysis, reduced cortical blood flow, polyneuritis, and Marchiafava-Bignami disease. Cerebral lacerations and subdural hemotomas due to traumatic injury while intoxicated are common. There is no question that some degree of brain damage is a major hazard of alcoholism. In fact, some degree of impaired brain function is likely to be found in the majority of diagnosed alcoholics. The likelihood may prove even higher with the employment of new techniques for brain scanning by computerized axial tomography (CAT), positron emission tomography (PET), and nuclear magnetic resonance (NMR).

MENTAL HEALTH CONSEQUENCES

Alcoholism is also a cause of major mental illnesses, including acute alcoholic dementia, delirium tremens, alcoholic hallucinosis, and Wernicke's encephalopathy. Permanent psychotic states, such as Korsakoff's syndrome, and other, less well-defined deteriorative dementias are related to prolonged heavy usage. Alcoholism is diagnosed at the time of admission in 20 to 30 percent of first admissions to American state mental hospitals, and in several states it leads all other diagnoses in mental hospital admissions.

Even though gross intelligence quotient (IQ) scores may not be significantly lowered, a slow and insidious thinking disorder (cognitive dysfunction) in heavy drinkers is now recognized. It is characterized by significant decline in memory, and decline of abilities in several visual-spatial and perceptual-motor tasks, nonverbal abstraction, and problem solving. These deficits have been found in cross-national studies and occur in both sexes. The degree of functional impairment varies directly with the magnitude of alcohol intake and the drinker's age; mild impairments have been found even among immoderate social drinkers.

ACCIDENTS AND VIOLENCE

In addition to its more or less direct medical consequences, alcohol consumption appears to increase substantially the likelihood of injury or death in accidents. With regard to home, industrial, and recreational accidents, one study found that 36 percent of regular drinkers, but only 8 percent of nondrinkers, reported two or more accidental injuries within the previous year. Approximately 70 percent of those who died as a result of falls (which account for more accidental deaths than any other cause except motor vehicle injuries) had been drinking. Fires are another major source of alcohol related death and injury. Alcohol is involved in 90 percent of all burn cases admitted to general hospitals and 83 percent of deaths by fire in the United States. Alcoholics are ten times more likely to die in fires than are members of a standard comparison population. Alcohol is involved in three times as many deaths from cigarette-caused fires as in deaths by fires resulting from other causes. Various studies also show 50 to 69 percent of drowning victims had been drinking. Compared to nonalcoholics, alcoholics are almost four times as likely to have accidents that require absences from the workplace of nine days or more. There is a high correlation of alcohol abuse with every type of trauma. For example, a 1980 study by Israel et al. reports that routine radiography found that fractures of the thorax were nearly fifteen times more frequent in alcoholics than in nonalcoholics. More than 33 percent of patients entering one general hospital's trauma department had blood alcohol levels above 0.08 percent.

In addition to alcohol's involvement in accidental death and injury, it also plays a significant role in suicide. Various studies (Noble, 1979; DeLuca, 1981) have found that 15 to 64 percent of those who attempt suicide and 30 to 80 percent of those who die by suicide had been drinking at the time.

Alcohol intoxicated behavior is arguably the largest, or at least the most ubiquitous, law enforcement problem in many Western nations (see chapters 4 and 6). In the United States roughly 50 percent of all arrests are alcohol related, and alcohol appears to be involved in approximately 80 percent of homicides, 70 percent of serious assaults, 50 percent of forcible rapes, and 72 percent of robberies annually. About 50 percent of family dispute cases handled by police involve alcohol. Available data indicate high rates of alcohol intoxication in husbands who abuse their wives, as well as wives who are abused. Alcohol is involved in 65 percent of child abuse cases; investigations of battered children who have died or required hospitalization reveal commonly that the parent was drunk at the time of abuse.

MOTOR VEHICLES

Motor vehicle accidents are the largest single cause of violent death in the United States; in 1977 alone, over 49,000 people were killed and another 2 million injured. Additionally, more than 16 million collisions involved significant property damage. Very recently the totals and the rates have declined somewhat, perhaps because of the national adoption of the fifty-five-mile per hour speed limit and the increased use of seat belts. Various studies show that 35 to 73 percent of the drivers in fatal and 6 to 25 percent of drivers in nonfatal accidents had been drinking prior to the accident; additionally, 29 percent of the passengers in fatal accidents showed blood alcohol concentration in the legally impaired range. Individuals with drinking problems comprise 48 percent of drivers responsible for their own fatal injuries, 41 percent of those who survived but were responsible for another's fatality, and 31 percent of those who fatally injured a pedestrian. Of those pedestrians who died within six hours of an accident, 74 to 83 percent had been drinking, and 33 percent had blood alcohol levels of 0.15 percent or higher.

The propensity for high school aged youth to engage in sporadic bouts of heavy drinking away from home and in motor vehicles may help to explain findings that 45 to 60 percent of all fatal automobile collisions involving a young driver are alcohol related. Younger drivers are considerably more likely to have been drinking prior to an accident than are older drivers, and the probability of alcohol involvement increases with the severity of the collision, as it also does for older drivers. Among American youth in general, no other cause of mortality approaches traffic accidents in terms of numbers, and no other cause is as predictably associated with traffic accidents as is alcohol. Among some of the most underprivileged American youth—blacks age fifteen to thirty —homicide has recently become the leading cause of death, and the majority of these violent episodes are also alcohol related.

Blood alcohol content is positively correlated with both the relative probability and relative severity of traffic accidents. The increased risk is found in all categories—rural and urban, fatal and personal injury, single and multiple vehicle. Motor vehicle accidents involving drunken drivers cost the nation more than $5 billion annually. Altogether, alcoholism in the United States probably reduces life expectancy of its 10 million victims by an average of twelve years.

A Note on Prevention

It must be emphasized that primary prevention must involve the education and protection of the consumer (see chapter 7). In an effort to avoid problems of substance abuse, an international emphasis on prevention is emerging. This is due to the realization that treatment systems alone are inadequate to deal with dependency disorders such as alcoholism; that acute, as well as chronic, intoxication can lead to serious social and medical problems; and that prevention is the most desirable approach in this as in all serious disease syndromes.

The DHHS notes that three major models for alcohol or drug abuse prevention may be distinguished.

1. *The public health model* involves three points of access: the drinker or *host* (the individual: knowledge, behavior, attitudes); the *agent* (the drug: content, distribution, availability); and the *environment* (the setting and context in which alcohol use occurs, including community mores). The major point of access for prevention, through "demonstration projects," is the host. Unfortunately, many such projects have been generated at considerable cost without showing very promising results to date. However, this does not mean that educational approaches are useless; it only means that greater effort should be made to devise and test better methods.

2. *The distribution of consumption model* presumes that there exists a relationship between per capita consumption and prevalence of heavy use. Prevention in this model generally calls for government action to restrict availability. Naturally there are resistances to this approach. Nevertheless, recent studies of this model indicate that effective controls on accessibility can lead to lower consumption and fewer related problems. So do other interventions that reduce consumption, such as raising the drinking age or increasing prices (usually by taxation) (see chapter 3).

3. *The sociocultural model* emphasizes the relationship between alcohol related problems and normative patterns of alcohol use within a society. Social problems are most likely to appear when norms conflict with changing practices. The challenge is to strengthen the appeal of an abstinent, abstemious, or more moderate norm. To the extent that norms can be influenced by educational programs, by counter-advertising, by changes in content of dramatic entertainment, by celebration of abstemious role models, etc., this model continues to offer promise.

Treatment

DIAGNOSIS

The treatment of alcoholism is one of the most vexing problems in clinical medicine. In the emergency room, alcoholic patients are more frequently misdiagnosed or mismanaged than any other group. The patient who comes (or, more likely, is brought) to the hospital in a drunken state is probably a chronic alcoholic. Therefore, medical personnel must be alert to the increased likelihood of associated nutritional deficiencies, infections, subdura hematomas, and malignancies, as well as chronic diseases of the liver, stomach, heart, and brain. The effects of mixing drugs must always be suspected. Barbiturates, antihistamines, tranquilizers, and various street drugs are common offenders. These may further complicate the already complex problem of the acutely ill and alcohol intoxicated patient. In recent years polydrug abuse increasingly has affected the diagnosis and treatment of alcoholism and most other addictions as well.

Alcoholics are so numerous and so frequently dirty, smelly, and noisy that hospital emergency service personnel tend to reject or neglect them. However, the odor of alcohol may disguise stupors or confusional states that are due to hypoglycemia, hepatic or renal failure, subarachnoid bleeding, schizophrenia, or other major mental illnesses. Furthermore, alcoholic analgesia ("feeling no pain" because of alcohol's potency as an anesthetic) may obscure the presence of fractures, dislocations, or severe internal injuries.

EXTENDED TREATMENT

The treatment of acute alcoholic episodes has improved greatly at competent hospitals in recent years, accompanied by a decrease in death rates from complications such as delirium tremens. Intensive short-term treatment of acute alcoholism may require all the resources of modern emergency medicine. Yet it is relatively straightforward and standardized in comparison with long-term treatment. Extended treatment and rehabilitation of the chronic alcoholic patient pose an enormous problem to the health related professions, the health care delivery system, and the public well-being in general.

Chronic alcoholics, like other chronic patients subject to high risks of relapse, can be a formidable challenge. Nevertheless, despite controversies and frustrations about their extended care, the challenge is not nearly as hopeless a matter as most laypeople—and many physicians—believe. Modern and well-integrated medical, psychiatric, and psychosocial treatment programs have shown short-term improvement rates (abstinence for six months) of 50 to 80 percent or better. Long-term improvement rates (abstinence for more than a year) of 50 percent or better are not uncommon in some clinics in the United States, the United Kingdom, and Europe, although the average improvement rate is probably closer to 25 percent. It should be kept in mind that most of the available data are from studies of chronic alcoholic patients in designated public clinics or treatment programs and are not cases primarily identified in general hospitals or general medical practice. The prognosis for the latter groups should be significantly better if diagnosis and treatment are prompt and appropriate.

The best comprehensive treatment of alcoholism should begin with a strong confrontation of the detoxified patient by a knowledgeable physician. As soon as possible the alcoholic's family members should be involved—the spouse or significant other person, the parents, the children, etc. Other significant persons (employers, friends, attorneys, clergymen) should also be included when appropriate. The nature and hazards of the illness must be clearly and firmly stated, and powerful emphasis should be placed upon the importance of total and permanent abstinence from alcohol. Authoritative advice of this sort may be the single and most effective element of early treatment (Edwards and Orford, 1977). It is properly enhanced by relatively intense experiences in specialized inpatient or outpatient settings capable of providing educational presentations, films, lectures, dynamic psychotherapy, behavior therapy, group therapy, family therapy, brief individual psychotherapy of the crisis intervention type, and introduction into Alcoholics Anonymous (AA). There are, as yet, few studies that adequately evaluate the efficacy of these procedures. However, AA is known to have helped hundreds of thousands of alcoholics to maintain sobriety. Other alcoholics, even without the help of AA, have also been able to remain sober through personal resolve reinforced by family support, religious conversion experiences, psychotherapeutic intervention, and effective contact with medical facilities and health personnel.

ADDITIONAL THERAPIES

Extended care can further enhance the likelihood of sobriety by the use of a variety of therapies, including psychosocial support, special diets, and dietary supplements. Short-term prescription of tranquilizers, antidepressant or mood stabilizing medications, and other agents may be useful. However, extended prescription of these agents should occur only when compelled by indication of psychiatric disorder and should be employed only on a case-by-case basis since not all alcoholics are alike. However, it is essential that they all be understood to suffer from a variable symptom complex resulting from prolonged, severe ethanol abuse, and that as patients they should be identified as ill rather than as wicked, weak, self-indulgent, or depraved.

Aversion therapy, which is based on a conditioned negative response created by linking alcohol to a powerful nauseant or emetic chemical, has been used in some treatment centers with good results reported. One widely employed aid is disulfiram (Antabuse). In most cases, when taken daily, it is essentially inert

unless alcohol is ingested. If even a small amount of alcohol is
swallowed by someone taking disulfiram, an extremely unpleasant
reaction will be experienced, resulting from a sharp rise of acetaldehyde in the blood. The reaction occurs almost immediately and
peaks within thirty minutes. For this reason the patient must be
carefully supervised and instructed in advance of the dangerous
consequences of drinking while medicated with disulfiram. These
consequences include intense flushing, coughing, shortness of
breath, nausea, and vomiting.

Metronidazole (Flagyl), used in the treatment of trichomoniasis
and, less often, amebiasis, sometimes produces milder effects
similar to disulfiram. It also frequently alters the taste of alcohol
in an unpleasant way and has been used as a deterrent to drinking
even though its manufacturer does not make any such claim for it.
Other antimicrobials occasionally found to produce similar effects
in some patients include chloramphenicol, furazolidone, griseo-
fulvin, isoniazid, and quinacrine.

ORIENTATION TO TREATMENT

Every modern medical center should provide a well-organized
inpatient and outpatient program of treatment for alcoholics,
employing special units with trained personnel to provide instruction and psychotherapy during detoxification and rehabilitation.
Such a program will properly provide authoritative medical advice
to patients and their families; multimodal short-term therapy; and
individually selected additional medical, psychiatric, psychological,
and social methods. The fact that this is generally not the case
in many countries—including the United States—despite the im-
mensity and urgency of the problem, is an indictment of our health
care delivery systems. It is also a reflection of continuing rejection
of the concept of the alcoholic as a sick person rather than as a
sinner or merely an obnoxious citizen with a nasty habit.

Ironically, the latter viewpoint has been given impetus by the
recent introduction of the proposition that many alcoholics will
do better if abstinence from alcohol is *not* the goal. Instead,
"controlled drinking," inculcated by purely behavioral methods,
is offered as a more reasonable and achievable outcome of intervention. Alcoholic patients characteristically cling to the hope
that they can return to normal, moderate, or controlled drinking,

despite the failure of many efforts to do so and the evidence that their alcohol intake is causing progressive deterioration of life and health. Needless to say, the "controlled drinking" approach has great appeal for many alcoholics.

Many experienced clinicians in this field believe that the "controlled drinking" option, widely touted as innovative and progressive, is essentially a throwback to the old and rather simple-minded view of alcoholism as a bad habit. It may be that "controlled drinking" is feasible for certain individuals who, while they have had some drinking problems, are nevertheless not *gamma* alcoholics in Jellinek's sense (those showing physical dependency) and, in fact, are not really alcoholics by almost any modern medical definition.

It has been argued that a few individuals who were once diagnosed as alcoholics by presumably competent observers have been known subsequently to become moderate or social drinkers. Even if such rare cases were accurately reported, they would not justify *advocacy* of "controlled drinking" rather than abstinence as a general goal for alcoholic patients. Such advocacy began with a series of reports by Sobell and Sobell starting in 1972. They asserted that *gamma* alcoholic patients at Patton State Hospital in California, randomly assigned to a behavioral therapy program with a special goal of "controlled drinking," were *less* likely to revert to uncontrolled drinking than were patients receiving either conventional therapy or behavior therapy with a goal of abstinence. The Sobells' reports were followed by numerous publications by both themselves and their followers hailing the success of the new method.

The proposition that "controlled drinking" is a feasible goal in the treatment of alcoholism received reinforcement with the 1976 publication of the "Rand Report" (Armor et al.) in which a nationwide U.S. survey appeared to reveal that a considerable number of former alcoholics were found capable of drinking moderately or in a successfully controlled fashion. However, a follow-up Rand Report in 1980 (Polich et al.) sharply modified the earlier claims.

As a result of the claims by Sobell and Sobell and their followers, there are many articles, textbooks, and monographs that now recommend programs of "controlled drinking" for alcoholics. Consequently, an increasing number of physicians, psychologists, and other health professionals have been led to believe that "controlled drinking" through behavior therapy is a feasible and desirable treatment that is superior to all others—even for *gamma* alcoholics. A number of clinics and hospitals are already providing such programs, and others are preparing to do so.

Meanwhile, contrary findings have appeared. John Ewing, an early advocate of the "controlled drinking" approach, published a follow-up study of his own cases with the conclusion that the method was a failure. Paredes et al. (1979) completed a careful Rand-type study in Oklahoma that disputes the Rand findings and concludes that for those alcoholics who attempted the moderate drinking option, the risk of relapse was significantly higher than for those attempting total abstinence. Foy et al. (1982) reported a careful replication of the original experimental procedure of Sobell and Sobell, avoiding a number of methodological errors that they identified in the Sobells' work. The study by Foy et al., probably the best of its kind to date, clearly demonstrates that a large sample of those alcoholic veterans who were trained in "controlled drinking" had, within six months, significantly *poorer* outcome than a matched group of patients who received comparable clinical care but with a goal of total abstinence. Eventually (after a year) there were no significant differences between the groups.

A ten-year follow-up of the original patient population reported by Sobell and Sobell was carried out by Pendery et al. (1982). A number of serious methodological flaws in the original Sobells' research were identified. It was discovered that most of the Sobells' original experimental subjects who were "successfully" trained in "controlled drinking" had, in fact, failed from the outset to drink safely or in a controlled fashion. Most of those called "successful" were drinking out of control within a year. Only one subject, clearly not a *gamma* alcoholic in the first place, was able to maintain a pattern of controlled drinking. All of the others failed. Eight of the patients continued to drink excessively, either regularly or intermittently, despite repeated damaging consequences. Four died from alcohol related causes. Six others finally abandoned their efforts to engage in "controlled drinking" and became abstinent. The remaining one, already certified as gravely disabled because of drinking within a year after discharge from the research project, was missing.

It now appears clear that the risks involved in advising patients with a life threatening illness such as alcoholism to continue to expose themselves to the causative agent—alcohol—cannot be justified. In the light of recent findings, even the continuation of experimental studies with a "controlled drinking" alternative should be challenged on ethical grounds. Alcoholic patients should be encouraged to achieve and maintain a goal of total abstinence. This view is supported by a growing body of relevant biopsychosocial knowledge and technique. The health related professions have an important role to play in this approach. They also have a clear responsibility to accept that role more fully, willingly, and effectively than has been the case in the past.

Insurance Coverage

Treatment for complications of alcohol abuse is covered by both public and private insurance, but treatment for the underlying alcohol problem itself is covered only partly or not at all (Saxe et al., 1983).

Medicare characterizes alcoholism as a psychiatric disorder, therefore providing less coverage than for physical illnesses (see Table 1). Medicaid plans vary from state to state, but the level of Medicaid reimbursement for treatment of alcoholism is still generally low. Greater reimbursement is obtainable for the physical complications of alcoholism than for the basic disease.

Medicare and Medicaid have generally encouraged inpatient, medically based treatment (over outpatient or partial hospitalization methods) even though inpatient care is more expensive and not necessarily more effective in many cases.

Private health insurance plans generally excluded treatment of alcoholism prior to 1972. Since then there has been limited coverage. Very few private insurance companies offer as much coverage for alcoholism as they do for other illnesses. Private and nonprofit plans often cover inpatient detoxification in a general hospital, but rarely in a psychiatric hospital. Free-standing rehabilitation facilities are not often covered or are covered only if a special "rider" is purchased. Blue Cross/Blue Shield's Federal Employee Health Benefits Program dropped its coverage for alcoholism rehabilitation in 1982 as a cost-saving measure without

TABLE 1.   MEDICARE COVERAGE

Medicare: Part A (Hospital Insurance Component)

Psychiatric hospital:	
Inpatient services	190 days/lifetime
General hospital:	
* Psychiatric ward services	90 days coverage per benefit period:
	$304 deductible,
	25% copayment after 60 days,
	60 days plus $50 copayment as
	lifetime reserve.

Medicare: Part B (Supplemental Medical Insurance)

** Outpatient services:	50% coinsurance,
	$250 maximum reimbursement
	per year.

* Standard reimbursement for physical ills.
** Partial coverage, unlike that for physical ills.

publishing cost-benefit figures or other data on which to base their decision. Bureau of Labor Statistics data show that only 37.9 percent of American workers have *any* alcoholism coverage.

As of January 1984, all Blue Cross/Blue Shield plans across the nation are required to include coverage for alcohol and drug abuse as part of their package to national accounts. The Substance Abuse Rehabilitation Benefit includes 60 days inpatient services, lifetime maximum (with detoxification separately covered); 180 days residential rehabilitation, lifetime maximum; and 180 outpatient visits, lifetime maximum (one day of residential rehabilitation cancels one outpatient visit and vice versa). Because this benefit was endorsed by the National Blue Cross/Blue Shield Association, resistance felt by other carriers may lessen.

The present situation created by insurance coverage patterns tends to encourage treatment of complications only. This practice results in (1) almost certain relapse, (2) treatment of alcoholism under other diagnoses resulting in less than adequate treatment planning, (3) the so-called "revolving door" (frequent relapses of alcoholic patients resulting in repeated detoxifications without adequate rehabilitation), (4) the continuation of a tendency for medical practitioners to ignore alcoholism and their own failure to diagnose and treat conditions not covered by insurance, and (5) extreme financial hardship for those alcoholics who undergo treatment.

The Need for Change

Although social attitudes toward alcoholism and alcohol related problems are changing, the enduring stigma attached to such problems remains a formidable barrier to successful intervention. Efforts for treatment face other barriers that include the patients' resistances through denial and rationalization; their lack of motivation to question their own drinking behavior or to seek help during early stages of problem drinking; the lack of guidelines against which to evaluate their drinking habits; inadequacies of referral treatment networks; and negative attitudes and lack of expertise within the health professions.

The magnitude of the alcohol problem is increased because it is still relatively unrecognized by many health professionals and others who should be taking responsibility for corrective action. This failure of vision can be found even at the highest levels of health planning. Relative to its estimated economic impact, support for alcohol related research is extremely low. In fact, only about 10 percent of the amount spent by the United States on heart disease or respiratory disease research and only 1 percent of the amount spent on cancer research is invested in research on alcoholism. Furthermore, recent national health policy decisions in America have led to shocking cuts in the NIAAA budget with marked reduction in services. Educational programs, improved prevention techniques, and other sorely needed approaches to this growing problem are poorly developed and seem to have a chronically low priority in the American public value system. Unfortunately, this view is not limited to the general public; it includes the health professions as well.

It is well known that alcoholics who request treatment at general hospitals, either in the emergency room or elsewhere, are prone to minimize their alcohol consumption and deny their dependence on it. This is often cited as the principal reason that the majority of cases are undetected and undiagnosed until disease is far advanced. However, health professionals are very likely to collude with the alcoholic in this game of denial. A recent study of a large medical center reveals that most of the doctors and nurses regularly failed to take adequate histories of alcohol or other drug use, often did not identify a patient's alcohol or drug dependency as a medical problem even when it was known, and did not get involved in recommended treatment regimens even when the problem was identified.

It must be added that most physicians have taken very little interest in new developments in the field of alcoholism. For example, the Michigan Alcoholism Screening Test (MAST) requires ten minutes to administer and is highly reliable and effective in identifying alcoholics in a general hospital. It has been available for more than ten years but is still not widely used.

Furthermore, the growing mass of information about the physiological effects of alcohol steadily is advancing prospects for objective laboratory verification of the clinical diagnosis of alcoholism. One rather elegant study (Ryback et al., 1980) recently tested a diagnostic algorithm employing multiple discriminant analysis of a number of routine chemical and hematological laboratory tests of hospitalized men. This technique correctly classified 100 percent of alcoholic patients on the medical wards as alcoholics, 94 percent of those in an alcoholism treatment program as alcoholics, and 100 percent of the medical control group as nonalcoholics.

Clearly the time has come for all physicians to become as sensitive to—and responsible about—the presence of alcohol abuse as they regularly are to the presence of such cardiovascular abnormalities as might be suggested by chest pain, shortness of breath, fatigue, heart murmurs, and high blood pressure. However, to accomplish this, it seems clear that considerable resistance within the medical profession must be overcome, beginning with the undergraduate medical curriculum, and extending through residency training in all clinical fields.

Intervention Efforts

Currently, the best developed and most extensive intervention efforts in the United States are aimed at three groups.

OCCUPATIONAL OR INDUSTRIAL ALCOHOLISM PROGRAMS

These programs are based on four assumptions: (1) the most effective mechanism for identifying problems related to alcohol use is the supervisor's awareness of impaired performance, (2) alcoholism should be regarded as a medical problem in the workplace, (3) regular disciplinary procedure for poor performance should be suspended while an employee conscientiously seeks assistance for the problem, and (4) returning to adequate job performance is a sound criterion for judging successful outcome. Since their advent in the 1940s, the number of occupational alcoholism programs (sometimes called "employee assistance programs" or EAPs) in the United States has grown to 5,000 or more. In the private sector, a steadily increasing proportion of companies have adopted such programs. In the public sector, implementation has been somewhat slower; more than 80 percent of all federal employees now have access to EAPs, but access for state employees varies greatly.

PROGRAMS FOR THE CHILDREN OF ALCOHOLICS

Children of alcoholics are considered a high-risk group for the development of abusive alcohol and other drug habits. In addition they appear to suffer from high rates of psychological and physical health problems and are prone to drop out of school. Unfortunately, fewer than 5 percent of the 12 to 25 million children of alcoholics in the United States receive help, coming mostly from AA derivatives such as Alateen. A wide variety of interventive programs exists, but their specific goals are usually unclear, and their interventive efforts are hampered by legal issues, especially those regarding parental authority.

DRINKING DRIVERS PROGRAMS

These programs are offered to or required of driving-while-intoxicated (DWI) offenders through a variety of interventive strategies by the court system. Police efforts that increase the likelihood of arrests have been shown to be only transiently effective in reducing the DWI rate. Increases in severity of punishment have proved relatively ineffective, due to extensive plea bargaining and the reluctance of courts to impose harsh penalties. Public information and education campaigns also have not yet proved to be very effective. Raising the drinking age appears to help, but the rationale for designating a specifically approved drinking age is unclear and fraught with political difficulties.

Conclusions

Alcoholism and related problems may well embody the nation's most vexing set of health policy issues (see chapter 8). Clearly required are more effective prevention strategies that, in part, include education regarding the dangers of alcohol and its abuse and that emphasize populations who are at especially high risk, such as adolescents, persons with family histories of alcohol abuse, and pregnant women. Also sorely needed are more and better clinics, employee assistance programs, special hospital facilities, and other similar operations, all staffed with more and better trained personnel. Decriminalization of drunkenness and provision of appropriate health care facilities instead of jails for the intoxicated have already been instituted in some European countries. Such an approach may be more expensive initially, but it is likely to save money, lives, and misery in the long run. The alcoholic patient is more likely to receive proper and timely care if insurance policies provide treatment coverage for alcoholism even at an early stage. Most important of all is the need for a far greater national investment in research on alcoholism at every level from the most basic to the most clinical.

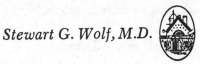

Stewart G. Wolf, M.D.

2

Alcohol and Health:

The Wages of Excessive Drinking

> *Bacchus, that first from out the purple grape*
> *Crushed the sweet poison of misused wine.*
> John Milton, Il Penseroso

This chapter will review the effects that ethanol (ethyl alcohol) produces in the health of body, mind, person, and society. Alcohol's short-term and long-term effects on the brain will be emphasized. Some original work undertaken in collaboration with the Laboratory of Metabolism of the National Institute on Alcoholism and Alcohol Abuse (NIAAA) will be described. The health hazards of rapid social change and the abandonment of tradition will also be documented, and the salubrious nature of social equilibrium and social supports will be shown. The need for expanding the horizon of research with fresh and creative

STEWART G. WOLF, JR., *is the director of Totts Gap Medical Research Laboratories, professor of medicine at Temple University School of Medicine, and Regents Professor of Medicine at the University of Oklahoma. Throughout his distinguished career he has held over thirty positions at eminent institutions, received many national honors, and served on federal government advisory committees as well as those of national organizations and associations. Dr. Wolf has published 26 books, contributed more than 65 chapters in various volumes, and written over 300 scientific papers.*

efforts and suggested ways of encouraging contributions from a broader range of disciplines will be offered. In addition, American social attitudes toward greater cohesion and a wider sharing of values will be recommended.

Alcoholism as a Disease

There is no doubt that alcohol abuse causes several diseases and often a concatenation of bodily disorders. Whether or not alcohol dependence should be classified as a disease is, however, the subject of continuing debate, although more and more this dependency is being accepted as such. Unequivocal identification of alcoholism as a disease awaits the discovery of a marker that sets it apart from other forms of overindulgence in alcohol. A possible candidate for such a marker in the form of a metabolic abnormality is the proclivity for forming diols (higher alcohols) during the metabolism of ethanol, which is discussed later.

The concept of alcoholism as a disease was proposed nearly 200 years ago by pioneer medical scientist Benjamin Rush, and yet, until recently, it remained submerged under the weight of cultural pressures. Drinking, even heavy drinking, was associated with celebration, sophistication, the good life. Alcohol abusers were the skid row bums or, perhaps, the daily workers who squandered their wages at the corner saloon, but it is surely the securely employed and leisure classes, the successful and affluent beautiful people, who actually account for over 90 percent of alcoholics (according to the studies of the Yale school). In the 1950s, the American Medical Association and the World Health Organization officially recognized alcoholism as a disease.

It should be emphasized that alcoholism is more than a disease of an individual. It disrupts the equilibrium of the family structure and, in one way or another, affects every family member. New equilibriums must be established when the alcoholic stops drinking, and there are adjustments to be made throughout both the drinker's period of recovery and after the establishment of long-term sobriety.

Despite the growing awareness of the medical significance of alcohol abuse, it was difficult to obtain hospital admission for the treatment of alcoholics until very recently when understanding began to replace public disapproval and disgrace. Today, at long last, at least some third-party payment policies at least partially cover the rehabilitation of alcohol and drug abusers.

Causes of Alcoholism

The basic reason for the alcoholic's alarming proclivity toward addiction has remained a mystery, although a metabolic explanation has been proposed based on a putative link between alcohol and opiate addiction through a class of alcohols called tetrahydroisoquinolines (Davis and Walsh, 1970; Cohen and Collins, 1970; Melchoir and Myers, 1977). This notion is still highly speculative since Sjoquist et al. found salsolinol, a closely related tetrahydroisoquinoline, in the brain and spinal fluid of non-alcoholics who had not been drinking, as well as in both drinking and sober alcoholics (Sjoquist, Eriksson, and Winblad, 1982; Sjoquist, Borg, and Kuande, 1981). The values were generally lower among the sober alcoholics than among the intoxicated alcoholics and normal controls. The values from the latter two did not differ significantly.

Rutstein and Veech (1978) provide evidence indicating that alcohol addiction may be genetically determined. Michael Bohman (1978) reports a twenty-five-year study of 2,000 children of alcoholic fathers who had been raised by nonalcoholic adoptive parents; he also studied criminality in similar fashion. With impressive statistics, he shows that criminality was learned at home, but alcoholism occurred four times as frequently among boys adopted by nonalcoholic parents whose real fathers were alcoholic than among those whose real fathers were nonalcoholic. At the present time, unfortunately, there are no data relating to the etiologic mechanism or the presumably neural structures involved in such a mechanism.

There has been much dispute, but no consensus, about the various parts played by genetic inheritance, the social pressures, special features of individual growth and maturation, and the insidious effects of ethanol itself in the cause of alcoholism. Apparently all are pertinent, and the behavioral characteristics of alcoholics are partly innate and partly shaped by learning or practice.

Bodily Effects of Ethanol Consumption

There is hardly a tissue or a function of the body that is immune to the damaging effects of large amounts of ethanol. Ethanol has been called an ambivalent molecule since it can both provide calories and serve as a poison. As Frank Lundquist (1975) puts it, "Alcohol is both a rapidly metabolized nutrient and a dangerous drug, depending on the amount consumed and the duration of the exposure to the substance."

It is necessary to be somewhat technical in order to explain what is known of the way alcohol affects the brain and the body, because alcohol abuse affects virtually all the tissues of the body, disrupts their normal regulatory mechanisms, and produces disease in nearly every organ. As more and more has been learned in recent years about the widespread depredations of alcohol abuse, alcoholism is rapidly becoming the number one disease in our culture—already it is the number two killer.

FATE OF ETHANOL IN THE BODY

The mechanisms of alcohol poisoning are both direct and indirect, either damaging cells and tissues of the body or distorting their function in some way so that control of secretions, the behavior of the circulation, and the absorption of nutrient or other aspects of the bodily economy are disrupted. Individual susceptibility to alcohol's effects appears to vary with genetic inheritance, with nutritional state, and in other lesser understood circumstances.

The small ethyl alcohol molecule is rapidly absorbed from the upper gastrointestinal tract into the blood where it diffuses across capillary membranes into the tissues of the body, including brain and placenta. Its direct metabolic effects are manifest chiefly in the liver (and, to some extent, in the intestinal mucosa and elsewhere) where alcohol dehydrogenase, an enzyme, catalyses the conversion of ethanol to acetaldehyde, which circulates throughout the body and is further degraded by the action of other enzymes to carbon dioxide and water. This process requires the removal of large numbers of hydrogen atoms, thereby preempting cellular energy normally engaged in metabolizing fat and glucose as fuels for the body. There are many chemical chain reactions and cycles of energy expenditure and regeneration of energy that regulate the enormously complex body economy of a healthy person, and the need to dispose of ingested ethanol disrupts most of them— the more ethanol, the more disruption. While waiting to be metabolized, ethanol itself, like its relatives ether and chloroform, can directly disturb the normal traffic of chemical substances among the cells and hence disrupt secretory and absorptive activities that are required for nutrition or other tasks in the dynamic processes of the body.

NUTRITION AND DIGESTIVE DISTURBANCES

Many of the tissue disturbances caused by alcohol are accentuated by malnutrition, a frequent accompaniment of alcoholism. Indeed, in severe alcoholics the nutritional deficits may be responsible for the worst of the symptoms and disabilities. Ethanol can impair the intestinal absorption of vitamins B1, B12, and folic acid (Tomasulo, Kater, and Iber, 1968; Lindenbaum and Lieber, 1969; Halsted, Griggs, and Harris, 1967). Other nutritional disturbances associated with alcoholism include magnesium, zinc, and copper deficiency, the consequences of which are poorly understood.

The liver, essential to life, is the body's busiest and most versatile chemical factory, converting a vast array of nutrients into materials to build, maintain, and repair. Like the kidney, it is also a major excretory organ and removes substances from the blood that are not readily soluble in water, especially the residue of old and damaged red blood cells.

Because it causes impairment of the ability to metabolize fats, fatty liver is an almost universal consequence of ethanol ingestion. The other liver disorders, hepatitis and cirrhosis, appear to occur only in suitably susceptible people and are positively correlated with the duration and amount of ethanol consumption (Pequignot, 1978). The transition from alcoholic hepatitis to cirrhosis appears to be determined by an immunological mechanism that interferes with the normal maintenance and replacement of liver cells (Leevy, Chen, and Zetterman, 1975).

Cirrhosis and other alcohol related liver diseases account for a level of lost productivity, illness, medical costs, and death comparable to the combined impact of gastrointestinal cancers. Carefully gathered epidemiological data from Canada show that death due to liver diseases, 80 percent of them alcohol related, is rising more rapidly in that nation than any other cause of death (Senior, 1983).

Pancreatic secretion is initially stimulated by ethanol, but its access to the intestinal tract may be obstructed because of associated smooth muscle constriction at or near the sphincter of Oddi, its point of entrance (Menguy et al., 1958). Alcohol may also be responsible for an inflammatory condition in the pancreas in which ducts are obstructed due to the formation of protein plugs in the pancreatic juice itself (Sachel and Sarles, 1979). These plugs may later calcify and produce chronic pancreatitis, causing scarring, destruction of pancreatic function, and further impairment of intestinal absorption with severe diarrhea and fatty stools; diabetes may also be a consequence (DiMagno, Malagelada, and Go, 1975).

ENDOCRINE ALTERATIONS

Among endocrine effects other than diabetes are hypogonadism and feminization in the male, which are related to suppression of male hormones and an excess of female hormones consequent upon impaired liver function (Lieber, 1982). The usually associated testicular atrophy (Bahnsen, Gluud, and Johnsen, 1981) may occur in the absence of liver disease; indeed, the testis, a tissue with a high glucose requirement, can be directly affected by alcohol (Van Thiel, 1983). Other hormone disturbances include suppression of the secretion of growth hormone even by moderate alcohol ingestion. Growth hormone is normally secreted during a phase of sleep in which slow waves are recorded on the electroencephalogram. Despite the fact that alcohol increases the periods of slow-wave sleep, growth hormone is, nevertheless, suppressed (Prinz et al., 1980).

HEART AND SKELETAL MUSCLES

Alcohol abuse has serious deleterious effects on both heart and skeletal muscle that appear to be due to the impairment of energy metabolism already mentioned (Eckhardt et al., 1981; Slavin et al., 1983). Alcohol damage to muscles is manifested by weakness and, ultimately, by the destruction of muscle fibers. Skeletal muscle damage is reflected in the blood by an elevated concentration of creatine kinase, a muscle enzyme. In severe cases, myoglobin, a muscle protein, may appear in the urine (Hed, Larsson, and Wahlgren, 1955). In the heart, alcohol affects the mechanisms that regulate the heartbeat, producing a variety of rhythm disturbances that may result in sudden death (Gunnar et al., 1975).

Until recently, heart disease associated with alcoholism was thought to be another manifestation of vitamin B1 (thiamine) deficiency. It is well known now, however, that, even in well-nourished alcoholics, the consequences of alcohol metabolism in the heart lead to destruction of heart muscle fibers and the deposition of fat and scar tissue that ultimately lead to congestive heart failure (Lange and Sobel, 1983; Talbott, 1975). Cardiac output is reduced in alcoholic cardiomyopathy in contrast to the high output type of heart failure characteristic of nutritional cardiomyopathy (beri-beri heart disease). Of course, the effects of the two may be combined and even supplemented by poisoning from chemical contamination of alcoholic beverages as, for example, from cobalt sulfate that at one time was used in the manufacture of beer (Eckhardt et al., 1981).

BLOOD AND BONE MARROW

Extensive disturbances in the blood formation system are attributable to the metabolic disruptions, as well as to the direct effects of excessive alcohol ingestion (McColl et al., 1981). Apart from reducing absorption of vitamin B12 and folate, indispensable for red cell production, alcohol directly impairs red cell maturation through effects on pyridoxine, folic acid, and iron metabolism (Hines, 1975; Herbert and Tisman, 1975). Through its effects on the red blood cell membrane, it shortens red cell life span (Hillman, 1975). An anemia similar to pernicious anemia may develop independently of folate deficiency because of direct effects of alcohol on the developing young red cell (Cumming and Goldberg, 1978). Either too little or too much blood clotting that produces bleeding or thrombus formation may result from alcohol's effects on the development of megakaryocytes, the producers of blood platelets (Haselager and Vreeken, 1977). Inhibitory effects on the production of other types of blood cells, macrophages, lymphocytes, and leucocytes may also occur, impairing resistance of alcoholic patients to infections (Herbert and Tisman, 1975).

RESISTANCE TO INFECTION

The lowering of resistance to infection by alcohol was discovered over a hundred years ago by Robert Koch in guinea pigs exposed to cholera vibrio (Williams, 1975). Since then it has been shown that even modest amounts of ethanol may impair the mobilization of polymorphonuclear leucocytes that engulf bacteria and decrease the bactericidal activity of blood serum. Larger amounts interfere with glottis closure that shuts off the windpipe during swallowing and ciliary activity that clears debris in the bronchial passages. Both of these effects are accentuated in the presence of hepatitis and cirrhosis (Johnson, 1975).

CANCER SUSCEPTIBILITY

Alcohol abuse has been implicated in promoting the development of some forms of cancer, especially of the mouth, pharynx, larynx, esophagus, and liver, and possibly pancreatic, colonic, and prostatic cancer as well (Eckhardt et al., 1981). These neoplastic effects appear to be enhanced by heavy smoking.

SKIN MANIFESTATIONS

Alcohol abuse manifests itself in changes in the skin. Through what appear to be capillary effects, the eyes and the face—especially the nose—become red, the conjunctivae suffused, and the skin of the eyelids edematous. Other skin manifestations, including red palms and porphyria cutanea tarda, are secondary to hepatic cirrhosis (Woeber, 1975). Spider nevi, small red blemishes often accompanied by breast development in males, are attributable to the hypogonadism and feminization already mentioned. Often, failure of severe alcoholics to eat properly may lead to the skin lesions of multiple vitamin deficiencies.

SURGICAL PROBLEMS

There is an impressive list of surgical consequences of alcoholism such as the cancers referred to earlier and esophageal varices secondary to hepatic cirrhosis (Orloff, 1975). Surgical emergencies include sudden rupture of the esophagus or the junction between esophagus and stomach that results from the trauma of violent vomiting. In addition, there are traumatic injuries of all sorts from fights and traffic and other accidents.

EFFECTS ON THE BRAIN

Of greatest concern are the changes in the brain attributable to overindulgence in alcoholic beverages. As alcohol diffuses freely across intracranial capillaries, the cells of the brain must accommodate the membrane effects and other actions of alcohol and its breakdown products. One of the most vivid and often frightening mental consequences of heavy drinking, delirium tremens, is due not to the alcohol, but to sudden alcohol withdrawal that requires the brain cells to accommodate rapidly to a new chemical environment. The alarming manifestations of delirium tremens can be quickly halted by reestablishing the former equilibrium among brain strictures with another drink—"the hair of the dog."

As a consequence of drinking, a seemingly fully alert person may display severe impairment of judgment without evident memory loss at the time, but perhaps with no recollection of the event the following day. More long-lasting effects on the person, including persistent impairment of judgment due to actual brain damage, are discussed later.

Alcohol induced delay in reaction time, weakening of social restraints, and impairment of judgment are reflected in an immensely high association of accidents and injuries with drinking (Holt et al., 1980). Assaultive and criminal behavior are also highly correlated with excess alcohol consumption (Mayfield, 1971).

Several devastating neural consequences of alcohol abuse, including degenerative changes in the brain and optic nerves, are basically nutritional and due either to inadequate diet or to the effects of alcohol on intestinal absorption or intermediary metabolic processes, or to a combination of all these factors. Alcohol inhibits the gluconeogenesis, the synthesis of sugar required when liver glycogen is depleted, and seizures or even death from severe hypoglycemia may be precipitated by drinking following a prolonged fast (Field, Williams, and Mortimore, 1963).

In 1881 Carl Wernicke, a German neuropsychiatrist, described mental deterioration accompanied by ataxia and paralysis of eye movements in alcoholic patients. A few years later Sergei Korsakoff, a Russian psychiatrist, described in an alcoholic patient a syndrome characterized by loss of recent memory and confabulation, usually associated with peripheral neuritis; the manifestations of the two disorders have often been seen together with or without polyneuritis since that time. The Korsakoff-Wernicke syndrome and other serious neurological disturbances are caused by deprivation of vitamin B1. This thiamin deficiency and probably other components of the B complex are responsible for degenerative changes in the optic nerves associated with blind spots, or even total blindness, as occasionally seen in alcoholic patients.

There are other degenerative disturbances in the brain that are not so clearly attributable to nutritional deficiency but, if related to 2,3 butanediol, may nevertheless reflect neuronal damage from blocked glucose metabolism or, on the other hand, may represent the more directly toxic effects of alcohol. Most often encountered are cortical atrophy in the cerebellum manifested by loss of muscle coordination and in the frontal lobes by the gradual loss of intellectual assets—especially judgment, capacity for abstraction, visual-motor and visual-spatial functions, visual memory, and social restraint (Draper, Feldman, and Haughton, 1978). Ron and associates (1982) have observed that radiological evidence of cortical atrophy associated with high consumption of alcohol appears after a shorter time in older than in younger drinkers. They also observed decrease in ventricular dilation and in frontal sulcal widening after prolonged abstinence from alcohol. Whether or not there is associated recovery of intellectual functions accompanied by neuronal regeneration has not been determined.

Psychological, Cognitive, and Behavioral Effects

DEPRESSION

Among psychiatric syndromes associated with alcoholism, perhaps the most common is depression (East, 1936). The etiologic relationship, if any, between depression and alcoholism is not clear, although a sizable cohort of depressed patients gives a history of alcoholism among relatives. By the same token, many alcoholics give a history of depressive episodes prior to the onset of alcohol addiction (Winokur, 1974). Nevertheless, studies have failed to correlate depression, especially bipolar manic-depressive depression, with subsequent manifestations of alcoholism (Vaillant, 1983). Therefore, while the association of depression with alcoholism is frequent, it is not clear that the depression comes first. Suicide is also frequent among alcoholics, and alcohol is said to be implicated in about 30 percent of all suicides (Eckhardt et al., 1981).

Abnormal Diols Associated with Depression—In a study of over a hundred patients admitted to an alcoholic detoxification center, a diagnosis of depression was associated with the presence of abnormally higher alcohol (2,3 butanediol) in the blood serum following ethanol ingestion (Felver et al., 1980; Wolf et al., 1983). Together with 2,3 butanediol, 1,2 propanediol appeared in the blood of approximately 85 percent of the patients in the detoxification center whose blood also contained ethanol. The other 15 percent whose blood did not contain the diols had, nevertheless, consumed the same type of alcoholic beverages in similar quantity and for similar periods of time. The blood of control subjects did not contain the diols, even after ingestion of large amounts of ethanol.

The complications of alcoholism—hepatic disorders, pancreatitis, cardiomyopathy, and Korsakoff-Wernicke syndrome—were just as prevalent among those patients whose blood was free of diols as among those containing high concentrations. Only one of the independently diagnosed conditions, manic-depressive depression, set the two groups of patients apart. Depression had been entered on the charts of only those patients whose blood was subsequently found to contain 2,3 butanediol associated with the presence of ethanol.

CONCLUSIONS OF THE DIOL STUDY—POSSIBLE INVOLVEMENT
IN INTELLECTUAL IMPAIRMENT

When metabolizing ethanol, the presence of large amounts of 1,2 propanediol and 2,3 butanediol in the blood of some alcoholics, not in the blood of others, and not in the blood of normals, clearly indicates a characteristic difference in the control of the pathway of ethanol metabolism among the majority of alcoholics. Two studies have confirmed these findings, one by Rolf Blomstrand in Stockholm, not yet published, and another widely publicized study by Rutstein et al. (1983). The latter claims that the different metabolic handling of ethanol provides an indication of a genetic etiology of alcoholism. It does not, of course. It merely strongly suggests—but by no means demonstrates—a genetic peculiarity among some alcoholics for a metabolic proclivity for the formation of 1,2 propanediol and 2,3 butanediol.

The observed association between presence of 2,3 butanediol and independently diagnosed depression may reinforce the speculation about genetic differences and also suggest an effect of the differences on brain function. Therefore, in an attempt to trace the in vivo metabolic pathways of the diols, Veech and his collaborators (1981) were able to show in rats that acetaldehyde was converted in testis and brain to acetoin, which outside the brain was converted to 2,3 butanediol. The consequences of such an alteration in brain metabolism are not as yet evident, but, as Veech suggests, since fatty liver is a consequence of the cessation of beta oxidation of fatty acids due to excess mitochondrial NADH during ethanol metabolism, there must be some similar compensation for this interference in the brain. Indeed, in the brain the diversion of pyruvate normally involved in the formation of acetyl CoA for the Krebs cycle to the formation of acetoin would result in the loss of forty-eight molecules of ATP per glucose molecule utilized in acetoin production rather than in Krebs cycle activity. This would constitute an intracellular equivalent of insulin coma or hypoglycemic shock with a consequent possibility of neuronal damage. Whether or not the atrophic changes demonstrable by CAT scan in the frontal lobes in some alcoholic patients are attributable to this metabolic aberration remains to be explored. In any case, if there are serious consequences, one would expect them in the frontal lobes, the site of the highest resting rate of glucose utilization.

POSSIBLE CONNECTION TO FETAL ALCOHOL SYNDROME (FAS)

Finally, as the ethanol molecule can diffuse freely through the vasculature of the placenta, innocent offspring may be affected by its poisonous properties. The manifestations of FAS include impairment of intellectual development and skeletal developmental disturbances that involve the bones and other tissues of the face, conferring a strikingly similar appearance on its victims. Ulleland et al., as early as 1970, identified among infants of alcoholic mothers a high incidence of defective skeletal and intellectual development. Susceptibility to FAS appears to be as genetically determined as some other of the consequences of alcohol abuse (Rutstein and Veech, 1978). The fact that 20 percent of women will produce infants that are unaffected by FAS, despite alcohol consumption as large and as lengthy as that of mothers whose offspring are diseased, suggests an inquiry into frontal lobe development among affected infants and the possible presence of 1,2 propanediol and 2,3 butanediol in their mothers.

EFFECTS ON THE PERSON

> *There are among us those who haply please*
> *to think our business is to treat disease.*
> *And all unknowingly lack this lesson still*
> *'tis not the body but the man is ill.*
> S. Weir Mitchell
> *Cited in A. T. Schofield,* The Force of Mind

The effects of drinking on the brain are reflected not only in intellectual capacity but in attitudes, values, beliefs, and patterns of thought and behavior. Initially, alcohol suppresses inhibitions —*in vino veritas*. Plato contended that heavy drinking reveals the goodness of the good and the badness of the wicked. Is it, however, the real person whom alcohol reveals? In part, perhaps it is, because without restraint speech may become incautious, less diplomatic, and more frank. An individual's characteristic attitudes and behaviors are usually accentuated, sometimes to the point of caricature. On the other hand, alcohol may cause distortions in brain function that actually change the person, therefore not revealing the real person at all.

SIMILARITIES IN ATTITUDE AND BEHAVIOR AMONG ALCOHOLICS

The most frightening effect of alcohol is its assertion of dominance over the person. Subservience to ethanol-containing drinks is the hallmark of the alcoholic. The vast experience of Alcoholics Anonymous (AA) has led to the identification of a constellation of behavioral, cognitive, and emotional features encountered frequently enough among alcoholics to become targets for rehabilitation efforts. They include, often from early childhood, a sense of being "different," of not fitting in with peers, accompanied by hunger for support, attention, and approval. Childhood and youthful behavior may be marked by intense efforts to gain praise and recognition by extraordinary achievement in meeting challenges at school and elsewhere. Coupled with a prominent self-centeredness are a relatively fragile and vulnerable sense of self-esteem and a sensitivity to slights, sometimes bordering on the paranoid. The paranoid style of thinking is evident in an unusual ability to rationalize behavior, to shift blame to others or to outside circumstances, and to excuse failure. Associated with a remarkable capacity for self-deception is a stubborn immunity to advice and an obsession with "doing it my way." With the passage of years, as alcoholics find themselves failing to meet their own standards and failing to gain the recognition they need, they nevertheless persist in this refusal to accept advice or help. Their response now may be to shun responsibility and avoid challenges. At this point alcohol may have become the center of their life, while assured access to their increasingly unreliable solace is equated with survival. Threats to the alcoholics' schemes to maintain that access are met with arrogant and intransigent behavior. Emotional responses include being "touchy" or explosively angered by trifles, cycles of rage, frustration, guilt, resentment, and depression. There may also be sudden feelings of invincibility, equally suddenly succeeded by self-doubt and depression.

Whether or not these attitudes, emotions and vulnerabilities, perceptions, and behavior are antecedent or subsequent to clinical alcoholism has not been clearly established by either retrospective or prospective studies of alcoholics (Vaillant, 1983). The constellation, however, recognized retrospectively, is almost monotonously familiar in the life stories of alcoholics speaking at AA meetings. The lack of resolution in the studies of the premorbid personality of alcoholics may be due partly to the penchant of young prealcoholics to play-act, to dissemble, and to conceal their feelings, often fantasizing omniscience and omnipotence and being outwardly self-confident while inwardly there persists those childhood feelings that they don't "fit-in" with others.

Bandura (1969) and others have suggested that the common personality and behavioral features encountered among alcoholics are largely conditioned by their experiences and their repetitive behavior in coping with life. The drink that initially allows uninhibited self-expression and relieves apprehension and self-consciousness gradually assumes greater and greater importance, but it is ultimately useful only in dulling a sense of guilt and remorse, justifying failure, and rationalizing a long chain of complicated and protective beliefs. The presumption is that alcoholics adopt similar psychological and behavioral maneuvers to serve as a protective shield and also to assure continued access to their life line—alcohol. As the disease progresses, the range of interest of the alcoholic becomes narrowed and increasingly focused on the need for a steady and reliable source of drink. When deprived, there are no limits to what alcoholics have done to themselves and to others to satisfy their craving.

Although some of the common behavioral features may still be evident after years of sobriety, successful recovery from alcoholism is often accompanied by impressive emotional growth. The recovering alcoholic may undergo a metamorphosis from callous indifference to the needs of others, typically found among lifelong sociopaths, to a generous concern for others and a strong sense of social responsibility. This remarkable consequence of achieving sobriety suggests that the stereotypic features of alcoholics are attributable to interference with specific brain connections that may be congenitally absent in the sociopath. In other words, normal modulators of attitude and behavior may be disrupted or distorted by the many chemical, pharmacological, and nutritional consequences of alcohol abuse, but they are capable of recovery nonetheless.

Social Implications of Alcohol Abuse

There is no social role for alcohol among the large and geographically widely separated Arab ethno-religious cultures. On the other hand, among French and Italians, wine drinking is as essential to the daily ritual as eating itself. Indeed, in 1951, France, despite one of the highest rates of alcoholism in the world, attempted to have wine drinking excluded from the World Health Organization criteria for alcohol abuse. In most western societies, drinking is accepted but drunkenness is scorned. Among ancient thinkers, Plutarch, Socrates, Plato, Seneca, and Horace all inveighed against drunkenness. Religious Jews use wine for ritual occasions but reject drunkenness with the expression "Shikker is a Goy"—the drunkard is a gentile. Jews, however, are by no means immune to alcoholism. Indeed, as Sheila Blume has observed, alcoholism has become a serious problem in Israel. Blume and her collaborators (1980) have identified among alcoholics in this country a significant number of Jews, chiefly those with the weakest religious identification. The ancient Chinese poet Li Po has suggested that peer pressure is a major basis for alcohol abuse: "These days continually fuddled with drink I fail to satisfy the appetite of my soul. But how can I, alone, remain sober with all men around me behaving like drunkards." In Russia, Sweden, and Australia, being a bit tipsy is a sign of congeniality and absence of threat—a bit like the peace pipe of the American Indians or marijuana to the Rastafarians of Jamaica.

The role of alcohol in rituals of human courtship and other aspects of human bonding has been explored by Derek Denton of the Australian National Health and Medical Research Council. In *Medical Aspects of Wine Drinking* he writes:

> The loyal toast, at least in ancient times, is consistent with a psychoanalytical view of ritual, as binding instinctual energy into a pattern of mutuality and bestowing simplicity on dangerously complex matters. The rituals of drinking are part of the style of a particular cultural ideology, and part of the process of establishing a psychosocial identity in the young may involve participation with the elder generation in drinking customs and ceremonies with resultant sense of bonding to a tradition. Drinking ceremonies may ratify precedence and peck order as with the Royal Kava ceremony of Tonga. As well as drinking behavior being learnt and reinforced in these deeply persuasive circumstances, the manual and oral displacement motor activities which drinking provides in other circumstances are of great importance, as with similar activities such as cigarette smoking. When the man invites the new girl friend to his flat for a drink and to hear some records, both parties are, consciously and unconsciously, very grateful of all the manual activities with glasses, ice cubes, uncorking bottles and reaching for and putting down drinks, etc. These provide a motor superstratum of activity to the conflicting feelings of fear, hostility, and attraction which would generate quite different gestures, in relation to what might be the mutually understood main business of the evening.

The ambivalence of the ethanol molecule in cellular metabolism which, depending on the amount ingested, acts both as food and poison, is matched by its social impact. In modest quantities its contribution to relaxation, human communication, and conviviality has inspired poets, musicians, artists, and scholars. It has long had a ceremonial importance for occasions serious, joyful, and collegial. In some religions wine is indispensable to certain sacraments. In other religions and in some cultures, as already mentioned, alcohol plays no part.

The medical use of alcohol goes back at least to the Sumerians whose records of 4,000 to 5,000 years ago contain references to the medicinal use of wine. The early Hindus were among the first to use wine as an anesthetic. Hippocrates recommended that wounds of gladiators be dressed with wine-soaked bandages to avoid putrefaction.

Wine's importance to medicine was summed up by Dr. Salvatore Lucia (1954) of the University of California Medical School in San Francisco:

> The elixirs of the grape are precious ammunition and offer a balm to the therapeutist whose genius can call upon them to brighten a dulled psyche, to cajole a wayward appetite, to pacify an overwrought bowel, tc banish the foes of Hypnos, and to bring hope reminiscent of youth to the autumnal years of those enfeebled by the execrations of old age.

All true, but bear in mind the role of wine and spirits as agents of disease and death. And bear in mind the words of Chaucer in "The Pardoner's Tale": "For dronkenesse is verray sepulture of mannes wit and his discrecion." Ultimately, of course, drunkenness is the sepulcher of the man himself.

Public Policy Issues

HEALTH CARE SERVICES

Alcohol related illness is an enormous burden on health care services of all sorts, including emergency services, general medical and surgical services, psychiatric services, and community health services. Detoxification and rehabilitation facilities for alcohol and other addictions have only recently been covered by government insurance such as Medicare and, in some states, through Blue Cross and other private insurance carriers. Inclusion of drug abusers in alcohol rehabilitation centers has been necessary because a high percentage of young alcoholics are "polyaddicted" to drugs, both prescription agents and illegal street drugs. It is too early to make an assessment of the human and economic savings achieved by modern rehabilitation facilities, but it is likely that the savings will amount to far more than their cost. Since more third-party payments have become available for financing and rehabilitation of the alcoholic, privately organized facilities have cropped up like mushrooms. Such "for profit" clinics have grown to a $400 million a year industry. Some of the companies are already on the stock exchange. Thus there appears to be enough incentive for rehabilitation facilities to become widely available.

Beyond the strengthening of health care services there is a dire need for emphasis on public education and a thoroughgoing commitment to research.

EDUCATION

The challenge to the nation is to mitigate the outrageous health, psychological, social, spiritual, and economic costs imposed by continually emerging new crops of alcoholics and alcohol abusers. Rescue and rehabilitation are costly, time consuming, and only partly successful. The desirability of early detection of alcohol abuse among employees is rapidly becoming recognized by U.S. corporations. Programs designed to recognize early the effect of alcohol on the performance of individual workers, to encourage those becoming impaired to seek help, and to assist them in obtaining it have proliferated in major U.S. companies. In 1974 there were 300 such programs—in 1984, nearly 6,000. An initial fear that the unions would object on the basis of infringement on their members' privacy was unwarranted. Instead, the overall success of the programs has led to the formation of an Association of Labor-Management Administration and Consultants on Alcoholism (ALMACA).

The characteristics of the programs are interesting and significant. They include (1) a clearly stated policy concerning detection and management uniformly enforced, (2) no fear of dismissal if treatment is entered into and maintained, (3) acknowledgment that alcoholism is not a character weakness but a disease requiring treatment, (4) guaranteed confidentiality, and (5) inclusion of care for alcoholism in insurance coverage.

As in AA, these treatment programs involve teaching and learning from one another. Experiences of fellow alcoholics that touch a chord of recognition and responsiveness provide important lessons for other individuals trying to recover.

The National Council on Alcoholism presents a "National Industrial Alcoholism Award" to companies whose high-quality programs for alcoholic employees are visible in their community. The E. I. DuPont de Nemours Company, a recent recipient of the award, declares that their "program is not only the humane way to deal with this disease, but that it is a sound business practice." The next step is to go beyond early detection and prompt treatment toward a feasible route to prevention.

INVOLVEMENT OF RECOVERED ALCOHOLICS IN EDUCATION
FOR PREVENTION

Effective prevention will require an inspired strategy for educating young people long before their work years. Although AA as an organization would not be likely to sponsor such an undertaking, the experiences of recovered alcoholics are a vast human resource that might be well directed toward prevention as well as rehabilitation. The personal dedication and generosity of AA members toward helping others toward recovery have endowed many of them with enormous power. As AA has designed and developed its recovery program for alcoholics, it should be possible for successfully rehabilitated alcoholics to develop a similarly successful and vastly more economical educational program for primary, middle school, and high school youth. In fact the National Council on Alcoholism is already providing such an educational service, and in some communities recovered alcoholics already have been recruited to teach youngsters in the regular school curriculum (Deutsch, 1982). This program needs to be extended more widely.

Because of a generally perceived need for sex education, such programs are already in place in most states and communities. Prevention of alcoholism is hardly less of a public challenge. Indeed, problems of sexual behavior are often linked to alcohol. From a medical perspective, venereal disease, teenage pregnancy, and sexually related emotional disorders are highly important but of far less magnitude than the problems engendered by alcohol that endure well beyond the period of youth. Sex education programs in schools vary enormously in content, emphasis, and style. The teachers do not come from any established or common educational experience. Recovered alcoholics do, and they should be able to tailor their teaching to the needs and understanding of schoolchildren. Shaped over time through trial and error, such curricula (including presentations by AA members) could make a difference and preserve a substantial human potential, especially among children of alcoholics who are at increased risk of becoming alcoholic themselves. Assignment of recovered alcoholics to this important task would, of course, require very careful selection. The children should be handled according to the special characteristics of their family unit, including attitudes and behavior of parents and siblings and the degree and nature of the social turmoil.

As noted earlier, there is increasing evidence that susceptibility of at least some people to alcoholism is genetically determined. If so, at some time in the future, a genetic marker may become available. When it does, those who are genetically susceptible will be able to be identified and exposed to especially enriched and focused educational efforts by appropriately selected recovering alcoholics.

Research

A good many people, deeply interested in the problems of alcohol and alcohol abuse, do not believe that research should be the principal way of attacking these problems. Others would argue that although treatment and rehabilitation must continue to be supported, their efforts should be strengthened and improved through the fruits of research. Research has certainly triumphed over many other crippling diseases. Eighty years ago William Osler contended that an understanding of typhoid fever would confer an understanding of all the pathology of medicine. Years later, typhoid fever had been conquered, and the disease that was recognized as manifesting itself in every organ of the body was syphilis; later it was diabetes; and now it is clearly alcoholism.

To explore the protean features of alcoholism and alcohol abuse will require the recruitment and generous support of creative investigators in genetics, intermediary metabolism, neuroscience, physiology, pathology, psychology, and many other disciplines. Alcohol studies have thus far attracted only a few first-class investigators.

The Advisory Council of the NIAAA might profitably launch an intensive effort to cultivate interest in alcohol studies among top scientists through specially designed conferences that include researchers from various fields that may not be involved at present in alcohol research. This approach was demonstrated to be highly useful by the National Institute of Arthritis, Diabetes, Digestive and Kidney Diseases for the recruitment of scientists for the study of digestive diseases and by the Muscular Dystrophy Association for the study of neuromuscular diseases.

Effective recruitment of new and talented investigators to alcohol research will not be achieved by clubby gatherings of investigators already involved in the problems of alcoholism. And neither will fresh ideas and cogent questions emerge from such meetings. On the other hand, bringing together creative people from a variety of relevant disciplines to listen to and communicate with already established alcohol researchers may prove fruitful indeed.

Examples of such productive efforts are found in the planning, organization, and conduct of a series of colloquiums that has been held at the Totts Gap Institute in Bangor, Pennsylvania, on a variety of biomedical topics with important social implications. These meetings are small, but interdisciplinary and international. Their objective is a fresh look at the issues, the reconciliation of disparities in data interpretation, and the identification of areas of ignorance to conquer and crucial questions to answer. These meetings have served to shed new light on old problems, to challenge and often correct longstanding assumptions, and to excite interest and seek new approaches from scientists previously not active in the particular field of research under discussion. The participants in these colloquiums have been selected not only on the basis of their expertise and achievement, but also on the breadth of their viewpoints and abilities to listen as well as to speak. In short, the meetings are not for advocacy but for inquiry. Since the aim is for synthesis and new insights, there is no audience to inhibit free exchange. Instead, the proceedings are given wide distribution through publication, and ten books have thus far emerged from these colloquiums.

COST-EFFECTIVE STRATEGIES FOR RESEARCH FUNDING

Strong public support is clearly needed for a vigorous and imaginative attack on the health problems of alcoholism and alcohol abuse. But strategies to reveal the unknown should not be devised by committees, institutions, or research administrators. Instead, the keepers of the coffers must be advised by relatively objective, disinterested, and tough-minded creative scientists who are responsive to new ideas, to an applicant's previous record of generating new knowledge and not merely to a conventional view on the part of competitors as to what questions should be asked and how to ask them.

Collections of planners and new layers of bureaucracy will not strengthen alcohol research. The model that works was operative long before the vast public funds for biomedical research became available. Before the days of National Institutes of Health grants, one man—Alan Gregg—by visiting investigators in their laboratories in the United States and around the world, made highly successful granting decisions for the Rockefeller Foundation for several years. Gregg required only brief descriptions of proposed work for application, but he informed himself of the backgrounds and records of the investigators. He did not want them to waste precious time in paperwork. He used to say, "Don't send me any reports. Send me the reprints." Alan Gregg was able to spend Rockefeller funds in a brilliantly cost-effective way that contributed mightily toward reversing the traffic of young student scientists from the eastward to the westward direction across the Atlantic Ocean.

AREAS FOR STUDY

Human Genetics—A full-scale genetic study is needed in which detailed information will be gathered from kindred. Such research is needed because often several members in the families of alcoholics are affected and because of the burgeoning evidence on adopted children. The information discovered from alcoholic relatives of the propositus may provide for establishing an inheritance pattern. Ultimately, chromosomal studies will be indicated and, with them, attempts to establish markers that lead to the identification of genes and gene products. Hints concerning possible markers may come from the widely divergent susceptibility of racial, cultural, and/or national groups.

Intermediary Metabolism—To understand the depredations of alcohol and its metabolic consequences, far more extensive studies of intermediary metabolism are indicated. The work with the abnormal diols 1,2 propanediol and 2,3 butanediol needs to be continued and vigorously pursued in a clinical setting where (under controlled conditions) large amounts of alcohol can be administered to nonalcoholic subjects over a period of several days and where metabolites may be traced using strategically placed arterial and venous sampling and, possibly, radioactive tracers.

Frontal Lobe Studies—There is a rich opportunity to explore problems of alcoholism with the tools of the neuroscientist. Neural circuits involved in certain types of behavior—defense, escape, aggression, submissiveness—already are being tied to the neurotransmitters that subserve them. The extraordinary imagination and resourcefulness of modern neuroscientists need to be focused on the problems of alcoholism. Major objectives should be to ascertain the basic mechanism and neural circuitry responsible for the alcoholic's inability to control drinking and to explain the startling similarity of thought and emotional patterns among alcoholics.

Behavioral Studies—The generally salubrious effects of social support systems for other diseases have been documented in numerous studies (Kaplan, Cassel, and Gore, 1977; Pilisuk and Froland, 1978; Lynch, 1977; Wolf, 1981). The contribution of each element of the therapeutic effects of AA can be sharpened and strengthened. AA's powerful emotional support is marked by trust, warmth, love, and fellowship. Intensive education, repetitive training, and the important elements of spirituality and reliance on a higher power are also stressed. At the same time there is an almost brutal demand for honest self-examination and frank acknowledgment of powerlessness over alcohol. Such a stern requirement is apparently needed to counteract the almost universal proclivity on the part of the alcoholic for easy self-deception and self-pity. All of these elements are woven into the firm, clearly explicit, and relatively unyielding fabric of AA. This whole phenomenology needs to be understood in the context of the process of becoming alcoholic. Application of the knowledge derived from research on these matters surely will transcend the field of alcohol studies and contribute to work on human development and maturation as well as toward the understanding of deviant and addictive behavior. A major challenge will be to develop and design reasonably precise new instruments capable of detecting and measuring the characteristic cognitive and emotional patterns of the alcoholic.

These are but a few areas of needed study; there are many others. If society is not to be limited by what is now known, a fresh commitment to promoting research in alcoholism is urgently demanded.

THE NEED FOR CREATIVE EFFORT

To achieve this fresh commitment, a shift in current public policy may be required. At this time America seems to have lost the concept of leadership, vainly hoping to find magic in management—even creativity in consensus. On the other hand, long experience has taught that intellectual progress has usually been brought about by often unusual and unconventional individuals committed to their mission. An alarming decline of U.S. heavy industry and manufacturing during this period of management worship has been witnessed when the captains of industry—the decision makers—could move from one company to another in an entirely different field without any knowledge of the business. They need not have creative ideas about perfecting the product as long as they act as effective managers. It is hardly surprising, therefore, that industrial innovation, once the hallmark of American industry, is now to be found in Europe and Asia. Fortunately for America there are the new burgeoning "high-tech industries" that, like the old Ford Company and the original General Motors, are governed by the creators and not the managers.

It appears that research planning in the alcohol field, as in heavy industry, has been somewhat parochial and unresponsive to new ideas. Perhaps widely held and powerful dogmas relating to cause and treatment of alcoholism and alcohol abuse have inhibited the emergence of freshness and flexibility in alcohol related inquiries. The NIAAA began as a division of the National Institute of Mental Health. Now as a full-fledged institute in the Alcohol, Drug Abuse, and Mental Health Administration (ADAMHA), it is still largely under the wing of mental health. A couple of years ago the Institute of Medicine, with the help of multidisciplinary panels of scientists, noted that many important areas of research in alcoholism are left unexplored and attributed the finding not to limitations in technology or talent but to lack of money. In 1983 Congress increased its appropriations for alcohol research from approximately $23 million to more than $33 million, an increase that should enable the NIAAA to seek the talent needed and to approve more investigator-initiated research proposals.

Not merely to provide an additional source of funding, it may be useful to create a privately supported foundation to supplement the efforts of the NIAAA. Such an organization should operate with voluntary service from senior scientific advisors and employ minimum administrative staff. The aim should be to launch a strong program of recruitment of top scientists and to support their research. The extraordinary success of Alan Gregg of the Rockefeller Foundation shows this to be feasible. There now exists a similar, but updated, model for the efficient purchase and support of research talent—the Howard Hughes Medical Institute. Interestingly, Alan Gregg inspired its formation and served as a consultant during its organization in 1951. For the first three years, Hughes contributed $100,000 a year for the support of specially selected research fellows. The institute was incorporated in 1953, and for the next three years spent less than $500,000 a year. Annual support for its investigator program has grown to approximately $30 million. The accomplishments of the Hughes investigators are immensely impressive. Considering the accomplishments of these and similar approaches, a new private foundation devoted to alcohol studies should, with its more sharply defined target, be able to match or exceed that level of success.

Other Issues of Public Policy

SOCIAL VALUES AND SOCIAL EQUILIBRIUM

Beyond education and research are broader and more controversial public policy issues—banning alcohol advertising, raising taxes on alcoholic beverages, drunken driving laws, and raising the minimum legal drinking age. However, there is doubt that such measures will work without a clear shift of social attitudes in America.

From time to time such attitudes can and do change in a major way, illustrated by the shift in the public's perception of alcohol research and the work of Alcoholics Anonymous over the past twenty-five years. Dr. Howard Haggard of Yale complained in 1945 that "the conflict between 'wets' and 'drys' has invaded the neutral ground of both the 'humanitarian', who wants to aid the alcoholic, and the scientist, who wants to study the problems of alcohol." He observed that the "wets" as well as "drys" regard both the humanitarian and the scientist with suspicion and tend to denigrate AA programs in which recovered alcoholics devote themselves to efforts for rehabilitation of others.

Toward the end of his article, Haggard predicted that public attitudes would change, lifting the barriers to progress:

> In spite of obstacles the growing numbers of scientists interested in the problem and the growing numbers of rehabilitated alcoholics, in close cooperation, will—in spite of opposition—gain the needed public support. The Forgotten Man will make himself heard, and the way will be opened to realistic solutions of an important social and medical problem.

Haggard's prediction seems to have been largely correct. The National Council on Alcoholism and multiple state and local programs have contributed substantially to public education and thus to change in social attitudes.

SOCIAL UPHEAVAL AND SOCIAL STABILITY

There is little doubt that social disruption is a contributor to alcoholism (Carrere, 1972; Gillis and Stone, 1973; Knapp, 1971; Ripley, 1973; Wanberg and Horn, 1973). It seems to have been a factor in the near pandemic of alcoholism among Eskimos and American Indians (Foulks and Katz, 1973). The principal forerunner of social disruption is rapid social change. Not only alcoholism, but a variety of other illnesses begin to spread and intensify during the disequilibrium characteristic of rapid social change. Social stability, on the other hand, has been identified with the effective operation of social controls on alcohol consumption and with a lower incidence of other chronic and debilitating diseases as well.

Social stability does not imply a lack of change or movement in society but, rather, the absence of social disruption and disillusionment, the presence of faith and trust in social institutions, roots in meaningful traditions, and shared involvement with others in the day's business. As this author commented in a Jessie and John Danz lecture delivered at the University of Washington in 1979:

> An effective social equilibrium, like bodily homeostasis, requires a neat balance of expressive behavior and restraint. Perturbations in the form of social change challenge the established interrelationships and adaptive capability of people in a society. To some extent, the continued stability of a tree in a windstorm will depend on the depth of its roots. Social systems are rooted in the past, in traditions, in shared values and goals. Rejection of the past and contempt for traditional values is hazardous to the health of the community and of the individuals themselves. When social change is so great as to amount to upheaval, the society is to an extent uprooted so that relationships become chaotic until new shared values and goals allow the establishment of a new equilibrium. Nearly twenty-five centuries ago, Hippocrates reminded his contemporaries of the risk of such drastic changes when he said, "Those things which one has been accustomed to for a long time, although worse than things one is not accustomed to, usually give less disturbance." While rapid change may be potentially noxious, nevertheless change is as essential for the growth of an individual as it is in the growth of social systems. The history of the world has been characterized by a continuous round of change and adaptation. At each point along the way, the quality of man's performance has reflected the validity of his values, his aims, his goals. In terms of social as well as bodily health, he has often been more unadapted, more sick than well.

More than thirty years ago René Dubos (1951) showed that vulnerability to infectious diseases may be enhanced in a setting of rapid social change. After a lifetime of study of tuberculosis, he concluded that unsanitary conditions, crowding, poverty, and so forth were less significant in outbreaks of the disease throughout the world than what he referred to as "social disruption"—rapid social change. Many other scientists have added confirmation to the concept that the quality of social adaptation is pertinent to health. Since antiquity this basic proposition has surfaced repeatedly. Nevertheless, it is still not wholly acceptable to the biomedical community and has yet to be incorporated in currently prevailing thought regarding medicine and public health.

The increasing emphasis on the significance of homeostatic

mechanisms of all sorts has made it easier to accept the proposition that perturbation of an established system may set in motion a destructive chain of events. Thus, an organism adapted to past circumstances is always, to some extent, maladapted to new circumstances.

SOCIAL SUPPORTS

The antidote for maladaption in the alcoholic was clearly identified by Bill W., cofounder of AA, to consist of emotional support from others, a sharing and caring relationship engendering in both parties a sense of personal worth, and a sense of belonging and of contributing to others (Thomsen, 1975). The salubrious nature of such human interactions extends far beyond alcoholism. A few years ago an opportunity arose to make a prospective study of heart disease in a small Italian-American town in eastern Pennsylvania (Bruhn and Wolf, 1978). This community, which had clung to its "Old World" culture from immigration in 1882 until the mid–1960s, had enjoyed relative freedom from heart attacks. In fact, the death rate from heart attack in Roseto was less than half that in neighboring communities. Interestingly, the prevalence of usually accepted risk factors for heart attacks—consumption of animal fats, smoking, lack of exercise, hypertension, and diabetes—was at least as great in Roseto as in the neighboring towns where this death rate was similar to that of the United States at large. What distinguished the residents of Roseto from the surrounding towns were there close family and community ties; their deep religious convictions; their deference and respect for the elderly; the subordination of the women to their men; and the high value placed on community, conformity, and the maintenance of symbols of their Italian heritage that included the egalitarian and classless attitude of villagers *(paesani)*. The result was a remarkably cohesive social structure where no one was ever emotionally abandoned and where everyone had a well-defined place in the scheme of things.

An important element in such a salutary environment appears to consist of a sort of social consensus consisting of shared traditions and beliefs—a clear identification and acknowledgment by the group of both taboos and acceptable behavior.

There is considerable published evidence that a healthy community is cohesive, mutually supportive, and interdependent with good individual and group morale (Insel and Moos, 1974). To achieve such social cohesion and to inculcate "adaptive stability" into American society poses a formidable challenge to the ingenuity of national policy shapers.

CODA

The involvement of alcohol with the affairs of humanity goes beyond historical reach. Drunkenness is probably as old as drinking, and there have been major changes from time to time in the public attitude toward alcohol abuse. Until recently in the United States, alcohol abuse was simply thought of as bad behavior and/or defective moral fiber. The idea that alcoholism was a physiological addiction and, therefore, a disease was probably not recognized—and certainly not accepted—until the founders of AA recognized it in themselves and their fellow alcoholics who together established this organization. Denial of the disease was prevalent among the alcoholics, their families, the public, and even the medical profession. In hospital records and on death certificates, evidence of alcoholism was ignored and euphemisms were substituted for any mention of its involvement in fatalities. Most in the medical profession took little interest in the shrewdly perceptive insights concerning alcoholic behavior that had been documented in the literature of AA. It is not surprising, therefore, that further understanding of the disease has progressed so slowly. However, one principle of AA was quickly adopted as self-help sharing groups emerged to help strengthen self-confidence and adaptive capability in a variety of diseases and handicaps. Finally, physician and scientist members of AA and many enlightened laypeople backed the efforts of Senator Harold Hughes in the Congress and Roger Egeberg, then assistant secretary for Health, in their successful effort to establish the National Institute on Alcoholism and Alcohol Abuse.

America is now faced with the challenge to do something sensible to mitigate the scourge of alcoholism and alcohol abuse. We cannot expect much from coercive measures. Greatly enhanced efforts in education and research are clearly indicated, but the most urgent need is for workable strategies to influence the American social ambience. A unification of public attitudes in the world has happened in the past. Certainly the present is again another propitious time.

Philip J. Cook, Ph.D.

3

The Economics
of Alcohol Consumption and Abuse

While the production and sale of alcoholic beverages constitute a relatively minor component of gross national product (GNP), the adverse economic consequences of alcohol consumption are enormous—lost productivity, property damage from alcohol related accidents, etc. These and related concerns engender public support for the pervasive governmental role in regulating the production and marketing of alcoholic beverages and the relatively high excise taxes traditionally imposed on these commodities. The nature and extent of government involvement in this area have always been controversial.

In what ways can economists help inform the public debate over alcohol control policies? First, there are a number of relevant factual questions that fall naturally into the economists' domain. What effect will an increase in alcohol tax have on consumption, the prevalence of heavy drinking, expenditures, and tax collec-

PHILIP J. COOK *is professor of public policy studies and economics at Duke University. A noted authority in the areas of health and safety regulation, preventive effects of punishment, and weapons and violent crimes, Dr. Cook has published many articles and spoken before distinguished forums on these topics. He also serves as associate director of the Institute of Policy and Public Affairs at Duke University.*

tions? What effects would result from changes in other control policies such as raising the minimum legal drinking age (MLDA) or eliminating a state's monopoly in retailing liquor? Second, economics offers a normative framework for evaluating such policy changes, given some prediction about their likely effects. This framework subsumes cost-benefit analysis and cost-effectiveness analysis, techniques that, at the very least, can aid in structuring the argument over any policy proposal.

This chapter begins with a brief statistical characterization of alcohol consumption in the United States. The next section considers the consequences of heavy drinking. A brief review of the adverse effects of intoxication and chronic excess drinking is followed by a summary and critique of recent efforts to place a dollar value on these adverse effects. The third section characterizes the array of alcohol control policies that regulate the market for alcoholic beverages and then presents a more detailed evaluation of two such policies—excise taxes and the minimum legal drinking age.

Alcohol Consumption

The $56 billion spent on alcoholic beverages in 1981 amounted to 2.8 percent of total consumption expenditures in the United States. This percentage has declined more or less steadily since World War II and is now less than half the 1946 level of 5.9 percent of total consumption expenditures. While consumers are spending less of their income on alcohol, they are drinking more now than in previous years. Figure 1 depicts the postwar trend in the adult per capita intake of beverage alcohol (ethanol); the most notable feature is the sharp increase in consumption between 1960 and 1972. Currently adult per capita consumption is about 2.8 gallons of ethanol annually, or approximately two drinks per day per person. (A "drink" is defined as four ounces of wine, twelve ounces of beer, or one ounce of spirits—each of which contains about the same amount of alcohol.) Beer is the preferred source of alcohol among U.S. consumers, with spirits a close second. In comparison with other Western nations, the U.S. consumption level falls in the middle range together with other countries where beer is the most common alcohol source—Canada, Denmark, the United Kingdom—and far below countries such as Portugal, France, and Italy, where wine predominates.

Fig. 1. *Apparent U.S. Consumption of Alcoholic Beverages in Gallons of Ethanol Per Capita of the Drinking-age Population, 1950 to 1978*

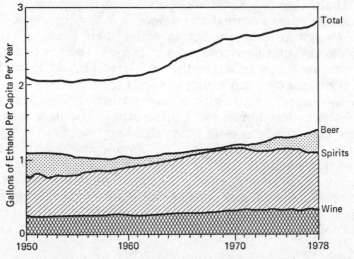

Source: Fourth Special Report to the U.S. Congress on Alcohol and Health, January 1981.

DIVERSITY OF DRINKING PATTERNS

Per capita consumption statistics tell us nothing about the broad diversity of individual drinking habits within the U.S. population. This diversity has been measured by a number of national surveys in recent years. Based on these surveys, it would appear that 90 percent of adults drink less than one ounce of alcohol (two drinks) per day—including approximately 33 percent who abstain completely. Unfortunately, survey respondents tend to understate their true alcohol consumption by a considerable margin; survey-based estimates of total U.S. consumption tend to be only 40 to 60 percent of true consumption. Hence, the true 90th percentile of the alcohol consumption distribution is unknown, but it is doubtless higher than two drinks per day. A generally accepted belief is that 10 percent of the population consumes 50 percent or even more of the beverage alcohol sold in the U.S. each year. Dean Gerstein (1981) vividly characterizes this highly concentrated distribution of consumption:

> If we were to reduce the overall U.S. consumption curve to a representative sample of 10 drinking-age adults, their annual consumption of absolute ethanol would not be very different from the following rough

approximation: 3 nondrinkers, 3 drinking a gallon among them, and others drinking 1.5, 3, 6, and 15 gallons, respectively. . . .

Thus, most adults in the U.S. drink alcohol on occasion, but a relatively few account for most of the sales and consumption of alcoholic beverages. The heaviest drinkers are of greatly disproportionate importance to the alcoholic beverage industry; for example, if the top decile (10 percent) somehow could be induced to reduce their consumption level to that of the next lower group (the ninth decile), then total ethanol sales would fall by over 33 percent. This rather startling fact can be explained using Gerstein's image. His ten representative drinkers consume a total of 26.5 gallons, and the heaviest drinker's share is 15 gallons. If this person reduced consumption to 6 gallons (the consumption level for the ninth person), then total consumption would fall by 9 gallons—over 33 percent of the group total. Alcohol related problems, including dependence, inebriation, and health and social problems, are highly concentrated within this top decile.

REDUCING CONSUMPTION

However one chooses to define the "drinking problem," it seems clear that its solution would likely entail a substantial reduction in overall sales and consumption. A primary concern in what follows is the evaluation of policies intended to reduce alcohol related problems by control of the availability of alcoholic beverages and the direct reduction of overall consumption. These policies, most notably alcohol taxes and MLDA restrictions, are controversial for a number of reasons. They pose a direct threat to sales and profits of suppliers, impose burdens on problem-free drinkers as well as abusers, and are of uncertain effectiveness in controlling abuse. The evaluation of alcohol control policies is prefaced by a general discussion of the social cost of alcohol consumption, with particular attention paid to the widely noted estimates of the total cost of alcohol abuse in the United States.

The Social Cost of Alcohol Abuse

ECONOMIC COST

Special regulations and taxes imposed on the alcoholic beverage industry have long been justified, in part, by the adverse consequences of alcohol abuse. There have been several notable attempts to translate this array of consequences into a single dollar figure—an estimate of "the economic cost of alcohol abuse." Such estimates are subject to several levels of critical attack, ranging from quibbles about the particular numbers employed to challenges to the basic conceptual justification for such estimates.

THE ADVERSE CONSEQUENCES OF ALCOHOL ABUSE

The immediate consequence of too much drinking is intoxication, with attendant changes in mood, alertness, and dexterity. These acute effects of drinking are variable and differ with the individual and environment. Alcohol can be a stimulant or depressant, a euphorigen or soporific, an irritant or tranquilizer. Depending on circumstances, intoxication may increase the likelihood of a number of adverse consequences: accidents; poor performance at work or school; and failures in judgment that lead to suicide attempts, decisions to commit a crime or foolishly provoke a violent attack, and other acts harmful to the individual's well-being or reputation.

In addition to these consequences associated with individual drinking bouts, there are adverse effects associated with chronic excessive consumption. The medical effects include a reduction in mental capacity, damage to the liver and other organs, reduced resistance to infectious disease, and early death. Chronic excessive consumption may also produce psychological dependence on alcohol, neglect of responsibilities at home and work, and financial ruin. Heavy drinkers are also frequently exposed to the various acute consequences of intoxication described earlier.

The number of deaths associated with alcohol is one indicator of the medical risks associated with its abuse. There are approximately 5,000 deaths yearly in the U.S. attributed to alcoholism and alcoholic psychosis and an additional 30,000 deaths from cirrhosis of the liver (chiefly the consequences of chronic heavy drinking). Most accidental deaths related to alcohol occur on the highway—approximately 50 percent of the more than 40,000 highway fatalities each year are the direct result of inebriation on the part of a driver or pedestrian. To this figure must be added approximately 10,000 alcohol related deaths resulting from falls, fires, or other accidents and some difficult to determine number of homicides and suicides. The total almost certainly exceeds 60,000 deaths per year and may be as high as 100,000. Other nonmedical consequences of alcohol abuse are not as readily quantified, but are nonetheless important.

POSSIBLE BENEFITS

On the other side of the ledger is the recent evidence suggesting that there may be adverse medical consequences associated with drinking too *little,* that there are hidden benefits to moderate drinking as opposed to abstinence. Alcohol appears to elevate high-density lipoprotein cholesterol (HDL-C) in the blood when taken in quantities that do not damage the liver. Elevated HDL-C is in turn associated with reduced risk of heart attacks caused by arteriosclerosis. Several field studies, summarized by Ashley (1982), report that moderate drinkers are indeed at reduced risk from heart disease even when other important causal factors are taken into account. This possible "protective" effect of moderate drinking is far from proven, but the evidence is strong enough to demand serious consideration.

Estimates of the Economic Costs of Alcohol Abuse

Ralph Berry, James Boland, and their associates (1977) estimate that the economic cost of alcohol misuse and alcoholism in the U.S. was $42.75 billion in 1975. This number is cited frequently in discussions of the alcohol-abuse problem, and probably has gained increased credibility through repetition. Leonard Schifrin (1983) has recently published a revised estimate using methods similar to those of Berry and Boland; Schifrin points out some omissions in Berry and Boland's work and reports that accounting for these omissions generates an estimated social cost of $73 billion for 1975. Updating this estimate to 1979 results in an increase to $113 billion. These numbers are impressively large and indeed are typically used as evidence that the alcohol-abuse problem deserves greater public notice and government action than it currently receives.

In Schifrin's estimate for 1975, 66 percent of the total social cost of alcohol abuse results from lost production. Of this lost production, $46 billion is the result of the reduction in the quality and quantity of work effort, both in paid and unpaid (at home) production. The principal source of evidence for this figure is

survey data on the income differential between families with and
without a male alcohol abuser present. Schifrin adjusts this differential to take account of a number of other factors.

The other major component of Schifrin's estimate is excessive
health care cost, pegged by him (and by Berry and Boland) at
about $13 billion in 1975—about 10 percent of that year's total
U.S. health care cost. Other important sources of economic cost
include the damages resulting from alcohol related motor vehicle
accidents and productivity loss due to excess mortality rates among
heavy drinkers. It should be noted that these estimates take no
account of the *reduction* in mortality that possibly results from the
alleged protection against heart disease provided by moderate
drinking.

Estimates such as those provided by Schifrin, and previously by
Berry and Boland, are generated from data and assumptions that
are subject to considerable error—a fact that these economists
readily admit. Thus, Schifrin's estimate of $113 billion for 1979
may well vary by a factor of 50 percent in either direction. Such
imprecision is a routine matter in policy oriented empirical work
and, at least in this case, does not undermine its usefulness. Of
greater concern is a more fundamental criticism of these "eco-
nomic-cost" estimates—the conceptual basis for such estimates
is not at all clear. What is most needed at this point is *not* more
precise data, but rather a clarification of the proper role and
purpose of such estimates. The next two sections attempt this
clarification.

CRITIQUE I: THE EXTERNALITIES QUESTION

The objective for producing an estimate of the "social cost of
alcohol abuse" is to quantify the magnitude of "the problem" and,
ultimately, to help make the case for greater public attention and
government action in this area. But the fact that a particular
activity is costly (in some sense) is not sufficient by itself to justify
government action; it would also be useful to know who is currently bearing these costs. In the liberal tradition that dominates
discourse on normative issues by Western economists, there is an
important distinction between costs of individuals' actions that
are borne by individuals themselves and those that are involun-

tarily borne by others. If individuals are "rational" and well informed, then they will take proper account of costs that they themselves must bear in deciding whether an action is worthwhile, but they may ignore those costs that result from their actions if the costs are borne by others. Hence, there is a stronger case for government action if the costs of a particular behavior are borne by society collectively than if the costs fall entirely on individuals who engage in this behavior. This is, of course, an ancient distinction in ethical discourse, and John Stuart Mill and other liberal philosophers have not convinced everyone that it is meaningful or important. Nevertheless, this question of "who bears the cost?" needs to be addressed in considering the ethical basis for government action.

A trivial example helps illustrate the point. One common consequence of inebriation is the withdrawal syndrome known as a "hangover." Hangovers are often so sufficiently unpleasant that many people would pay a substantial sum for an instant cure the "morning after." Thus, the aggregate cost of hangovers may be substantial, but since it is borne almost entirely by the drinkers themselves—and no doubt even anticipated when the decision was made to drink excessively—the economist would conclude that the benefits of the drinking bouts exceed the cost of the consequent hangovers. Hence, the liberal policy maker should ignore the cost of hangovers in assessing the alcohol-abuse problem. Indeed, Schifrin and Berry and Boland do not include hangover cost in computing their economic cost estimates.

However, it can be argued that a large percentage of the cost estimates reported earlier is borne, like hangovers, by the drinkers. For example, the economic cost of lost productivity is calculated on the basis of data that reflect the reduction in earnings resulting from chronic alcohol abuse. The primary "losers" in this case are obviously the drinkers and not society at large. Liberals may have some qualms about the fact that the chronic drinkers' dependents will also share in this loss, but government intervention to protect family members from each other is almost as ethically troublesome as intervening to protect individuals from themselves. This same liberal line of thought would suggest excluding a large percentage of economic cost of injury and death resulting from highway and other accidents because the drunken drivers themselves, or people who voluntarily elect to ride with them, constitute a high percentage of the victims.

A Neglected Issue—Finally, there is a more subtle point to be made about who bears the costs of alcohol abuse. Chronic heavy drinkers incur high medical and disability costs, much of which is borne by third parties via social welfare programs and private insurance. However, it is also true that chronic heavy drinkers tend to die at younger ages, thereby sparing society the high medical and pension costs associated with old age. Indeed, it is not at all clear that a reduction in alcohol abuse would be a financial boon to the medical, old age, and disability payment systems, either government (Social Security) or private.

A Response—There are a number of responses to this liberal perspective. The most powerful one is based on the claim that alcohol abuse is often the result of consumers' being poorly informed about the consequences of chronic excessive consumption. Though such arguments have considerable weight, the basic question remains "which costs should be included in calculating the social costs of alcohol abuse?" If the accounting principle that only those costs borne collectively should be counted is deemed too simplistic, then what alternative principle is preferable? The estimates that are currently available and widely cited are not guided by any clearly stated principle and, hence, are of uncertain applicability.

CRITIQUE II: FOR PURPOSES OF INTERVENTION

The purpose of developing an estimate of the economic cost of alcohol abuse has been defined in different ways. The main use for the cost estimate in the Institute of Medicine's report (1980) was to demonstrate that federal funding for alcohol related research is disproportionately small compared to federal funding for cancer or heart or respiratory disease research because the ratio of research funding to total social cost was estimated to be relatively low for alcohol problems. In most other cases where an estimate of social cost is cited it is as one datum supporting a general argument that alcohol abuse is a serious problem deserving greater public concern and government attention.

As such, the cost estimate simply supplements statistics on alcohol related morbidity, mortality, etc.

There is a general belief among economists who have studied alcohol related problems that the most appropriate use of economic cost estimates is in the context of evaluating a specific, well-defined government action or program, rather than as a device for indicating the overall impact of alcohol abuse on society. Since there is no conceivable program that would eliminate the adverse consequences of alcohol abuse, there is no specific context in which estimates of total cost acquire meaning or have direct application. From this perspective, the correct procedure by which the Institute of Medicine could have made an economic case for increased funding for alcohol related research would have been to estimate the likely reduction in alcohol related costs resulting, for example, from an additional billion dollars of research funding in this area. This benefit could then be compared with likely gains from increased research funding in other health areas. Such estimates would obviously be subject to a great deal of uncertainty, but this type of marginal analysis has the great advantage of being conceptually correct and directly relevant to the problem at hand. Such economic analysis and evaluation have been made of two specific alcohol control policies, namely alcohol taxation and MLDA laws.

Alcohol Control Policies

In an era characterized by extensive government regulation of commerce, the alcoholic beverage industry is still exceptional for the comprehensiveness and stringency of federal, state, and local regulations. The current array of regulations reflects diverse objectives that include revenue collection, maintenance of an "orderly" trade in alcoholic beverages, and promotion of temperate drinking practices.

LEGACY OF PROHIBITION

Current public attitudes toward alcohol control policies continue to be heavily influenced by the legacy of the "Great Experiment." The modern-day conventional wisdom concerning Prohibition is that it was an unmitigated failure—a clear historical lesson that it is impossible to effectively "legislate morality." The truth is more complex. Clark Warburton (1932) demonstrated that consumption declined considerably, especially among the working class. The most reliable statistical indicators of alcohol abuse—mortality rates due to cirrhosis of the liver and to acute alcohol overdose—dropped dramatically during the early years of Prohibition and stayed at historically low levels until after Repeal. The alcohol control measures enacted during the 1930s were motivated in part by the hope of maintaining more temperate drinking practices while eliminating crime and public corruption engendered by Prohibition. But modern-day legislators, alcoholic beverage control administrators, and the public at large have been generally skeptical about the effect of regulation on the incidence, patterns, or circumstances of use.

FEDERAL AND STATE EFFORTS

The Twenty-first Amendment left primary responsibility for regulating alcoholic beverage commerce to the states. However, the federal government does play an important role in assessing taxes, suppressing illegal production, regulating advertising and labeling, and licensing manufacturers and importers. It also regulates sales on military reservations, where the drinking habits of millions of men and women are first established.

States establish the MLDA; impose excise taxes; and legislate restrictions on advertising, hours of legal sale, selling on credit, etc. Eighteen states opted in the 1930s to create a public monopoly over the wholesale and (except in Wyoming) retail trade in distilled spirits and, in most cases, some other types of alcoholic beverages as well. The remaining states have established alcoholic beverage control boards to license and regulate wholesale and retail dealers with an eye to the control of density and location of package stores and to the elimination of criminal elements in the business. In an effort to discourage practices that promote excessive drinking and rowdiness on the part of patrons, state and local governments have imposed a wide variety of regulations on the nature and operation of establishments that sell drinks.

During the 1960s and 1970s there was a marked trend toward more liberal controls on alcoholic beverage commerce. Restrictions on the place and time of legal sale were eased, the effective levels of tax rates were eroded by inflation, and minimum drinking ages were reduced in a majority of states. The policy pendulum appears to be swinging back, accompanied by a growing body of scientific evidence indicating that alcohol taxes, MLDA laws, and related controls are effective in reducing alcohol abuse and promoting public health.

Alcohol Taxation

Alcoholic beverages have long been singled out for special tax treatment. Indeed, a liquor excise in 1791 was the first internal revenue measure enacted by the U.S. Congress, which provoked Shay's Rebellion and was a severe test of the new federal government's powers. Alcohol tax revenues continued to figure prominently in federal tax collections until World War II and accounted for 80 percent of internal tax collections in 1907 and 10 percent in 1940. But times have changed. Federal alcohol tax revenues in recent years have been on the order of $6 billion—about 1 percent of total revenues. Taxes continue to have an important influence on the price of alcoholic beverages and are, therefore, an important determinant of alcohol availability to the consumer.

THE EFFECT OF ALCOHOL TAXES ON CONSUMPTION

In 1982, the retail price paid for a fifth of 80-proof liquor averaged $6.74; federal tax was $1.67 (25 percent), and state and local taxes were $1.28 (19 percent). Although taxes figure less prominently in the cost of beer and wine, they are not insignificant. The federal liquor tax was a much larger percentage of retail price in the 1950s and 1960s. Federal tax rates were last changed in 1951, when they were set at $10.50 per proof gallon for liquor, $.29 per gallon for beer, and between $.17 and $3.40 per gallon for wine depending on alcohol content and type. Since the overall price level for consumer items increased by a factor of 3.8 between 1951 and 1983, it is reasonable to say that this levy has been largely nullified by inflation. State and local tax rates have increased during this period, but they too have lagged behind inflation. Partly as a result of the declining real value of alcohol taxes, the prices of alcoholic beverages have trended sharply downward relative to the prices of other goods and services, especially during the inflationary period beginning in the mid–1960s. Between 1967 and 1983 the real price of alcoholic beverages, adjusted for overall inflation, declined 27 percent. Distilled spirits have led the way with a 48 percent decline in average price, followed by beer with a 25 percent fall and wine with a 19 percent reduction. The greatly increased availability of alcohol resulting from these reductions in relative price has the effect of promoting alcohol consumption and thereby increasing the incidence of alcohol related problems.

An increase in taxes on liquor or beer would cause an increase in the average price of these commodities, thereby inducing a reduction in alcohol consumption. More precisely, consumption would be less as a result of the tax increase than it would be without the increase. This result has been established quite conclusively by a number of econometric studies using data from the United States, Canada, and other countries. More important and controversial is the question of how taxes and prices influence the alcohol consumption of the heaviest drinkers. It is logically possible that the heaviest drinkers may be immune to economic incentives and that average consumption would fall as a result of a tax increase solely due to its effect on moderate drinkers. An argument supporting this possibility can be stated by the following chain of propositions: (1) a large portion of the heaviest drinkers are alcoholics in the sense that they are addicted to alcohol; (2) alcohol addicts will drink nearly the biological maximum every day with little regard for the cost of obtaining their drinks; (3) therefore, because the heaviest drinkers will not respond, it must be the more moderate drinkers who adapt their drinking practices to the price of alcoholic beverages.

This argument may seem plausible to many. In reply, an economist would point out that a price increase has greater economic impact on alcoholics, who may already be spending a third or more of their income on alcohol, than it would on moderate drinkers, and, if anything, this greater impact would be expected to yield a greater response in consumption behavior. Furthermore, there is considerable clinical evidence that alcohol consumption by alcoholics is responsive to experimental manipulations of the cost of a drink (Mello, 1972; Nathan and Lisman, 1976). In any event, this issue is better resolved through careful empirical analysis than through unsupported generalizations.

THE EFFECT OF ALCOHOL TAXES ON CIRRHOSIS MORTALITY

Statistics on the prevalence of chronically heavy drinking are not routinely available. However, there is a widely accepted proxy measure—the mortality rate due to cirrhosis of the liver. Liver cirrhosis death rates have provided the basis upon which nearly all alcoholism prevalence rates have been estimated.

Most people who die of liver cirrhosis, especially after age thirty, exhibit a history of chronically intense drinking. Schmidt (1977), for example, found that 80 percent of all cirrhosis deaths in Ontario were alcohol related. The typical victim of alcohol related cirrhosis has consumed an enormous amount of alcohol. Lelbach (1974) estimates that drinking approximately twenty-one ounces of 86-proof liquor every day for about twenty years yields a 50 percent chance of contracting liver cirrhosis in a primarily healthy subject weighing 150 pounds. Thus, for any individual there tends to be a long lag between the onset of heavy drinking and death from liver cirrhosis. This cirrhosis mortality rate, therefore, is not a direct indicator of the current proportion of alcoholics in a population, but it does give a good indication of the proportion who have been drinking heavily for a decade or two. It should be kept in mind that cirrhosis mortality rate is of interest in its own right, as well as being a proxy for the prevalence of alcoholism. Cirrhosis is one of the leading causes of death in the United States, Canada, and most European nations.

Using this statistical indicator of the prevalence of chronically excessive consumption, it is possible to explore the relationship between alcohol taxes and excessive drinking. A study of this relationship (Cook, 1981) was based on annual observations of thirty states for the fifteen-year period 1960–74. During this period there were thirty-eight instances in which one of these states increased its liquor tax by a substantial amount (more than $.24 per proof gallon). Each of these tax increases was viewed as a "test case" in a "natural experiment." For each of these test cases, the percentage change in the state's cirrhosis mortality rate was calculated. (The test statistic was defined as the difference in mortality rates between the three years following the tax increase and the three years prior to the tax increase, divided by the mortality rate around the time of the tax increase.) The

control groups for each of these test cases were the other states in
the corresponding years. The study found that states that raised
their liquor tax had a greater reduction or smaller increase in
cirrhosis mortality than other states in the corresponding year
(Table 1). Indeed, 63 percent of all test cases fell into the bottom
half of the distribution with respect to the test statistic—a result
that would occur by chance alone with probability .072—fairly
strong evidence that, at least in the short run, the tax increase
reduced the cirrhosis mortality rate.

TABLE 1. EFFECT OF STATE LIQUOR TAX INCREASES ON CIRRHOSIS MORTALITY
RATES, 1960–74

Number of Rank Order	Number of Test Cases	Percent of Test Cases
1–5	9 ⎫	
6–10	9 ⎬	63.2
11–15	6 ⎭	
16–20	3 ⎫	
21–25	9 ⎬	36.8
26–30	2 ⎭	

Source: Cook (1981)

Note: Each year during the sample period, the thirty states are rank ordered
with respect to percentage change in cirrhosis mortality. The state with the largest
reduction is ranked first. States that raised their taxes were usually at the low end
of this distribution in the year of the tax increase.

Why did 37 percent of the tax-increase states experience a relative *increase* in cirrhosis mortality? One interpretation is that
cirrhosis mortality fluctuates from year to year for a variety of
reasons besides changes in liquor prices. In some of the test cases,
these chance fluctuations happened to be positive and large enough
to more than compensate for the consumption-suppressing effect
of the tax increase. The fact that 63 percent of the states exhibited a relative reduction in cirrhosis mortality suggests that this
consumption effect does exist.

The Influence of Cirrhosis Trends—The principal challenge to
the validity of this interpretation is that a state legislature's decision to raise the tax is influenced, directly or indirectly, by
cirrhosis trends in the state. For example, if a sudden increase in

cirrhosis mortality led to a tax increase and was followed by a natural regression to the cirrhosis mortality trend, then the tax increase would be followed by a reduction in mortality but not cause it. This possibility was tested by Cook (1981) and in a subsequent study. The evidence from these tests does not support this principal challenge—tax increases apparently *are* largely exogenous.

A Further Test—Although this quasi-experimental approach to studying the effect of liquor taxes on heavy drinkers has the virtue of simplicity and ease of interpretation, it does not generate a usable estimate of the *magnitude* of the effect in question. Primarily for this reason, a subsequent study was undertaken (Cook and Tauchen, 1982) that applied an estimation technique (an analysis of covariance estimated by generalized least squares regression) to annual data from the same thirty states for the period of 1962–77. Preliminary to this estimation task, the annual state-level cirrhosis mortality data were refined; the variable was the age-adjusted mortality rate for state residents aged thirty and over. The tax variable in the regression was adjusted for inflation as measured by the consumer price index; and the results given here are converted to October 1981 dollars. The principal result showed that, other things equal, a $1.00 per proof gallon increase in a state's liquor tax will reduce the state's cirrhosis mortality rate by 1.9 percent in the short run. The 95 percent confidence interval for this estimated reduction is .4 percent to 3.5 percent; thus, this parameter estimate is statistically significant by the usual standards of social science. Further, this parameter estimate suggests that the tax effect is far from trivial.

Long-range Effects—Given the normally long lag between the onset of heavy drinking and death from cirrhosis, it may not be obvious how an increase in the liquor tax could cause an immediate reduction in cirrhosis mortality. This reduction is possible because the cirrhotic process is interruptible. When alcohol consumption stops, the liver ceases to deteriorate; if the rate of consumption slows, the deterioration process also slows. At any one time, there is a "reservoir" of people who are within one year of death from cirrhosis at their current rate of consumption. If some of them reduce their consumption in response to a tax increase, then not all will die in that year. Therefore, the mortality rate will decline the first year. In the long run, the mortality rate will gradually decline after the initial drop as the size of the "reservoir" gradually shrinks. The total effect of the tax increase will not be realized for many years. The ultimate reduction in mortality rate due to a tax increase will exceed the initial reduction. Thus the previous estimates actually underestimate the full effect.

In conclusion, there is considerable statistical evidence that a liquor tax increase causes an immediate and substantial reduction in cirrhosis mortality. If cirrhosis mortality rates are a reliable indicator of the prevalence of alcoholism, then it can be inferred that alcoholics' drinking habits are quite sensitive to the price of liquor.

THE EFFECT OF ALCOHOL TAXES ON AUTO FATALITIES

There is also some direct evidence that accident rates are responsive to changes in liquor taxation. The effect of state liquor tax increases on the automobile fatality rate was tested in a 1981 study (Cook) using the same sample and technique as in the cirrhosis study. Between 1960 and 1974, most states (twenty-five of thirty-eight) that increased their liquor tax experienced a below-average change in automobile fatality rates compared with states that did not increase their tax.

Unfortunately, there is no comparable evidence on the effect of beer prices on automobile fatalities. Beer is particularly important since it is the beverage choice of youths—the demographic group that is the greatest risk on the highways.

SUMMARY

Available evidence suggests that increases in alcoholic beverage taxes cause reductions in per capita consumption, consumption by chronically heavy drinkers, and the incidence of drunken driving. It seems safe to conclude that the sharp decline in alcohol prices during the last fifteen years has exacerbated alcohol related public health problems. Fortunately, there appear to have been countervailing forces at work during this period, such as increased societal emphasis on health and fitness, that have prevented a large increase in drinking. Indeed, adult per capita consumption has changed very little since 1970. If alcohol prices had kept pace with inflation, the per capita consumption would probably have declined rather substantially during this period.

EQUITY CONSIDERATIONS IN ALCOHOL BEVERAGE TAXATION

Alcohol control policies, including taxation, have been criticized by some as overly blunt instruments, reducing the enjoyment of the many for the sake of curtailing the alcohol related problems suffered by the relatively few. Gusfeld's (1976) image is that these policies fall "like sober rain from heaven upon the problem and problem-free drinkers alike." There are two comments to be made in response to this critique.

Problem-free Drinkers—First, much of the social cost of excessive drinking falls not only upon "the problem and problem-free drinkers alike" but also the abstainers. Private automobile and health insurance premiums and taxes to support government social insurance programs reflect, in part, the costly consequences of drinking. The drunken driver puts everyone at increased risk of injury or death on the highway. Thus, it can be argued that an *effective* alcohol control measure will indirectly benefit the "nonproblem" drinkers, as well as those who abstain, by reducing the collective costs generated by problem drinking.

Second, the incidence of the direct cost of alcohol control measures, such as taxation, is more or less proportional to the amount of alcohol an individual consumes. The "sober rain" falls on all drinkers but with much greater intensity on the chronically heavy drinkers than on others. As stated earlier, in the United States it is estimated that the 10 percent of the adult population who are the heaviest drinkers consume about 57 percent of all beverage alcohol sold each year. To the extent that alcohol taxes are proportional to ethanol content, this group of drinkers will also pay 57 percent of the taxes. Thus, the relatively small group of drinkers who have the highest incidence of alcohol related problems also pay the bulk of the alcohol taxes.

To summarize, alcohol taxes, if effective in reducing the costly consequences of excessive consumption, reduce the burden alcohol imposes on society at large. Furthermore, whether or not alcohol taxes are effective in reducing the costly consequences of excessive consumption, they do have the characteristic of exacting payment both in proportion to consumption and in rough proportion to the social costs generated by drinking. If drinkers should pay, at least in an actuarial sense, for the social costs related to their drinking, then the excise tax on alcohol receives fairly high marks for fulfilling this purpose.

Poor Households—A second equity issue concerns the burden imposed on poor households by alcohol taxes. Unlike the income tax, such taxes are not adjusted to the household's ability to pay. By a traditional measure, alcohol taxes appear regressive in the sense that middle-class families will spend a smaller percentage of their income on alcohol taxes than lower-class families. While this may be true in the aggregate, it is interesting to note that adults living in poor households are much more likely to characterize themselves in national surveys as abstainers than are adults in middle-class families. The proportion of adults who report moderate or heavy drinking styles increases markedly with family income.

It is certainly possible that an increase in alcohol taxes will actually prove beneficial to the children of heavy drinkers in poor families. For example, if a household's demand for alcoholic beverages is elastic (price elasticity greater than 1.0), an increase in price will cause a reduction in total expenditures on alcohol, thereby leaving more money for other expenditures. Certainly there are considerable differences among poor households with respect to price elasticity of demand. Available evidence suggests that the average household's demand for liquor is quite elastic, and the poor household's demand would tend to be more elastic than the higher income household's. Therefore, for some proportion of poor households, an increase in alcohol tax rates would reduce expenditures on alcoholic beverages. It is also quite possible that a tax-induced reduction in drinking by heavy drinking household heads will benefit other family members insofar as reduced drinking yields improved health and higher earnings.

EMPLOYMENT EFFECTS

The alcoholic beverage industry, broadly defined, employs over 800,000 full-time-equivalent workers. Any alcohol control measure that reduces total alcohol consumption may be faulted because of the reduction in industry employment that would inevitably follow reduction in sales. This prospect is especially troublesome in times of high national unemployment rates. However, economists do not accept the view that jobs eliminated from one industry due to industry-specific causes (increase in tax, change in consumer tastes, etc.) are lost to the national economy. Total United States employment is determined by macroeconomic factors, in particular, the aggregate demand for goods and services by government, consumers, and investors. Employment reductions in the alcoholic beverage industry caused by tax increases would ultimately result in employment increases elsewhere in the economy. For this reason it is not accurate to view employment reductions in this industry as a "social cost" of raising excise taxes. Of course there will be individuals associated with the industry, such as stockholders and some employees, who will be adversely affected by the tax increase. Many government policies cause changes in the distribution of wealth, and alcohol taxation is no exception.

CONCLUSION

Alcohol taxes are properly viewed as policy instruments that have a direct influence on public health. An increase in alcohol taxes may impose a burden on some poor families, but it may ultimately help others. In any event, the claim that alcohol taxes are highly inequitable or regressive is not defensible. Finally, while a tax increase would probably damage industry stockholders and some employees, it would not cause a net loss of employment in the economy.

These observations do not constitute a complete evaluation of an alcohol tax increase. However, the net current evidence indicates that an increase in alcoholic beverage taxes should lead to a decrease in alcohol related problems.

Minimum Legal Drinking Age

Every state prohibits the sale of alcoholic beverages to minors. The MLDA differs among states, but for a number of years no state has set this minimum at less than eighteen or more than twenty-one. The enactment in 1970 of the Twenty-sixth Amendment, which gave eighteen-year-olds the right to vote in federal elections, touched off a wave of legislated reductions in the MLDA; between 1970 and 1975, twenty-nine states lowered their minimums. Since 1975 the pattern has reversed, and a majority of states have raised their MLDAs. This reversal was partly the result of mounting evidence that earlier reductions had caused an increase in the number of highway accidents involving teenage drivers. One estimate, based on automobile fatality rates of young people for the period 1970–77, is that a reduction in MLDA from twenty-one to eighteen increases the automobile fatality rate of youths aged eighteen to twenty by about 7 percent (Cook and Tauchen, 1984). There is also evidence that even younger teenagers (aged sixteen to seventeen) are affected by a reduction in MLDA and that their fatality rate increases by approximately the same percentage. By 1975 the annual cost to the nation of the legislated reductions in MLDA was several hundred lives, a number of serious injuries, and substantial damage and loss. Several evaluations of the more recent increases in MLDA have demonstrated that they have been effective in reducing highway casualties.

An economist would quickly point out that raising the MLDA also imposes some cost on youthful drinkers—when barred from legally purchasing alcoholic beverages, it becomes more difficult for them to obtain drinks. That is presumably why the increased MLDA is effective in reducing drunken driving. Whether this cost should be countered in the evaluation of an increased MLDA depends upon one's view of whether or not eighteen-year-olds' preferences on this matter should be given consideration. If the answer is affirmative, then an estimate of the magnitude of the cost involved is relevant. An illustration can be found in a recent study by Barbara Weinstein (1983) that estimates how much a youth would be willing to pay, on the average, for the right to drink legally. Her study examined the effect of beer taxes and the MLDA on beer consumption by youths. She found that for the relevant age group, increasing the MLDA has an effect on consumption equivalent to raising the tax by a certain amount. From these findings she was able to indirectly derive the cost to this group of an increase in MLDA. She compared the total of such costs to the number of lives saved by the MLDA increase. Her conclusion is that each life "costs" about $150,000, which is very "cheap" compared to other health and safety legislation.

Of the various types of alcohol control policies, the MLDA is unique in several respects. It has been subjected to numerous evaluations; these evaluations are nearly unanimous that the MLDA is effective in reducing drunken driving; and state legislators and the public at large have been persuaded of its effectiveness.

Concluding Thoughts

Public discourse on the "alcohol problem" has for several decades been dominated by the alcoholism perspective, which focuses both on individual victims and on those at risk of becoming victims of alcohol's addictive properties. The appropriate response from this perspective is public education coupled with individual counseling and medical assistance. An alternative perspective places greater emphasis on alcohol itself, rather than the individual drinker, and suggests a focus on regulation of alcoholic beverage availability as a means of reducing abuse. This perspective is paradoxically both older and newer than the alcoholism perspective; it characterized the thinking of temperance advocates before and during the early part of this century, the alcohol control advocates of the 1930s who were responsible for the creation of state regulatory systems following Repeal, and the resurgent advocates of more stringent controls (sometimes incorrectly labeled "neoprohibitionists") who are largely oriented by the public health viewpoint. Alcohol control policies attempt to intervene in and modify the outcome generated by a free market in alcoholic beverages, and it is appropriate for such policies to be subjected to economic analysis and evaluation. Indeed, economists have contributed substantially both to developing the rationale for such market interventions and to evaluating the likely effectiveness and desirability of particular interventions. This chapter has focused particularly on alcohol taxation and the minimum legal drinking age, two policy instruments that frequently appear on state and federal political agenda. While both of these instruments impose some costs on some drinkers, their potential benefits in reducing alcohol abuse and alcoholism are well documented and impressively large.

John Kaplan, LL.B.

4

Alcohol, Law Enforcement, and Criminal Justice

Alcohol and the Law

Several areas of the law impinge on alcohol use and alcoholism. Certainly the criminal law does not exhaust the areas where the law affects alcohol use and abuse. In fact, it can be argued that regulatory and tax policies have much greater an effect upon the course of alcoholism and its related problems in American society. These issues are dealt with at length elsewhere in this volume. Regulatory policy is generally aimed at lowering the availability of alcohol either to the general public or to certain segments of the population that are deemed especially vulnerable. These regulatory policies include restrictions on the sale of alcohol to young people (though the relevant age varies from state to state), laws preventing alcohol from being sold on certain days or hours of the day, laws regulating the number of alcohol outlets and sale by the drink, and laws attempting to guarantee that beverages are not sold to those already intoxicated.

JOHN KAPLAN *is the Jackson Eli Reynolds Professor of Law at Stanford University. Professor Kaplan is the noted author of ten books, including the recently published* The Hardest Drug: Heroin and Public Policy. *He served for four years as a member of the National Advisory Commission of the National Institute on Alcohol Abuse and Alcoholism.*

These laws are often enforced through a regulatory mechanism, through attempting to ensure that those who sell alcohol are of good moral character, and through the use of civil liability in cases of accidents or the like.

As a matter of theory one can argue that restrictions on the availability of alcohol, either to the population as a whole or to any group, should lessen the total problems related to alcoholism. However, very little effort has gone into determining how improvement in the design of the United States regulatory system or effective restrictions on alcohol availability would diminish the burden of cost that alcohol imposes.

Alcohol and Criminal Law

The many-faceted problems of alcoholism present two major issues that fall into the realm of criminal justice policy. The first relates to the criminal responsibility of those whose alcohol use was causally related to the commission of a crime—if they had not been drinking, they would have not committed it. The second involves the proper legal and social response to those situations where alcohol use or abuse is partly the essence of prohibited behavior.

Though the relationship between alcohol and crime is a complicated one, there is good reason to believe that alcohol use is a major causal factor in a wide variety of criminal behavior; for instance, a number of studies have derived impressive figures relating alcohol use to homicide. No study since has summarized data any better than the 1967 *Task Force Report: Drunkenness* of the President's Commission on Law Enforcement and Administration of Justice.

Homicide . . . is an alcohol-related crime. . . . Shupe (1954) in an Ohio study found 43 percent of the homicide offenders had been drinking. Spain et al. (1951) found 87 percent of a small sample of homicide offenders had been drinking. The most comprehensive study of homicides is that by Wolfgang (1958: see also Wolfgang and Strohm, 1956). Among 588 Philadelphia cases alcohol was *absent* from both victim and offender in only 36 percent of the cases. In 9 percent of the cases alcohol was present in the victim only; in 11 percent of the cases it was present in the offender only. In 44 percent of the cases it was present in *both* the victim and offender. Consequently in 64 percent of the homicide cases alcohol was a factor; and in the majority of these alcohol was present in both parties to the crime.

A recent National Academy of Sciences study has estimated that alcohol is involved in 49 to 70 percent of homicides. Alcohol has not only been implicated in general homicide statistics, but also in the type of murder weapon as well. A study by Professor Marvin E. Wolfgang furnishes valuable data on this subject. On the basis of an analysis of every criminal homicide in Philadelphia, 588 cases from 1948 to 1952, Wolfgang concludes:

> There is a significant association between alcohol in the homicide situation and the method of inflicting death. More stabbings occurred with alcohol present during the act of homicide than did any other assault method. Of 228 stabbings, 72 percent involved the presence of alcohol. Beating by fist, feet, or blunt instrument ranked second, for of 128 cases 69 percent revealed alcohol in the situation. The 194 shootings and 38 slayings by miscellaneous methods yielded no [statistically significant] association with alcohol, for only 55 percent of the former and 45 percent of the latter involved the presence of alcohol.

Professor Wolfgang is careful to caution against construing the relationships he reports as causal connections suggesting that "significant relationships only point a finger of inference at the presence of alcohol as a cause." In a more recent publication he suggests mechanisms that are consistent at least with a causal hypothesis. He states, for example, that "in considering the distribution of passionate murders, it should also be remembered that alcohol functions to release emotions and lower cortical control over manifestations of anger." In another passage, he reports that "alcoholism, whenever it reaches chronic pathological levels, can cause homicide through its violent motor outbursts or through its persecutory or jealousy delusional components."

If it is true that alcohol acts to release impulses and lower inhibitions that restrain individuals from aggressive behavior, it would be peculiar if such aggression manifested itself in homicidal crime only. Of course, this is not the case. Between March and October of 1959, a total of 2,324 new inmates in California's state penitentiaries were interviewed. Of these, 29 percent had been intoxicated at the time of their arrest. Even more significant is the fact that over 60 percent of those involved in crimes of great personal risk (aggravated assault, sexual crimes, etc.) had been drinking prior to the commission of the crime.

In another study, conducted by L. M. Shupe (1954), a chemist associated with the police department of Columbus, Ohio, this view is also supported. Shupe reports the urine-alcohol concentration of 882 persons arrested either during or immediately following the commission of a felony. Only 27 percent of this total showed no alcohol whatsoever; by comparison, 17 percent of those arrested for the thirty homicide offenses in the sample showed no alcohol. Moreover, Shupe found that alcohol was present more often in crimes of violence and less often in offenses against property that require a higher level of skill (e.g., 92 percent of knifings and concealed weapons arrests versus 60 percent of the forgery arrests). While this research is by no means conclusive, it is, nevertheless, highly suggestive since its results are typical of a large number of other studies.

Research has also been performed to establish the relationship of alcohol to sexual offenses. In a study published in 1940, Selling examined one hundred male sex offenders and reported that 8 percent were chronic alcoholics and 35 percent of them had been under the influence of alcohol at the time of the offense. While the fact that almost every member of this 35 percent blamed his crime upon alcohol is not probative, the fact that more than a third of them committed their offenses while intoxicated remains impressive. Similar results were obtained in England by Cruz in a study of sexual delinquents. Almost half of them were described as "constant" drinkers, and nearly a fifth were drunk at the time of their offense. While causality in all these areas is notoriously difficult to disentangle, alcohol abuse is undeniably a predictive factor in violent crime, and there are good reasons to believe it is a causal factor as well.

While some connection between alcohol use and crime is clear, the posture of criminal law toward the matter is less certain. Although the difference between alcoholism and alcohol use—or even occasional overuse—is extremely important for medical purposes, this distinction plays a relatively small part in the most important dilemma of criminal law—criminal responsibility. Indeed, the concept of alcoholism itself may be directly relevant only in rather small areas of criminal law—but insofar as alcoholism is obviously related to alcohol use on particular occasions, it bears an important relation to criminal law.

SPECIFIED ACTS

To understand the relationship between alcohol use and criminal responsibility, one must appreciate the overall structure of substantive criminal law. Criminal law typically is concerned with specified, illegal acts. Unlike other legal systems that often define status or conditions as subject to criminal sanction, the Anglo-American tradition focuses much more on narrow segments of behavior. Thus, rather than declaring the status of being a counterrevolutionary or a parasite as criminal, it typically provides punishment for behavior such as theft (the *act* of taking someone's property) and homicide (the commission of an *act* that results in death).

The requirement of an *act* in criminal law is not adhered to merely on the grounds of tradition. There are two major advantages in enforcing such a requirement. First, an act is generally easier to define than a status. Indeed, a classic Supreme Court case held a statute to be unconstitutionally vague when the statute declared it a crime to be a "gangster." Second, the requirement of an act gives citizens notice of precisely where the line is drawn so that they can avoid involvement with the most coercive institution of the state by simply not engaging in the prohibited conduct. For this reason, the narrower the conduct circumscribed, the greater the ambit of their autonomy.

BLAMEWORTHINESS

Though it is a necessary ingredient of virtually any crime, an act alone is not sufficient. Many acts are undertaken that cause social damage but, nonetheless, do not violate criminal law. For example, an individual, although driving carefully, may kill a child who darts out between two parked cars and into his path; or someone may accidentally take someone else's umbrella instead of her own after dining at a restaurant. In both these cases, the acts of killing or taking someone else's property are not sufficient for the attribution of criminal liability. Because criminal law has a strong moral base, it requires that the act charged be committed with a blameworthy state of mind. This requirement is extremely important since, like the requirement of an act, it helps to draw the line between the autonomy of the individual and the coercive power of the government. As a first approximation, it can be said that government intervention through criminal law—which carries with it not only moral condemnation but also sanctions of fine and/or imprisonment or, conceivably, even the death penalty —is inappropriate unless the accused can be convicted of a crime involving a blameworthy mental state.

Typically the mental states to which blameworthiness can attach are divided into four categories. The first category is purpose, the conscious object of the accused to commit an act or bring about a result that the law forbids. Second, there is the category of knowledge—the accused must have known, with a substantial certainty, that a forbidden result would occur, even if it were not desired. Third, there is recklessness, probably the most confusing of the blameworthy mental states. The accused is reckless with respect to a result when, even though it is neither desired nor known that an illegal result *will* occur, the accused apprehends that it *may* occur. In other words, the risk in the action is recognized and the action proceeds nonetheless.

The final blameworthy mental state is that of negligence. There is considerable argument as to whether or not the state is, in fact, morally blameworthy. Negligence occurs when the accused takes an action that involves an unjustifiable risk of forbidden result, even though the accused may not appreciate the risk. The important aspect of negligence is that the accused committed an act that was unreasonable since it involved a serious enough risk of a forbidden result, even though the accused may not have appreciated the dangerousness of the behavior at all. Moreover, under the circumstances, the behavior of the accused must be not merely less than could be expected of a reasonable person, but *considerably* less. In other words, to be criminally negligent, one must act not only stupidly, but very stupidly.

To determine criminal responsibility, the questions that the law asks are, as a first approximation, relatively simple. It asks merely whether or not the defendant performed the forbidden act and whether or not it was done in a state of mind that the legislature has deemed appropriate for the commission of the crime. Thus, if an individual were so drunk that he/she did not know he/she was aiming a gun at somebody, or that in shooting he/she was killing a human being, he/she could not be convicted of a crime requiring such knowledge. Similarly, if the defendant were so obtuse that he/she could not apprehend a risk which a reasonably perceptive person would have noted, he/she would not possess that appreciation of the risk which the definition of recklessness requires. In either case, however, the defendant could be convicted of a lesser crime requiring only negligence.

With respect to crimes involving recklessness, however, there are two theories under which a defendant, intoxicated at the time of a criminal act and hence not appreciating the risk, still may be convicted. Many jurisdictions hold—and juries are notoriously willing to accept—the view that someone who gets so drunk that the ability to apprehend the kind of risk that sober people recognize is lost is still committing a reckless act simply by getting drunk. Of course, in order to be truly reckless, the defendant would have had to disregard the risk that by getting drunk a chain of behavior might ensue resulting in the commission of a harm that the law has sought to prevent. Nonetheless, such a state of mind is conceivable, and, presumably, juries are willing to find it in some cases since they feel that getting drunk provides the kind of blameworthiness that is a moral requisite for criminal punishment.

The second, more direct, approach is simply to say—as has the Model Penal Code—that if, because of intoxication, the defendant does not appreciate a risk which would have been appreciated if in a sober state, the defendant may still be charged with that appreciation—even though it was not there. This avoids the difficult fact-finding issue as to whether or not someone about to get drunk could have anticipated the actual occurrence of the kind of situation in which intoxication later caused a failure to perceive the risk. This is probably more forthright than artificially creating a sense of risk in the defendant's mind that probably was not there. On the other hand, whenever punishment is administered for consciously disregarding a risk that was not appreciated or recognized, it is a departure from the general view that there is extra culpability attached when one in fact does appreciate a risk in conduct, but proceeds anyway. In a sense, making an exception for drunkenness treats it as an aggravating factor, whereas in most other areas of the law, it is either treated as irrelevant or a mitigation.

However, the disarray that characterizes these views toward recklessness is not repeated in the law's views toward negligence. Negligence involves an objective standard requiring no subjective appreciation of risk. The only issue is: should the person who is drunk be judged by the standard of a reasonable person or be held to a lower standard because of drunkenness? The courts have virtually unanimously rejected the standard of the "reasonable drunk" and have held that no account is to be taken of the defendant's intoxication. The sole question is: has the defendant met the standard that the law requires of a reasonable and sober person?

VOLITIONAL ELEMENTS

These relatively simple (by legal standards) rules, however, by no means capture the complexity of the relationship between drunkenness and criminal law. In addition to the cognitive elements in the concept of blameworthiness, there are volitional elements to consider. It is known—or at least believed—that, at any given level of cognition, inhibitions are lowered by alcohol; that is, an act may be committed by a drunken person which the same person would not have done if sober. In other words, even when an act was committed with the required knowledge or appreciation of the risk, a person might "not have been himself" at the time.

That is not to say that punishment under such circumstances is punishment for drunkenness rather than for the crime. An individual is not being punished merely for drunkenness when punished for committing a crime while drunk, even though it is admitted that the criminal act would not have been committed had sobriety reigned. A crime may have *many* causes, without any *one* of which it would not have occurred. A person might commit a crime because of anger, because of a sleepless night, or because of indigestion. Although the crime would not have happened had such conditions not been present, punishment, nonetheless, is for the commission of a crime.

However, it must be recognized that, regardless of alcohol's pharmacological effects and its effects in other cultures, in our culture, alcohol seemingly releases inhibitions in certain individuals. So long as this release is traced to a drug rather than a quality inherent in the individual, it is more difficult to blame the individual for the ensuing behavior. And, even if the individual properly can be blamed for the act of getting drunk, it typically will be regarded as a relatively venial offense, although the act for which criminal punishment is sought may be very serious.

Society's ambivalence about whether or not drunkenness is an aggravating factor or a mitigating one is probably caused by the extreme tension between the utilitarian desire to suppress dangerous behavior and the moral requirement of blameworthiness as a necessary condition of guilt. On utilitarian considerations, it is likely that involvement of alcohol is an aggravating factor since alcoholic behavior tends to be compulsive and repeated. Indeed, in addition to prior criminality and other such variables, alcohol use is one of the predictors of dangerousness that may be an important deciding factor when considering the extension of sentences for convicted criminals.

On the other hand, as noted before, society regards behavior performed under the influence of alcohol as more understandable and, under certain conditions, less blameworthy than behavior with no such "excuse." Certain legal systems have reacted to this, and crimes committed under the influence of alcohol are "excused" to the extent that those deemed to have been caused by the defendant's intoxication typically are provided with lesser sentences (e.g., in Spain, sentences are halved).

In considering the effects of drunkenness upon an individual's criminality, it has been assumed that drunkenness should be regarded as "voluntary." The problems of criminal responsibility are equally complex when drunkenness is, for some reason, involuntary. In such a case, blameworthiness cannot be attached to the act of getting drunk. The prototypical involuntary drunkenness case involves an extremely rare—indeed freakish—situation in which a defendant was consuming alcohol unwittingly because its taste had been disguised. In theory, the same problem would be raised when alcohol is administered to people against their will by physical force.

The term "involuntary" does not mean quite what one might think. Intoxication by an alcoholic, even one clinically addicted to alcohol, is not generally classified as "involuntary." Although the law is not clear on this topic because of the relative dearth of cases, it is assumed that someone who would not have committed a crime but for involuntary intoxication would not be a proper subject for criminal sanction, in spite of possessing the knowledge or purpose necessary for the crime. Though the formulations are different, this defense, cutting across all other rules in the criminal law, can be likened to the insanity defense. And, just like the insanity defense, it can raise thorny issues. Though the decisions are not by any means clear on the matter, it may be that the defendant should not be exculpated even when involuntary intoxication is a cause of the crime—any more than when insanity is a cause—unless the defendant's condition meets other requirements of the law.

As far as insanity is concerned, the crucial requirement in most jurisdictions is that the defendant's mental condition must deprive him or her of the ability to discern the difference between right and wrong. With respect to intoxication, however, when it is believed that the drug affects volition more than cognition, framing of a standard raises even more difficulties. Already, efforts to expand the insanity defense to cover volitional defects, such as the irresistible-impulse test or the ALI test (which requires that the accused "lack" substantial capacity to conform his or her conduct to the law), have produced serious difficulties. It is far easier to receive testimony on the issue of the cognition of the defendant than on the ability to control impulses. Operationally, there seems to be no difference between an irresistible impulse and an unresisted one.

By far the most difficult problem involving involuntary intoxication, however, is whether or not to consider drinking by alcohol addicts voluntary behavior. Application of the medical model to alcoholism would seem to require that, in this respect, the actions of alcoholics be treated no differently from those of the mentally ill, who are, in a large category of cases, beneficiaries of the insanity defense. Perhaps simply because of the huge number of alcoholics and perhaps because the courts are unwilling to distinguish alcohol addiction from heroin addiction, there has been virtual unanimity among courts that an alcohol addict's alcohol consumption is "voluntary."

Public Intoxication

In addition to the issues of criminal responsibility that alcohol use raises, a separate set of problems appears because efforts to prevent certain kinds of misbehavior involving alcohol use have placed an enormous strain on our criminal justice system. Perhaps this stress was at its greatest during Prohibition, when an effort was made to enforce laws against the production and marketing of alcohol. Today, it is the problem of public intoxication that places a substantial strain upon our criminal justice resources.

It is not known what percentage of the approximately 10.8 million arrests are due to public intoxication. While nationwide figures are out-of-date, in the late 1960s the matter was studied carefully by the President's Commission on Crime and Criminal Justice. Public drunkenness then represented a massive drain on law enforcement resources and an area where the criminal law seemed to do virtually no good for either its subjects or society. States handle these cases under differing laws. What is called "public drunkenness" in one state is called "vagrancy" in another and "disorderly conduct" in a third. Nonetheless, there is reason to believe that 2 million arrests a year are the direct result of alcohol abuse. For instance, in the city of Los Angeles, it is known that over 50,000 arrests per year are made for public drunkenness.

Numerous authors have expounded on both the expense and inhumanity of the "revolving door process" that characterizes the treatment of public drunkenness. A number of jurisdictions have attempted to provide a more public health oriented approach, but often this has failed to receive sufficient public support. Some of those concerned with the problem have turned to the courts for aid. At this writing, the California Supreme Court is considering —in the famous Sundance case—the appeal of an effort to declare the public drunkenness laws of California unconstitutional.

Interestingly, the National Academy of Sciences recently reported that neither the public drunkenness laws nor their replacements have been shown to have any effect on the health or human problems of those involved in public intoxication. Probably the most significant finding of this report was that public drunkenness was, in great part, an aesthetic problem that might be solved best by allowing places that are "inconspicuous and out of public view" for those who prefer to be drunk. The one thing that becomes clear from all the studies in this area—and, indeed, from the cases discussing the problem—is that public inebriates, particularly long-term public inebriates, are a matter far from the competence of criminal law.

There are indications today that the drain caused by public

drunkenness upon criminal justice resources has considerably diminished. Part of the reason for this change may be the vastly greater rate of more serious crimes that has caused public inebriates simply to be ignored by overworked police officers; part may be the impact of new efforts to treat public drunkenness more humanely outside of the criminal justice system; and, finally, part may be that many police and public officials have decided that, except when interfering with business, residential neighborhoods, or some public aesthetic, it is better to simply ignore the public drunk.

Drunken Driving

Another area where attempts to cope with a direct approach to alcohol use have placed great stress on criminal law is that of drunken driving. Here, demands for action are far more urgent. Although drunken driving is only one of the many kinds of dangerous behaviors which overburden U.S. courts and jails, it still is a very substantial one. In some European countries, particularly those in Scandinavia, drunken driving is the greatest burden on the criminal justice system.

The serious problem of drunken driving is discussed in more detail in another chapter. For this chapter's purpose, the problem appears as the cost and inefficiency of criminal law in this area. Part of the problem is the sheer number of offenders from all segments of society who pose a very serious threat to the lives and safety of the population. Indeed, by most computations, drunken driving accounts for at least as many deaths as intentional homicide. Indeed, with 1.5 million arrests per year, drunken driving dwarfs any of the less directly alcoholic offenses except for larceny, which it still overshadows by 25 percent.

There are several reasons why criminal law does not function well in the case of drunken driving. First of all, the number of drunken drivers on the road at any one time is so large that the chances of anyone's apprehension or involvement in an accident from a single episode of drunken driving are very small (between 1 in 1,000 and 1 in 2,000). As a result, many people do not regard the threat of legal punishment for this behavior to be significant enough to deter it.

Second, when one thinks that a serious accident would involve a more serious injury than the law would impose, it becomes reasonable to assume that those who are undeterred by the threat of personal injury also would be undeterred by the threat of criminal sanctions. In a sense, this is understandable because drunken driving laws must generally exert their deterrent effect upon those who are already intoxicated and, hence, the least likely to make the precise calculations of costs and benefits that the law would like them to consider.

Nor is isolation particularly effective with respect to drunken drivers, although, along with deterrence, it is the major mechanism by which criminal law exerts its function. Although the cases that are most likely to be circulated involve multiple publicized offenses of drunken driving over a long period and although alcoholics and problem drinkers are overrepresented among drunken drivers, the majority of drunken driving episodes appear to be committed by social drinkers—who vastly outnumber the problem drinkers and alcoholics. To try to promote safety on the road by locking them up would cause a staggering expense simply because of their enormous numbers.

Conclusion

When the problem of alcohol and its overuse has such impact on the criminal justice system, there is danger in regarding this manifestation as the most serious problem. In fact, those aspects of alcohol and alcohol's relation to criminality and its costs to the criminal justice system are only two of many consequences that this broad social and medical problem has for our society. Moreover, probably the most careful summation of the alcohol problem would indicate that criminal law has relatively little influence even on damages that alcohol related criminality causes. If for some reason the problem of alcoholism and problem drinking diminishes, as it has at various times in U.S. history, then the impact of behaviors that criminal law attempts to cope with will be lessened. Until then, criminal law cannot be looked upon as more than a palliative—and an inefficient, expensive, and not very effective one at that.

Robert G. Niven, M.D.

5

Alcohol and the Family

Introduction

The use of alcohol, the most readily available psychoactive drug other than caffeine, is an issue which affects virtually every family in modern industrialized society. Recent Gallup Poll data indicate that alcohol abuse is perceived as a growing threat to the family, a sentiment echoed by many health care professionals. This poll revealed that one-third of the persons interviewed felt that alcohol related problems had adversely affected their own families.

Combining these individual concerns with the widespread availability, use, and promotion of alcoholic beverages, and with escalating evidence of the adverse personal, economic, and societal costs associated with inappropriate or excessive alcohol use has led many groups and individuals to demand a reexamination of societal policies governing alcohol use and its attendant problems. Since the family is the basic unit of all societies, any threat of this magnitude must be examined seriously and effective steps taken to understand, characterize, and deal with it.

ROBERT G. NIVEN *is the director of the National Institute on Alcohol Abuse and Alcoholism. Formerly, he was a psychiatrist on the staff of the Mayo Clinic and served as director of the clinic's Adolescent Alcohol and Drug Abuse Service. Dr. Niven is a member of a number of medical associations and has written numerous articles in prestigious journals.*

This chapter will review four of the major ways in which alcohol has a direct and adverse effect on family life. It also will summarize some of the minor or less direct, but still important, alcohol related issues that face today's families. This chapter will focus on a descriptive overview of the various problems based on current research findings, and this will be followed by a listing of the more important research questions needing further study. Finally, important public policy questions derived from this review will be outlined.

It is important to note that there are numerous variables—age, sex, race, ethnicity, economic status, etc.—that affect the type, amount, pattern, and consequences of alcohol consumption. These variables, which cannot be addressed in this overview, are nonetheless very important from the perspective of prevention, treatment, and research. In addition, much of what can be said about the adverse effects of alcohol on the family applies also to the impact of other psychoactive drugs—a very important fact for prevention and treatment programs.

Scope of the Problem

In order to understand the impact alcohol has on the family, it is important to gain a general understanding of the extent of alcohol use, abuse, and dependence in American society. The following general data, therefore, should be considered.

1. According to the most recent survey of alcohol consumption patterns, in the United States, 2.81 gallons of alcohol are consumed per year per person aged fifteen or older.
2. Approximately 75 percent of males and 60 percent of females drink alcoholic beverages.
3. Of the total adult population, approximately 33 percent are abstainers, another third are light to moderate drinkers, and the remaining third are classified as heavy drinkers, consuming two or more drinks per day.
4. Of all high school seniors, 90 percent have tried alcohol, and 40 percent of male and 25 percent of female high school seniors report drinking every week. In addition, 25 percent of male and 10 percent of female high school seniors are considered heavy weekly drinkers.
5. The average age of first alcohol use reported by high school students who drink is 13.2 years.
6. Children under the age of six begin to form attitudes and opinions about alcohol and can recognize alcohol related media messages.

7. Users of alcohol are more likely to be smokers and to use other psycho-active drugs than are nondrinkers, and the more alcohol consumed, the stronger is the correlation with other drug use.

8. Symptoms of loss of control or dependence on alcohol are reported by 7 to 15 percent of adult males and 3 to 6 percent of adult females.

9. The economic cost to society of alcohol related problems is difficult to estimate with precision. In 1977 the annual cost was estimated to be almost $50 billion. Recent estimates of such costs, however, suggest that they may be in excess of $86 billion per year.

10. Excessive or inappropriate alcohol use, positively correlated with an estimated 61,000 to 97,000 deaths and over 200,000 injuries per year in the United States, is a major contributor to lost productivity.

11. More than 5,000 major American corporations have prevention, referral, and/or treatment programs for employees and their dependents with alcohol related problems.

Alcohol Related Accidents

Accidental injury and death are two major ways in which alcohol related physical trauma affects families. Since the issues surrounding alcohol related accidents will also be considered elsewhere in this volume, they will only be summarized here. Alcohol is implicated as a significant contributor to a wide variety of accidents resulting in the injury, disability, or death of over 200,000 persons annually, as well as the cause of immeasurable psychological trauma to their loved ones. Perhaps between 33 and 50 percent of adult Americans involved in major accidents, various types of crimes, and suicides had been drinking alcohol shortly before the event. While the specific contribution of alcohol to the accident is not often clearly defined, the vast majority of studies clearly show a positive correlation of alcohol to the event. In a recent representative study, it was shown that positive blood alcohol levels were present in 32 percent of suicides, 42 percent of homicides, and 61 percent of drownings. A substantial portion of these victims had blood alcohol levels that were at or above legally intoxicated levels at the time of their death (a level generally defined as blood alcohol content of over 0.10 percent). For example, 85 percent of the victims of falls, 85 percent of the victims of fires, and 64 percent of the victims of homicide had blood alcohol levels in the legally intoxicated range.

Other studies have shown alcohol to be involved in from 9 to 40 percent of industrial accident fatalities, from 1 to 63 percent of ✗ aviation accident fatalities, and from 4 to 83 percent of drownings. A similar range of alcohol involvement is usually found for non-fatal accidents. The involvement of alcohol in traffic accidents is one of the better studied issues, but even in this area knowledge is based on incomplete information. The issue has been studied from the standpoint of both fatal and nonfatal outcome and from those of drivers, passengers, and pedestrians. Numerous accident related variables also have been studied.

Depending upon the type of accident studied, the range of alcohol involvement may vary from 16 to 82 percent. The National Institute on Alcohol Abuse and Alcoholism (NIAAA) conducts specific analyses of the data from the Fatal Accident Reporting System (FARS), a national surveillance system of all fatal traffic collisions occurring in the United States. These data reveal alcohol use to be implicated in a large number of fatal collisions. The more severe the accident, the greater the probability that alcohol is involved. Based on currently available information, a reasonably accurate and commonly quoted estimate is that about 50 percent of all fatal automobile accidents are associated with alcohol. Examination of this data, focused particularly on youth and young adults, convincingly documents that these age groups are involved disproportionately in fatal alcohol related motor vehicle accidents. Additionally, and less well known, between 33 and 50 percent of pedestrians killed by automobiles have positive blood alcohol levels.

Evaluating the causal role that alcohol plays in some of these events is a difficult challenge. Most of the studies can only point to a statistical association and cannot definitively delineate a causal role for alcohol. Critics of these statistics maintain that many of the studies do not include comparison groups, do not use well-defined or measured variables, and tend to ignore the situational context of the event being reported. The NIAAA notes:

> The same studies are cited by those who want to enhance alcohol's role in serious events and by the studies' critics who want to minimize its role. The fact that these same studies can be used either to enhance or to minimize and question alcohol involvement is primarily because most of the research in these areas does not, and in some cases cannot, conform to the standards of the epidemiologic tradition in which it is rooted. In particular, it has been difficult to find appropriate control groups for events that are sudden, violent, and in many cases improbable.

Regardless of the precise contribution alcohol makes to these events, there can be little doubt that these untoward and tragic occurrences have a substantially adverse impact on family structure and function. The death or serious disability of a breadwinner can have a devastating influence on the economic well-being of the family unit. Continuing chronic disability can cause a heavy strain on the mental and emotional well-being of the victim and other family members. Yet a greater understanding of the implications of this trauma for the family remains elusive because research findings are largely anecdotal and less than ideal.

It is clear that a more complete understanding of the prevalence of alcohol related accidents of all types and the causal role that alcohol plays in each is necessary. Enhanced understanding of the nature and extent of the cognitive impairment associated with alcohol consumption and its influential variables is critical to development of successful prevention, early intervention, and treatment programs. Studies on the impact of new or changing laws and other implemented public policy devices are necessary to determine their effectiveness in minimizing alcohol related problems. Such data are essential to identification, implementation, and maintenance of effective long-term prevention, intervention, and treatment strategies and social policies.

The primary public policy issue regarding alcohol and accidents concerns the public's right to protection from the drunken driver. A related issue involves which costs of dealing with the drunken driver should be borne by society and which by the individual responsible. The outcome of these research efforts and considerations of public policy will be important in the design of laws and policies that govern alcohol use by those responsible for public safety, such as firefighters, police, and railroad engineers.

Genetics and Alcoholism

Over the years, one of the most debated issues in the alcohol field has been the role of inheritance. Does it play an important part in the development of alcoholism? If so, what are the predisposing factors? To what extent do environmental influences determine the expression and severity of the disorder? An answer to these questions began to emerge in the early 1970s. Impressive evidence now indicates that inheritable factors influence susceptibility to alcoholism as well as to a number of physiological and biochemical responses to alcohol consumption. Furthermore, research has documented that environmental and hereditary factors interact to produce the alcoholic condition in some individuals.

For centuries it was believed that alcoholism runs in families, although most early reports were primarily anecdotal. The most striking finding in a 1979 review of a large number of family studies was that, regardless of the nature of the comparison population, alcoholics were more likely than nonalcoholics to have an alcoholic father, mother, sibling, or distant relative. On an average, almost 33 percent of any sample of alcoholics had at least one parent with an alcoholism problem. Alcoholic patients were six times more likely than nonpsychiatric patients and twice as likely as psychiatric patients to report parental alcoholism. Thus the high rate of parental alcoholism appeared to be a specific correlate of alcoholism and not a general characteristic of a disturbed population. Alcoholism was reported to be more prevalent in male relatives, in families of female alcoholics, and in near relatives rather than in distant ones.

The results of family studies do not unequivocally support genetic transmission. A family shares a common environment as well as common genes, and familial patterns of alcoholism can be explained just as readily by behavioral and sociocultural theories as by genetic ones. Although evidence in support of environmental theories is more tenuous, environmental factors cannot be ignored. Some family studies have shown that at least 45 percent of the alcoholic subjects did not have an alcoholic parent or other relative. This suggests that environmental factors influence the expression and severity of the disorder for many individuals. To separate the influence of heredity from that of environment, studies have been undertaken with special populations in which the influence of either heredity or environment differs. These special populations include identical and fraternal twins, half-siblings, and adoptees. From key studies over the past ten years, a number of significant findings have emerged, and some observations have been replicated more than once. Other conclusions have emerged from analyses possible with only certain studies. The findings include the following.

1. On the whole, even if raised in an adoptive environment where alcohol problems are absent, adopted sons whose biological fathers are alcoholics are more likely to become alcoholic than are the sons of nonalcoholics.

2. Compared to those of nonalcoholics, the sons of alcoholics are more likely to develop alcohol problems at a relatively early age.
3. Nonadopted siblings raised in their alcoholic families of origin are no more frequently alcoholic than their adopted-out siblings raised in nonalcoholic environments.
4. Adopted sons whose biological mothers are alcoholics are twice as likely to become alcoholic as are the adopted sons of nonalcoholic mothers.
5. Adopted daughters whose biological mothers are alcohol abusers are four times more likely to become alcohol abusers themselves than those whose biological mothers are not.
6. A relationship between alcohol abuse by daughters and by their biological fathers has yet to be statistically established.

Some recent analyses of data from adoption studies have made it possible to draw inferences about the contribution of environmental factors to alcohol abuse and alcoholism, as well as to permit the delineation of differing subtypes of alcohol abuse. The findings include the following.

1. Two inheritable subtypes of alcohol abuse have been identified for men— *milieu-limited* (both congenital predisposition and appropriate postnatal environmental factors are necessary for development of alcoholism) and *male-limited* (congenital predisposition is from father to son only).
2. The milieu-limited form occurred in 13 percent of the adopted men studied. Either the biological father or biological mother typically exhibited mild alcohol abuse or abuse for which treatment was not obtained. The adoptive environment determined both the frequency and severity of the susceptible son's alcohol abuse. Possible contributing environmental factors include the occupational status of the adoptive father and the age at adoptive placement. The son's alcohol abuse is usually mild but can be severe. Depending upon the nature of the environmental provocation, the relative risk of developing alcohol abuse increases twofold; without it, the risk is the same as that of the general population.
3. Male-limited alcohol abuse occurred in 4 percent of the adopted men studied, representing approximately 25 percent of the alcohol-abusing subjects. Their biological fathers—not their mothers—had severe alcoholism requiring extensive treatment. The postnatal environment had no effect on the expected numbers of abusers. However, the environment may have influenced the severity of alcohol abuse. An estimated ninefold increase in risk of alcoholism or alcohol-abuse development was evident in the affected individuals, regardless of postnatal environment.
4. As for the interaction of genetics and environment in women, the small number of alcohol abusers (3.3 percent of the population under study)

made a fine-grained analysis difficult. The genetic risk appears, thus far, to be mother-to-daughter limited. Environmental factors, with possible precipitating factors such as the type of home placement and the occupational status of the biological father, appear to contribute to the risk.

Of all individuals studied, it is noteworthy that an average of 60 percent had no family history of alcohol abuse. Their alcohol abuse may have been caused by other psychiatric or behavioral disorders. Alternatively, they could represent, in part, a group whose parents were genetically susceptible to alcohol abuse but lacked the necessary environmental provocation to become abusers. This issue remains to be resolved in future research.

The demonstration that sociocultural influences are critically important in the majority of genetically predisposed individuals suggests that changes in behavior and social attitudes by and toward high-risk individuals can alter both the course and prevalence of alcohol abuse and alcoholism. These recent discoveries provide significant promise for future treatment and prevention strategies—as well as for future research on this important health problem—so that it will be possible to identify potential alcohol abusers through sensitive and accurate physiological, biochemical, and behavioral predictors of vulnerability to alcoholism.

In addition to studies demonstrating the role of genetics in alcoholism development, it has been shown recently that inheritance plays a role in determining some variations noted in the metabolism of alcohol in different individuals. Genetically controlled variation in the make-up of alcohol metabolizing enzymes may predispose some individuals to alcoholism by facilitating ingestion of large amounts of alcohol; other persons, however, may experience some immunity by the inability to ingest too much alcohol without experiencing an unpleasant cluster of symptoms referred to as "alcohol flush reaction." Further, there is emerging evidence that some individuals may be genetically susceptible to certain complications of alcoholism, such as cirrhosis of the liver and alcoholic dementia. Such human and animal research on related issues has great potential for enabling the early identification of individuals at risk for various adverse effects of alcohol consumption. Prevention efforts aimed specifically at such individuals could be designed with greater likelihood of success than with the current, broad-based approaches.

Fetal Alcohol Effects

Since ancient times, alcohol's adverse effect on the fetus has been suspected. In the mid-eighteenth century, the London College of Physicians successfully petitioned for reinstatement of gin taxes in an attempt to decrease gin's availability and use by pregnant women and, in subsequent years, issued many warnings about drinking during pregnancy. Another English study in the late nineteenth century noted higher infant mortality and stillbirth rates for the infants of alcoholic mothers and noted that such women subsequently gave birth to healthy children when forced into abstinence. In the United States, a few relevant studies in the early twentieth century identified fetal damage resulting from prenatal alcoholic exposure. Research on alcohol use during pregnancy, however, apparently declined during Prohibition, leaving only sporadic reports in the world literature for the next fifty years.

The modern era of investigation of alcohol's effects on the fetus began in 1973 when a paper reporting a specific cluster of abnormalities observed in the offspring of some alcoholic women was published in the medical journal *Lancet*. The authors coined the term "fetal alcohol syndrome" (FAS) to describe the condition that included prenatal and postnatal growth deficiency, small head circumference, unique facial characteristics, mental impairment, and a variety of other skeletal, kidney, and heart abnormalities. Over the next ten years, more than 1,000 papers appeared describing the effects of alcohol in pregnancy and reporting cases of FAS from all over the world. In 1980 the fetal alcohol study group of the Research Society on Alcoholism proposed specific criteria for FAS.

From these continuing research efforts, it has become clear that maternal alcohol use during pregnancy can be associated with a broad range of health compromises, and FAS—the most severe of these outcomes—represents only a small percentage of cases. These consequences of alcohol use have been termed "fetal alcohol effects" or alcohol related birth defects. It should be noted that some fetal alcohol effects do not, in their own right, constitute an adverse outcome but may be independently associated with risk to the fetus. Such effects include amniotic infections during pregnancy; birth related complications such as premature separation of the placenta, fetal distress, precipitous delivery, and preterm delivery; low birth weight; and poor Apgar scores at birth. Because these adverse effects are not unique to alcohol use, they can be ascribed to alcohol only after careful study in which the contribution to risk of other factors—smoking, nutrition, other drug use, and maternal illness—are controlled and accounted for as much as possible. Animal studies have been extremely valuable in corroborating findings on fetal alcohol effects, and they will play a major role in future studies by elucidating the mechanism(s) through which alcohol exerts its teratogenic effect.

Approximately 60 percent of adult American women drink alcoholic beverages, and an estimated 6 percent of all adult women in this nation are classified as problem drinkers. The reproductive years coincide with the heaviest average consumption of alcohol by females (consumption peaks in the late thirties or early forties, and declines thereafter). Fortunately, there is evidence that pregnancy is often associated with a decrease in the consumption of both alcohol and nicotine, another drug which adversely affects the fetus. During the peak reproductive age range of eighteen to thirty-four, an estimated 5 percent of American women consume an average of two or more drinks per day. Since alcohol readily crosses the placenta, yielding levels of alcohol in the fetus almost identical to those of the mother, it is reasonable to conclude that a significant number of unborn children in the United States are exposed to the equivalent of two drinks a day.

There is some encouraging evidence that women who do drink decrease their consumption during pregnancy, and there is some evidence to suggest that education of women about the risks of drinking during pregnancy can have a further positive effect. It is also clear, however, that many women, including many who are the heaviest drinkers—and likely have the greatest risk of bearing a fetal alcohol syndrome child—do not alter their drinking during pregnancy. It should be noted that women who drink heavily tend to be married to men who drink heavily, and the possibility that some fetal alcohol effects are related to paternal drinking has been examined. Although long-term heavy alcohol consumption by males can have a variety of adverse effects on sexual and reproductive functions, there is no convincing evidence to date that such effects are related to fetal alcohol syndrome.

Diagnostic problems, including incomplete forms of FAS, difficulty correlating the apparent syndrome with maternal alcohol intake (denied and minimized by many individuals), as well as reluctance to diagnose the syndrome have all contributed to difficulty in obtaining accurate estimates of its incidence. Prospective studies around the world have generally found that the incidence of FAS ranges from 1 to 3 infants per 1,000 births; this means over 1,800 babies are born yearly with this syndrome in the United States. Estimates of the frequency of FAS calculated on the basis of occurrence only among women identified as problem drinkers or alcohol abusers are higher, ranging from 23 to 29 cases per 1,000 births. Further, estimates of the prevalence of fetal alcohol effects far exceed the prevalence of the full-blown syndrome; these estimates among women identified as alcohol abusers have been reported as high as 50 to 70 percent.

In general, about 66 percent of developmental defects have been noted to be of unknown origin. One calculation has estimated that approximately 5 percent of all congenital abnormalities may be attributed to prenatal alcohol exposure. This suggests that alcohol may account for a significant proportion of previously unexplained anomalies and that it should be considered as a major contributor to abnormal fetal development. Clearly, the incidence of FAS falls in the same order of magnitude as Downs syndrome and spina bifida—three disorders that constitute the leading known causes of birth defects associated with mental retardation. FAS, though, is unique since it has a known teratogenic origin and is completely preventable.

While it is undeniable that heavy alcohol use in pregnancy poses a significant risk to the health of the fetus, the debatable issue concerns the potential risk posed by moderate alcohol use. Several studies have reported associations between alcohol consumption of two drinks per day and pregnancy outcomes such as decreased birth weight, preterm delivery, and increased spontaneous abortion. Other studies have reported an effect upon a variety of neurological and behavioral measures. An important part of the controversy concerning the effects of low levels of alcohol in pregnancy centers around the reliability of drinking histories obtained in the studies. The debate cannot be resolved with a single answer at this point, because the manner in which drinking information was obtained varies considerably from study to study. Research that is specifically designed to focus on an alcohol issue is usually more sensitive to problems surrounding the acquisition of drinking information, and confidence in the data is likely to be higher.

A related issue concerns the day-to-day variation in the normal drinking practices of people. These variations can be considerable, and they can make reduction to a single measure, such as two drinks per day, tenuous. As a result, some investigators question whether or not certain adverse outcomes, such as increased spontaneous abortion, truly occur at the levels of alcohol consumption of two drinks per day. Animal studies, so valuable for the study of heavy alcohol use in pregnancy, have not yet proved useful to study the effects of moderate alcohol use. While the potential for adverse effects of small to moderate doses of alcohol may be debatable, it is established that even small doses of alcohol reach the fetus and cause physiological responses. Thus, a single drink of alcohol has been shown to suppress fetal breathing movements. Whether or not such effects are pathological, however, is unknown at this time.

It is clear that women who abuse alcohol during pregnancy place their fetuses at significant health risk. For this reason pregnancy is an important period for intervention, referral, and treatment of the alcohol-abusing or alcohol-dependent mother. Preliminary evidence indicates that many such women can be confronted in a nonthreatening and non-guilt-provoking manner and be motivated to abstain from alcohol and deliver healthier babies. However, those women who do not accept appropriate treatment for their alcohol problems continue to place their babies at considerable risk of mortality or morbidity.

Public education efforts concerning the risks associated with alcohol use during pregnancy have been pursued since the mid–1970s. Broad coverage in the media has been obtained from public health advisory warnings issued by NIAAA, the Surgeon General of the United States, the American Medical Association, the March of Dimes, and several state governments. Indeed, most Americans have been exposed to such public health messages, and 90 percent of the respondents in a recent survey knew that drinking during pregnancy might be harmful. However, fully 75 percent of those who thought abstinence is unnecessary believed that an average of more than three drinks per day was safe—a belief not conclusively supported by available scientific evidence. These findings suggest that current public education and prevention programs may not be fully permeating the public consciousness. They also indicate the need for ongoing efforts such as the NIAAA's current FAS education program directed at physicians and other health care professionals.

Although knowledge of potential adverse effects of alcohol during pregnancy has changed and public attitudes have shifted since the 1970s, only recently has there been evidence that the drinking behavior of pregnant women is changing. In a recent survey in Seattle that compared drinking patterns during pregnancy over a six-year period, the proportion of women who drank during pregnancy was found to have decreased, although the proportion of women who drank at least an ounce of absolute alcohol (two drinks) per day was relatively constant. Because precisely this limited portion of the population incurs the highest risk for alcohol related birth defects, these findings again indicate cause for concern. Successful prevention strategies for alcohol related birth defects, including FAS, remain elusive. More information is needed about alcohol abuse and dependence in young women so that focused approaches for prevention can be developed. Professional education of physicians, nurses, and other health care providers gives promise of a rational and cost-effective approach to the prevention of alcohol related birth defects.

Of the many specific questions requiring further research, understanding the mechanism of alcohol's teratogenicity and the variables affecting it, including the timing and amount of alcohol intake during pregnancy, will be crucial to the development of more specific prevention, intervention, and treatment programs. The most frequently asked question at this time has to do with the safety of "moderate" drinking levels during pregnancy. Since there are many variables, including genetic ones, that may influence the impact of alcohol on the fetus, a definitive answer to this question is, undoubtedly, several years away. In the next few years, recommendations concerning the use of small amounts of alcohol during pregnancy must continue to be based on incomplete knowledge.

In addition to the morbidity and mortality associated with FAS, there is the economic cost to society. It has recently been estimated that the lifetime cost for caring for infants born in New York State in one year with FAS and alcohol related birth defects approaches $150 million. Therefore, it would appear that the most urgent policy issue surrounding this preventable cause of illness is the extent to which restrictions on alcohol consumption during pregnancy and the use of such devices as warnings about the risks of fetal alcohol exposure—including warning labels on alcoholic beverage containers and signs in establishments where alcohol is served—should be encouraged by society.

Alcohol Abuse and Alcoholism in the Family

The impact of one family member's alcohol abuse or alcoholism on other family members has been of interest to both clinicians and researchers for several decades. During this time, the primary focus of both treatment personnel and alcohol researchers has been on the spouse of the alcoholic—primarily on the female spouse of the male alcoholic. Much less attention has been paid toward the male spouse of the female alcoholic and even less attention toward understanding the psychological impact of parental alcoholism on children. Since the mid–1970s, however, this latter area has been addressed by numerous descriptive studies, and clinical and public interest in the children of alcoholics is expanding rapidly. This is due in part both to the formation of concerned national organizations and to the heightened visibility that media attention has given to the problems of these children.

Finally, there has been little research on the psychological impact of children's alcohol or drug abuse or dependence upon their parents or siblings, although these are areas faced daily by personnel involved in treatment of adolescent alcohol and drug abusers. Indeed, the prevalence of alcohol and drug abuse by young people (rising steadily until recently) has been a major factor in stimulating a reexamination of societal policies governing alcohol and drug use. Adolescent alcohol and drug problems have been described as epidemic, and specialized identification, treatment, and prevention programs have increased markedly in the past few years. Unfortunately, access to such treatment programs remains a problem in many areas of the nation.

Numerous groups of concerned parents and others have banded together for therapy and to influence laws and policies they see as fostering adolescent drug abuse and thereby threatening the lives of their children and stability of their families. The Department of Health and Human Services, through a Secretarial Initiative on Teenage Alcohol Abuse, has also sought to further stimulate and facilitate these local efforts, and the states have been actively involved in assisting local groups of concerned persons to address these problems.

SPOUSES OF ALCOHOLICS

The early focus of research studies on spouses of alcoholics was on understanding and describing the spouse's personality and motivation for beginning or continuing marriage with an alcoholic partner. One such early hypothesis depicted the female spouse of the male alcoholic as having significant psychopathology and sometimes even being responsible for her husband's drinking. Later studies refuted these notions. As it is presently known that there is no typical "alcoholic personality," it is also known that there is neither a "typical personality pattern" nor greater incidence of psychopathology in the spouses of alcoholics. Another hypothesis suggests that husbands of alcoholic women initiate divorce more readily than do wives of alcoholic men. Recent research has tended to focus on the role the spouse can play in coping with alcoholism in the family and in facilitating the recovery of the alcoholic partner. These studies, however, have been preponderantly descriptive in nature.

Controlled prospective studies of a variety of hypotheses and treatment strategies are clearly necessary. In addition, studies are needed to define precisely the prevalence and nature of problems experienced by spouses of problem drinkers, including those of alcoholics. A hypothesis that warrants further study suggests that there may be health benefits experienced by families who successfully deal with intrafamily alcoholism and participate regularly in long-term aftercare programs such as Al-Anon. Recent evidence has demonstrated that use of health care services by families of alcoholics declines following successful treatment of the alcoholic patient. This is an important finding that needs further verification and elaboration.

CHILDREN OF ALCOHOLICS

It is estimated that in the United States today there are 7 million children under the age of twenty—and millions more adults —with an alcoholic parent or parents. Studies to date on this population have focused predominantly on descriptions of the various psychological impairments or on assessment of the risk of alcoholism experienced by such children. Psychological problems attributed to them have been numerous and varied and include the presence of both major and minor types of psychopathology; impaired self-esteem and reality testing; impaired academic/vocational performance; and susceptibility to a large number of "acting-out" behaviors such as delinquency, running away, and alcohol and other drug abuse. Further, a variety of the mechanisms to cope with life that are seen in children of alcoholics have been identified; these include mechanisms that suggest that some of these children may become responsible and achieving adults, relatively free of long-term psychopathology.

Although currently there is intense interest in the development of large-scale intervention and treatment programs for children of alcoholics, there clearly is great need for studies to document the prevalence and nature of the psychological impact of parental alcohol abuse and alcoholism on children. This is of critical importance if cost-effective, successful, and large-scale intervention and treatment programs are to be implemented. In order to design, implement, and evaluate prevention programs, there is also a great need to identify children who may be prone to suffer serious pathological consequences of parental alcohol abuse and alcoholism. Another priority for research is better identification and understanding of those variables that influence both positive and negative outcomes for children. This type of research may be enhanced by involvement of social scientists who conduct research on victims of other problem behaviors or diseases. Such theoretical and practical research from various disciplines would greatly strengthen the ability to identify and treat families who are at risk.

FAMILY VIOLENCE

Alcohol abuse and alcoholism are often presumed to play a role in family violence. Although it has received increased attention in the media and has been a gradually increasing subject of professional study, there remain many unanswered questions about the nature and extent of family violence and much controversy about the role of alcohol abuse and alcoholism in such episodes.

A recent review of studies of spouse abuse notes that most studies cite alcoholism or excessive drinking in 45 to 60 percent of reported cases. Estimates of alcohol consumption at the time of abuse vary widely, ranging from 20 to 80 percent. Dr. Henry Kempe, a pioneer in the study of child abuse, estimates that approximately 33 percent of child abuse and neglect cases are associated with parental alcohol abuse or dependence. Recent analyses by the American Humane Association (AHA) of official child abuse and neglect reports found alcohol and drug abuse a factor in 15 to 20 percent of cases, with alcohol abuse or dependence generally accounting for 75 percent of these cases. Other studies report a range of alcohol problems in child abusers from 0 to 38 percent, and the most frequently reported figures are in the same range as those noted by the AHA. There are also data to indicate a positive correlation between higher frequency and severity of physical abuse and drinking by fathers. Other studies indicate that drinking fathers tend to be abusive rather than neglectful, whereas drinking mothers are more likely to be neglectful rather than physically abusive.

Research has led to several hypotheses to explain the role of alcohol in spouse and child abuse. The disinhibiting effect of alcohol has led to the suggestion that violence by alcohol consumers is really an expression of underlying aggressive impulses. Similarly, alcohol impairs memory, reason, judgment, and the ability to control a variety of behaviors; in the presence of intrapersonal or interpersonal stress, it may simply act as a facilitator of violence. Theorists have suggested that some individuals learn to expect to behave more aggressively when drinking and act so regardless of the disinhibiting effect of alcohol itself. More recently, it has been suggested that alcohol is used as an excuse for violent behavior—both in an attempt to deny and/or rationalize unacceptable behavior and/or in an attempt to escape legal punishment for violent acts. Beyond statistical correlation, the overall relationship between alcohol and violence is only beginning to be understood. The large number of questions to be answered and the difficulty in studying intrafamilial violence due to personal, family, legal, and professional obstacles suggest that comprehensive understanding is years away.

A most urgent research need is to better understand those variables that accurately predict individuals who are at high risk for alcohol related violence—either as a perpetrator or victim—including the extent to and manner in which problem drinking and alcoholism contribute to such violence. Attention must also be given to where and how the alcohol treatment system fits into the multitude of social, legal, welfare, and health care agencies mandated to intercede and protect victims of family violence.

The presence of alcohol abuse or alcoholism in a family—particularly, but not exclusively, if present in a parent—raises several important policy issues that only are beginning to be addressed. These include medical confidentiality, including the treatment of minor children; mandatory reporting of suspected, as well as confirmed, cases of child abuse and neglect; mandatory treatment for parents; civil and criminal liability for inadequate or inappropriate diagnosis and treatment; and the roles, and sometimes conflicting mandates, of the various social, health, welfare, and legal agencies involved in dealing with families.

Summary

The adverse consequences of excessive or inappropriate alcohol use constitute a major threat to many families. Though in recent years much has been learned about alcohol abuse and alcoholism, understanding of their scope, nature, and impact on the family is only beginning, and more years of intensive basic and applied research will be necessary to answer all the questions now posed.

In addition to investigating the prevalence and mechanisms of alcohol's effect on major problems such as accidents and child abuse, researchers should examine the relationship of alcohol to separation and divorce, childhood hyperactivity and learning disability, psychosomatic illness in family members, and general family attitudes and behaviors concerning health matters. Such investigations should focus not only on problems and pathology, but also should assess variables that may correlate with relative immunity or invincibility to alcohol related problems. Included in the latter category would be studies of individuals and families without alcohol problems, both drinkers and abstainers, to identify the process by which they avoid alcohol related problems.

Successful alcoholism treatment programs, although developed empirically, are now widely accepted and available. Self-help programs such as AA and Al-Anon are also widely available in the industrialized world. Although they appear to be cost-effective and provide an element of tertiary prevention, more refinement is possible. A major research need in the area of treatment concerns the extent of the need for and demonstration of the efficacy of family therapy in intrafamily alcoholism treatment. However, primary and secondary prevention programs are mandatory if a major reduction in the current level of alcohol related morbidity, mortality, and economic cost is to be achieved. While these prevention efforts cannot await definitive answers to current questions, they must be carefully conceived and evaluated and take into account the current state of knowledge as well as prevailing public sentiment and available resources.

History is replete with failed attempts in many cultures to control a variety of drug-related social ills. Why such failures have occurred is always debatable, as are the reasons for those few successful efforts. It is important to recognize that many people use alcohol and other psychoactive drugs and that a large percentage of alcohol users experience no problems with its use. This group of individuals, as well as families, combined with those who have an economic interest in alcohol consumption can be expected to keep strong sentiments about many alcohol related public policy issues currently under consideration. It is reasonable to assume that policies likely to be implemented, maintained, and successful for reduction of alcohol problems must be based on a combination of solid data, broad public support, and documented effectiveness. This will require extensive awareness and long-term commitment and involvement of diverse segments of society —whether or not they have been directly or adversely affected by alcohol misuse—including the family.

John A. Volpe

6

Alcohol and Public Safety

Alcohol is a substance with such a rich Biblical and cultural history that, despite its enormous national consumption, its use is not some unique American habit. If it is abused by altogether too many people, it is also avoided entirely for personal or religious reasons by a significant segment of society. However, the best available studies show that the majority of Americans who drink do so in moderation. Their choice is a highly personal one, and no amount of restrictive legislation should ever be designed to deny this liberty.

In the interest of the common good and public safety, it is necessary to address the results of alcohol abuse, but drinking itself cannot be redressed as an intrinsic evil—a bad habit to be shunned by reasonable people. At times, its use may be beneficial, but excessive consumption can prove harmful to drinkers themselves and damaging to innocent victims of irresponsible drinkers. Excessive consumption of alcohol creates problems in the home, at

JOHN A. VOLPE *was the chairman of the Presidential Commission on Drunk Driving and is chairman of the successor organization, the National Commission Against Drunk Driving. A distinguished public official, Mr. Volpe served as ambassador to Italy during the Nixon and Ford administrations. He served three terms as governor of Massachusetts and served as secretary of the Department of Transportation in the Nixon cabinet. Before seeking elective office, Mr. Volpe was commissioner of public works for Massachusetts and was the first federal highway administrator, serving under President Eisenhower.*

work, in recreational activities, and on the highway. Since alcohol is so common in all kinds of social settings today, the spillover effect puts public safety very much at issue in any serious discussion of alcohol abuse.

The tragedies associated with alcohol abuse and highway safety alone are of epidemic proportions. Even without mentioning figures for other kinds of alcohol related deaths, the highway fatality rate continues to be a leading public health hazard. Unfortunately, even with all the anxiety that the majority of American society shares about drug substance abuse, there is a great tendency to downplay or minimize the impact of alcohol—or even to think of it as a drug at all. Yet alcohol is the cause of more deaths than any of the controlled substances headlined in drug busts. This chapter, then, will focus principally on the issue of drinking and driving, while touching briefly on the overall problem of alcohol abuse and its effect on public safety.

Earlier means of transportation were not as sophisticated or swift as today's, but responsible drivers were still demanded. Drinking and driving is by no means a modern-day social happening. Legislative records show that the combination of the two prompted early laws regarding the manner in which a man drove his horse after overindulging at the local public house. Furthermore, as early as 1904, one published report cited drinking as the cause of nineteen to twenty-five accidents involving the novel horseless carriages. Fifteen people were killed and nearly as many more were injured in these collisions. In our more mobile society, the record shows both the private and public sector have sought to combat drunken driving. These efforts will be examined by tracing the development of, and demand for, effective alcohol countermeasure programs.

Moderation and Safety

To grow up in the average Italian family was to inherit a healthy attitude toward alcoholic beverages. Wine was very much a part of daily table fare, and additional alcoholic drinks were always available for special occasions. People old enough to recall the outbreak of influenza at the end of World War I may recall the daily "teaspoon treatment" of whiskey that parents administered to ward off that dread disease.

Whatever one's personal experiences with, or strong convictions about, alcohol may be, this nation cannot afford to return to any form of prohibition as a matter of social policy. The cries of those who seek a return to prohibition and thereby turn off the community at large cannot be heeded. Drinking is here to stay; this means that while moderation and responsible drinking should be encouraged, drunkenness should be met with understanding, education, treatment, and, yes in some instances, punitive measures.

By the same token, operating motor vehicles is one of the benefits of twentieth century living, and no one is so enamored of nostalgia as to want to return to the horse-and-buggy days. Next to a home, the automobile is a family's most prized possession and ranks first for many today who cannot afford to buy a home. As well as a great convenience, an automobile is often a necessity.

Nevertheless, in our progress from animal-drawn carts to high-horsepower automobiles, and from some simple alcoholic drinks to all manner of distilled spirits, wines, and beer, needed moral values have not been promoted. Nor has the nation's health been safeguarded any better with the increased mixture of these two creature comforts. When related to public safety, alcohol abuse is a national health problem with obvious side effects. Alcohol and gasoline have proven to be a frightening and deadly mixture.

At stake, then, is how to respond to those problems which arise when people drive after drinking. This is especially true when it is estimated that 80 percent of those who use alcoholic beverages do not hesitate to drive after drinking. "Don't drive after drinking!" is a neat sounding slogan, but it will remain just that until society's attitude changes about personal responsibility and public safety.

There is no magic formula that will serve as an antidote to drunken driving. No application of technological know-how or crash programs of innovative deterrents, including more severe sanctions, will remedy the situation. Nothing will change until society accepts the fact that *drinking and driving is socially unacceptable.* To achieve this acceptance in the long run demands education as a positive means of prevention. Society must give young people, perhaps as early as twelve years of age, information about alcohol; they must be told what it is and what it can do to them when it is abused. By such an educational approach, young people may arrive at the legal age to purchase and possess alcohol and to operate motor vehicles with a positive attitude toward the responsibility that they share for public safety. By exercising this attitude, young people could then give the lie to the misleading and all too prevalent macho feeling that it is socially acceptable to drink and drive.

Alcohol Abuse at Work

There is deep concern about the dangers associated with alcohol abuse in the workplace. For example, the construction trades involve the skilled use of heavy equipment; the work is hard, and the labor force must be safety-minded and constantly alert. The emphasis at every stage of the job must be on safety measures and quality control to protect both the crew's well-being and the project's successful completion. There is no time or place for workers who report to the job "under the influence," and supervisors are usually authorized to send them home. They could endanger the lives of other workers as well as their own; hard hats would be of little help if an operator's abilities were seriously impaired by reason of alcohol while controlling a crane, a lift, or some other heavy machinery.

This is also true in other types of employment where the working environment demands sobriety—airline pilots, train personnel, bus and boat operators, and all who are entrusted with the safe transit of millions of Americans every year. Regulations do exist as public law and/or company policy relating to the consumption of alcohol for those engaged in public transportation. Safety-sensitive functions cannot be performed properly when there are flagrant violations of rules that forbid drinking while on, or for a specified number of hours prior to, duty.

The Federal Railroad Administration held public hearings in 1983 on the control of alcohol and drug use in railroad operations. Fresh in the minds of many witnesses were accidents involving both freight and passenger trains. On September 28, 1982, a forty-three-car freight train derailed in Livingston, Louisiana, and fourteen of these cars were tank cars containing hazardous materials. The toxic gasses released into the atmosphere prompted the evacuation of some 3,000 people who lived within five miles of the accident; several homes were burned and destroyed, and the losses were estimated at $10 million. Less than a week later in Tennessee, one train collided with another; both the engineer and brakeman were killed; the damage estimate totaled $1 million. Investigating these two accidents, the National Transportation Safety Board found that crew members in both crashes had consumed alcohol either before reporting for duty or while working. On February 14, 1983, the engineer of a Maryland commuter train was escorted from the locomotive only two minutes before the train's scheduled departure from Washington's Union Station with 300 passengers aboard. A blood alcohol content (BAC) test showed he had an alcohol level in excess of 0.22 percent. In forty-one states, operating a motor vehicle at or above 0.1 percent BAC is considered to be "driving under the influence" (DUI) and per se illegal.

These cases demonstrate all too vividly the grave threat to public safety that exists when an individual displays a drinking problem on the job. Unions, management, and government must address this issue as a common concern. For too long there has been reluctance on all sides to confront this problem. Fear that a job might be lost or a jurisdictional dispute might arise has taken precedence over any thought that a tragic accident might occur.

Commercial airlines forbid alcohol use by pilots within the period of eight hours before flight time. Passengers have every right to believe that pilots adhere to this rule, and with the controls exercised at commercial airports, this seems to be true. Certainly, rail personnel and bus and boat operators should be bound by the same strict standards for passenger safety.

The Federal Railroad Administration, the Federal Aviation Administration, the United States Coast Guard, the National Highway Traffic Safety Administration, and the Urban Mass Transportation Administration, all operating under the Department of Transportation, should be able to harmonize safety regulations in the interests of public safety. The National Transportation Safety Board is the agency that investigates accidents, checks out reported violations of regulations, and makes needed recommendations. Surely, when its findings reveal alcohol as a contributing cause in *any* transportation accident, sanctions should not be any less than those invoked for highway tragedies. In fact, since the death and damage toll could be significantly greater, the penalties should be more severe.

PROBLEMS AT HOME AND AT PLAY

Nor can we overlook the increasing number of accidents related to the reckless use of all types of recreational vehicles and equipment on land and sea. While it is not appropriate to allege that alcohol is a major cause for deaths and injuries in work and play settings, as in the history of road accidents, it has been shown to be very much a factor. Statistics for these accidents have not been scrutinized as thoroughly as those relating to highway collisions.

It is worth noting that in 1982 Michigan passed a law prohibiting the operation of any boat or vessel by any person under the influence of alcohol or other *controlled* drug substance. This followed similar action taken in Michigan in 1981 regarding snowmobiles and other off-road recreation vehicles.

It is difficult, if not impossible, to establish the role of alcohol in household accidents. The tracking system used in reporting these does not emphasize BAC tests as highway accident reports do. Also, families are reluctant to admit to medical authorities and insurance investigators that alcohol is even involved in falls, burns, etc. Clinical tests may show that alcohol was present, but such information may not become public.

In its 1983 edition of "Accident Facts," the National Safety Council (NSC) reports 93,000 accidental deaths during 1982. Of this number, 46,000 resulted from motor vehicle accidents; 11,200 happened at work; and 21,000 occurred in the home. It should be noted that work and home totals included 4,200 killed in motor vehicle accidents. NSC also lists 19,000 as public, or all other forms of accidental deaths. Included in these figures are 1,100 victims of firearms. (The NSC figures for motor vehicle fatalities vary from those of the National Highway Traffic Safety Administration [NHTSA], which show 43,721 vehicle fatalities for 1982. The tracking time for actual and estimated statistics accounts for this variation.)

This marked the second time since 1962 that accidental deaths numbered less than 100,000—the fourth consecutive annual decrease. Of all NSC's breakdown on accidental fatalities, deaths from motor vehicles showed the greatest decrease, about 11 percent.

Highway Safety Up-front

There is a great need to lessen the frightening impact of alcohol related tragedies on our nation's highways. The issue of drunken driving was not up-front in the 1950s as it has been in the 1980s, but the fatality figures were increasing steadily. By 1959, there were over 36,000 traffic deaths—6,000 more than in 1949.

It is common and fairly correct to attribute 50 percent of the annual highway deaths to DUI. There is every reason to feel this same percentage was evident in the past, despite the lack of sophisticated tracking systems. For example, in 1952, there were 36,088 deaths for 5,135.81 million vehicle miles traveled, resulting in a fatality rate of 7.03 per 100 million miles. Contrast this with 1982 when there were 43,721 deaths for 15,710 million vehicle miles traveled. This breaks down to a fatality rate of 2.80—almost a 300 percent improvement when measured against increased highway use.

In 1982 the nation had the lowest recorded highway fatality rate in history and 5,580 fewer deaths than in 1981 (a total of 49,301), marking the largest annual decrease in forty years (except for the oil embargo year of 1974). No one reason can be advanced for this dramatic downturn. However, a heightened public awareness, aided by grass-roots citizen action groups that push legislation at state and federal levels, together with the work of the Presidential Commission on Drunk Driving, can be credited with this encouraging change.

Since chronic or problem drinkers account for a disproportionate share of highway accidents, not to mention other problems for society, treatment is very much in order today. Such an approach is not to be seen as a substitute for appropriate penalties for those who violate the law, but as a carefully chosen response in individual cases. Rehabilitation should not be ruled out, and for many offenders it needs to be intensified. Social drinkers must be distinguished from problem drinkers when treatment is considered.

In fifteen years a great deal has been learned about drinking patterns and their tragic consequences on the highways of the nation. Just as the nation cannot afford prohibition, neither can it afford to believe that punishment is a guaranteed remedy for the social ills caused by drunken driving. Education and prevention must be included in any ongoing attack on drunken driving. Likewise, tighter enforcement of existing laws or enactment of new legislation, coupled with swift, certain, and just prosecution, must be a part of the total package of alcohol countermeasures.

ESTABLISHING NEW PRIORITIES

During the early months after the formation of the Department of Transportation, all functions relating to driver and vehicle safety were handled within the Federal Highway Administration.

The principal interest of the Federal Highway Administration was the design and construction of highways; its highest priority was the completion of the 41,000-mile interstate system. Safety was more a highway design issue, and little attention was given to the issue of drinking and its impact on highway deaths.

In March 1970, the National Highway Safety Bureau became a separate agency within the Department of Transportation and reported directly to the secretary. In December Congress passed the Highway Safety Act of 1970, and the name of the Highway Safety Bureau was changed to its present title of National Highway Traffic Safety Administration.

Douglas Toms, the administrator of Motor Vehicles in the state of Washington and a nationally recognized expert in the field of public safety, headed the agency. After evaluation of the federal efforts to cope with the increasing highway death tolls, it was his task to establish a series of priorities. Traffic fatalities had topped 50,000 in 1966, reaching the frightening figure of 53,543 in 1969. Almost 10,000 fewer Americans were killed on our highways in 1982 than in 1969, an encouraging sign that cannot be overlooked in any evaluation of the anti–drunken driving campaign.

With the knowledge that at least 50 percent of these totals was the result of alcohol related accidents, a program was undertaken to integrate and improve enforcement, prosecution, and treatment countermeasures. The Alcohol Safety Action Project (ASAP) was developed, consisting of thirty-five local ASAPs. Each lasted over three years between 1969 and 1975, costing the federal government some $88 million. During the early 1970s, the National Institute on Alcohol Abuse and Alcoholism (NIAAA) funded eighteen problem-drinking projects to operate in conjunction with ASAPs.

This comprehensive ASAP program varied in size from one site to another, but, overall, it covered millions of drivers across the nation. In twelve of the thirty-five ASAPs, a significant statistical reduction in fatal night accidents occurred. These twelve projects averaged a 30 percent reduction in night accidents over the three years. Individual projects were able to double—and even triple—DUI arrests by using such new technology as roadside breath tests. These early experiences with driver checks paved the way for more sophisticated tests now used more widely by enforcement officials. To complement the arrest procedure, adjudication was accelerated to handle the heavier court caseloads.

It is estimated that 250,000 drinking drivers were referred for treatment. In any evaluation of the ASAP, the conclusion is that the program was successful in both raising the enforcement level and increasing public awareness in order to deter the social drinker from driving. It proved that drunken driving can be combated if society is ready to commit resources, publicity, and the required citizen involvement to make deterrence a reality rather than an abstract idea. The key to success is a continuing campaign on the local level, not merely a national one-week assault.

For example, one project in a midwestern city showed tremendous community involvement. It was given wide media coverage, and all the agencies working in the field of safety and alcohol treatment coordinated their efforts to deal with the drunken driving problem. The focuses were the evening hours and weekends because the incidence of impaired drivers increased during those times. While the rate of apprehension varied from 1 in 500 to 1 in 2,000, it was estimated in the ASAP program that in the late hours on weekend nights as many as 1 in 10, possibly 1 in 4, were impaired drivers.

There was no systematic approach to alcohol in relation to highway safety until NHTSA was created. Since 1970, however, the majority of states have made improvements in their law enforcement, adjudication, rehabilitation, and education efforts. Federal standards for alcohol safety, such as the legally defined DUI at 0.10 percent, have spurred the states to set similar standards. Later in this chapter a closer look at examples of high-interest legislation will be taken.

ALCOHOL ATTITUDES IN OTHER LANDS

In so many European countries, wine is something to be cultivated and appreciated, not a product to be abused. Though, for example, it is certainly socially acceptable to drink at home and in the cafes of Italy, and modern Italians love their motor vehicle, however modest it may be, DUI is not the problem there that it is in the United States (an observation made when I was U.S. ambassador there in 1973). An outside observer finds that even with all the bravura that characterizes Italians, *it is not socially acceptable for them to drink and to drive.* Their disposition to drink is by no means less than that of Americans, but their attitude toward alcoholic beverages is very different. It is said that Italians drink today with the idea that there will be more tomorrow. On the other hand, many Americans seem to drink as though the supply will be gone tomorrow.

Perhaps the Swedish system of voluntary abstention by the one selected to drive when a group is out for the evening should be encouraged in the U.S. This responsibility is then exchanged at another time, ensuring a spirit of conviviality at the party and competent driving upon departure. Such an approach avoids the danger that the driver has even "one for the road."

It is both ironic and tragic that in a nation with one of the best designed highway systems in the world, the United States has the worst record for alcohol related accidents. More than 50,000 persons were killed each year in eleven of the seventeen years from 1966 to 1982. It is estimated that 50 percent of all these fatalities were related to the excessive use of alcohol. Traffic deaths are now the single largest health hazard for all citizens up to age twenty-four, as well as a close second to cancer as the cause of death for all Americans up to age forty-four.

The carnage on our highways decreased in 1974 at the time of the oil embargo. Safety experts who study the data believe that the far-reaching effects of the oil crisis, the establishment of the fifty-five-miles per hour speed limit, and the positive effects of the ASAP program accounted for the downturn in deaths from 1974 to 1977. In 1978, the totals again exceeded 50,000, and remained at that high level through 1980.

The Presidential Commission

Little wonder, then, that President Reagan resolved to seek remedies for a social problem that had reached epidemic proportions. The grass-roots organizations played a significant role in his decision to establish the Presidential Commission on Drunk Driving (PCDD). Citizen action groups like Mothers Against Drunk Driving (MADD), Citizens for Safe Drivers (CSD), and Remove Intoxicated Drivers (RID) had prompted local, state, and federal officials to take a hard look at the problem and to propose some reasonable solutions.

This citizen insistence upon action together with vigorous bipartisan congressional support for stricter legislative measures proved to be a positive factor in founding the national body. More than 300 senators and members of Congress, including an absolute majority in each chamber, urged the President to take a firm public leadership role in the fight against drunken driving. They recommended that he appoint a blue-ribbon national commission to confront the issue and to enlist the American people in this campaign.

Established on April 14, 1982, the commission was not just another campaign with political overtones. From the very beginning it combined the voices of the victims and their families with a healthy participation of professionals and politicians. The call to action was not something new, but the response had never been so broad-based and insistent.

The work of this body of thirty-two men and women made it apparent that no one is in favor of drunken driving, not even drunken drivers themselves. The commission's members included doctors; law enforcement officials; leaders in the insurance, alcoholic beverage, and motor vehicle industries; the media; and citizen action groups. Four members of Congress represented the public sector, and the support personnel were drawn from NHTSA. Originally, it was intended that the commission would complete its presidential mandate in one year. However, as the expiration date drew near, the President extended the life of the commission until December 31, 1983.

The commission did not have the responsibility of conducting large-scale research on the problem of drunken driving. Comprehensive studies to determine the nature of the problem and the kind of alcohol countermeasures that should be initiated had been undertaken and already completed. Essentially, the commission's function was to provide a national forum to heighten public awareness and to encourage action by state and local governments.

While recognizing the insistent call for a change in attitudes, the commission did not disdain information or guideline suggestions that came from the data available to its members. It was imperative to balance the critical scientific approach with citizens' outrage at the continued slaughter on the nation's highways. From the outset, the commission realized the value of educating society to both the magnitude of the drunken driving problem and the need for both short-term and long-term solutions. To fulfill its mission, the commission did not limit its focus to the highway environment as the central cause of the problem; it concerned itself as well with society's values, attitudes, and behavior regarding the use and abuse of alcohol.

THE FUNCTIONS

When the composition of the commission was completed, three committees were created: education and prevention, enforcement and adjudication, and executive leadership. The commission made a determination of its role by agreeing on the following functions:

1. to encourage task forces in states, counties, and communities to examine their drunken driving control systems and to develop solutions to identified problems;
2. to serve as the catalyst in the promotion of public awareness of the issue;
3. to advocate the implementation of existing approaches and to recommend improvements where needed in the areas of legislation, enforcement, and adjudication; and
4. to identify long-term prevention and education programs.

THE NATIONAL DRUNKEN DRIVING SCENE

At its first meetings, the commission was briefed on the problem, available tools and resources, and state and local experiences. Many of the members had special expertise in the fields of safety or alcoholism and were well aware of the frightening damage caused by drunken driving. However, as a starting point, the entire commission found the following statistics sobering and extremely useful as an overview of the problem.

1. Each year 25,000 people are killed in alcohol related deaths.
2. Each year 1 million drunken driving collisions occur.
3. Over 65 percent of all fatal single-car accidents are alcohol related.
4. Relatively few problem drinkers (about 7 percent of the driving population) account for over 66 percent of all alcohol related fatal accidents.
5. It is estimated that one out of two Americans will be involved in an alcohol related accident in his or her lifetime.
6. Motorcyclists and drivers of light vans and trucks are more likely to be DUI than are automobile drivers.
7. Male drivers with previous convictions for DUI are more likely to be drinking than are drivers without such records.
8. The average drunken driver arrested on the highway has an 0.20 percent

blood alcohol concentration level—fifteen drinks of 86-proof, or a comparable consumption of beer or wine, in four hours for a 180-pound person—double the level for illegal per se intoxication in forty-one of fifty states.

9. Every year 708,000 persons are injured and 74,000 of these people suffer serious injuries in alcohol related accidents.
10. Alcohol related collisions are the leading cause of death for young Americans between ages sixteen and twenty-four.
11. Although those between ages sixteen and twenty-four comprise only 22 percent of the total population licensed to drive, they cause 44 percent of all fatal nighttime alcohol related accidents.
12. Of all fatal alcohol related auto crashes, 80 percent occur between 8:00 p.m. and 8:00 a.m. On weekends as many as 10 percent of all drivers are impaired or drunk. The most dangerous hours are those between 12:00 a.m. and 4:00 a.m.
13. The cost in damages of alcohol related accidents is estimated to be $21 to $24 billion a year. In 1981 serious crimes such as murder, assault, and robbery were estimated to cost $12 to $13 billion.
14. Most Americans drink, and over 80 percent admit to driving after drinking.
15. When drinkers are at the presumed level of intoxication, their risk of causing an accident is six times greater than that of nondrinking drivers.
16. An accident caused by drunken driving is the most frequent violent crime in the United States today.

On this last point, there is a definite relationship to the all too prevalent attitude that it is socially acceptable to drink and drive. For some unfortunate reason, Americans regard alcohol related deaths as "acceptable homicides." They do not perceive drunken driving as being as serious a crime as they do widely publicized homicides. In 1981 there were 21,000 headline homicides calling out for justice—or about 4,000 fewer deaths than the 25,000 caused by drunken drivers in the same year. For some strange reason, the American society seems to separate the violent forms of killing into "polite" and "vicious" by reason of the weapons involved. The automobile in the hands of a drunken driver is never thought to be as deadly as the automatic pistol in the hands of a killer.

This is rather sobering when it is realized that the latest available figures show a total population of 229,304,000 of which 147,-968,000 are licensed drivers. Even more striking is the comparison of registered vehicles to population. From 1980 to 1981 the population increased from 226,505,000 to the figure noted. The registered vehicles in 1980 were 157,291,431, and in 1981, there were 165,732,000. That is a remarkable increase of over 8 million vehicles, yet the population growth was less than 3 million. If the majority of drivers drink alcoholic beverages as previously indicated, the threat to public safety is unlikely to decrease unless, of course, the current national anti–drunken driving mood continues to prevail.

THE COMMISSION APPROACH

Individual members of the commission brought their own first-hand knowledge of the legal problems associated with DUI cases. Still others were familiar with the education and treatment of problem alcoholics. However, despite the skills of the commission as a group, it was imperative to obtain the views of a cross section of the American people. While the members appreciated the fact that alcoholism is an illness, they were appalled by the death and destruction that result from drunken driving.

From August to November 1982, eight public hearings were conducted in Oklahoma City, Denver, Boston, Chicago, Baton Rouge, Detroit, San Francisco, and Washington. During this same period the entire commission and/or the three committees held a number of meetings to evaluate the wealth of information that the oral and written testimony provided.

The commission listened to the victims of drunken driving collisions or to their families; law enforcement officials, prosecutors, judges, and probation personnel; business and industry executives; leaders in the fields of education, health, religion; and the media. The input from those who experienced the tragedy of drunken driving personally, as well as the insights provided by the professionals, placed the problem in bold relief. It was only natural that a different emphasis would result from the discussion of solutions, but there was no disagreement on the need for and value of a consensus if the commission's recommendations were to be acceptable and effective.

The information gained during these public hearings and from the added testimony submitted by recognized experts was considered by the commission in developing the fifty-three recommendations contained in its interim report to the nation. That report was presented to President Reagan on December 13, 1982, and then sent to the governors of the fifty states; leaders in Congress and federal department heads; task force directors; presiding justices of those courts handling drunken driving cases; state law enforcement and safety officials; insurance, alcohol, and motor vehicle executives; civic, fraternal, educational, and religious bodies; and print and electronic media outlets. In all, 5,000 copies were distributed.

Comments and suggestions were solicited from all these sources. The feedback was encouraging. The commission received over 600 thoughtful responses in a matter of weeks. Special credit must be given to the private sector, which accounted for the majority of replies. This confirmed the commission's opinion that grass-roots movements and private business interests have been prominent in the drunken driving campaign. No one should be surprised to learn that it is mainly the private sector that has encouraged and supported citizen action programs such as MADD, SADD (Students Against Driving Drunk), and RID.

NO MERE REFERENCE REPORT

While some criticism was voiced in the responses, the general feeling was one of enthusiasm and a pledge of support for a continuing national program to combat drunken driving. There was an implicit plea in most of the responses that the commission should not allow its report to become just another survey of a bad situation; the findings should not be used for reference purposes, gathering dust on the bookshelves of alcohol safety specialists. The message was obvious—this campaign against drunken drivers should not be allowed to falter!

The fifty-three recommendations offered a look at the overall problem of drinking and driving. It was not a narrow view focused on a single dramatic solution to the issue. The unity that the commission manifested must be attributed to its primary goal—to reduce the tragic toll of alcohol related deaths and injuries.

Essential to any successful countermeasure program is the need to change the deadly and widespread attitude that drinking and driving is socially acceptable. This demands involvement of the total community—within families, among friends, in the workplace, and at social settings. Above all else, the total message directed against drunken driving must not be obscured by indicting any one cause or any one age group. Abusive drinking and irresponsible driving are reprehensible whether the offender is young or old or is a social or problem drinker, and regardless of one's social standing or influence.

While the individual's right to drink must be upheld, public safety must be maintained. As a free society, the United States must be able to demonstrate its ability to balance personal freedom and safe movement by a system approach to the drunken driving problem. Our criticism must be directed at people's behavior, not at the bottle or the motor vehicle.

On September 26, 1983, the commission met in Atlanta for its last formal meeting. The original fifty-three recommendations were reduced to thirty-nine, the changes being a matter of style rather than substance. There was no modification of the position taken by the commission in its interim report. The chief concerns hinged upon the earlier recommendations relating to mandatory sentences and the age of twenty-one as the minimum legal age for the purchase and consumption of all alcoholic beverages. Both of these issues will be addressed later in this chapter.

At this meeting, the commission approved by an overwhelming vote (twenty-eight to one) a continuing, national, nongovernmental commission to monitor the drunken driving issue. This body was specifically charged with the implementation of the PCDD's recommendations and the coordination of future programs designed to halt the slaughter on the nation's highways.

COMMISSION GOALS

In the final analysis, the commission recognized that DUI is basically a state and local concern for which state and community solutions must be found. The report should serve both as a catalyst for this kind of action and a guideline for states and localities in the development of innovative and effective long-range programs. The wholehearted support given to the commission during its existence must continue if this nation is to realize a significant reduction in the number of lives wasted in alcohol related accidents.

The commission became convinced that any program seeking to solve the drunken driving problem must include some key elements.

Prevention—Most importantly, drunken driving must be recognized as socially unacceptable. The public must focus on changing the tolerance of drunkenness and drunken driving. It must realize the grave consequences of DUI that require all citizens to take personal responsibility for prevention in their own social circles.

Community Focus—Since the attitudes which mold drinking and driving behavior are largely shaped within the community and because the primary administrative responsibility for efforts to combat drunken driving rests with the groups and governments at that level, efforts must have a community focus.

System Approach—Because attempts to deal with this problem involve a large number of governmental agencies and nongovernmental groups, a system approach must be employed to ensure that the activities of these groups are coordinated and that they interrelate smoothly in order to enhance their effectiveness.

General Deterrence—In order to ensure that laws play their proper role in discouraging the largest possible number of potentially drunken drivers, states and localities should take a general deterrence approach in developing short-term remedies to the problem, focusing on increasing the perception of risk of arrest.

Grass-roots Support—To help develop personally responsible drinking and driving behavior and to build a community consensus behind effective countermeasure programs, citizen support through grass-roots groups must be encouraged.

Self-funding Programs—Because drivers under the influence are responsible for this problem with its great resulting human cost, it is appropriate that offenders should defray the costs of enforcement, prosecution, adjudication, treatment, and education. Budget constraints have been cited as a major reason for the inaction or delay by states or communities in enacting and implementing these programs. The commission felt that they can and should be made self-funding by way of offenders' fees. It also recommended an adequate system of funding by the federal government to states, local communities, and even the private sector. The commission recommended that the administration and Congress consider new dedicated funds, as well as traditional dedicated revenue funds, such as the Highway Trust Fund.

Supplemental Grants for States

It should be noted here that Federal Incentive Grants amounting to $125 million over three years became available for fiscal year 1983. In Section 408, Congress amended the Alcohol Traffic Safety Program Act of 1982 by providing for additional funds for those states that have in place, or adopt by legislation or regulation, and implement effective programs to reduce the drunken driving problem. The act established criteria that, if met, would qualify a state to receive up to an additional 50 percent of its Section 402 fiscal year 1983 allocation from the Highway Safety Act.

A two-tier grant system was established—basic and supplemental. In order to qualify for the 30 percent basic incentive grant, four requirements that square with similar recommendations in the report of the PCDD must be met. They are:

1. prompt license suspension for not less than ninety days for a first offender and not less than a year in the case of a repeat offender,
2. mandatory sentences that are not subject to suspension or probation,
3. an illegal per se blood alcohol concentration of 0.10 percent, and
4. increased enforcement of alcohol related traffic laws and increased efforts to inform the public of such enforcement.

To qualify for an additional 20 percent supplemental grant, a state must have a license suspension system in which the time from the date of arrest to suspension does not exceed an average of forty-five days. It must also have in place, or adopt and implement, eight of twenty-one supplemental criteria. To receive a 10 percent supplemental grant, a state must have this same suspension system but only four of the requirements. Again, these criteria reflect the substance of identical recommendations of the commission. The twenty-one requirements are:

1. to establish twenty-one years of age as the minimum for drinking any alcoholic beverages;
2. to coordinate state alcohol–highway safety programs;
3. to establish rehabilitation and treatment programs for persons arrested and convicted of alcohol related traffic offenses;
4. to establish state task forces of governmental and nongovernmental leaders to increase awareness of the problem, to more effectively apply

drunken driving laws, and to involve governmental and private sector leaders in programs combating the drunken driving problem;

5. to use a statewide driver record system readily accessible to the courts and the public that can identify drivers repeatedly convicted of DUI;

6. to establish in each major political subdivision a locally coordinated alcohol–traffic safety program that involves enforcement, adjudication, licensing, public information, education, prevention, rehabilitation and treatment, and management and program evaluation;

7. to establish prevention and long-term education programs on drunken driving;

8. to authorize courts to conduct presentence or postsentence screenings of convicted drunken drivers;

9. to develop and implement a statewide evaluation system to assure program quality and effectiveness;

10. to establish a plan for achieving self-support of the state's total alcohol–traffic safety program;

11. to use roadside sobriety checks as part of a comprehensive alcohol–safety enforcement program;

12. to establish programs to encourage citizen reports to the police of alcohol related traffic offenses;

13. to establish 0.08 percent BAC as presumptive evidence of DUI;

14. to adopt a one-license/one-record policy and to participate fully in the National Driver Register and the Driver License Compact;

15. to authorize the use of preliminary breath tests where there is probable cause to suspect a driver is impaired;

16. to limit plea bargaining in alcohol related offenses;

17. to provide victim assistance and victim restitution programs and require the use of a victim impact statement prior to sentencing in all cases where death or serious injury results from an alcohol related traffic offense;

18. to provide for mandatory impoundment or confiscation of license plates/tags of any vehicle operated by an individual whose license has been suspended or revoked for an alcohol related offense;

19. to enact legislation or regulations authorizing the arresting officer to determine the type of chemical test to be used to measure intoxication and to authorize the arresting officer to require more than one chemical test;

20. to establish liability against any person who serves alcoholic beverages to an individual who is visibly intoxicated; and

21. to use innovative programs.

This incentive grant system encourages state legislators to introduce the kind of bills that will guarantee compliance with the criteria. Surely, the passage of Section 408 prompted a larger volume than usual of state alcohol related legislation in 1983. In 1982, a total of 378 bills were introduced and incomplete figures for 1983 show that at least 763 bills had been introduced in state legislatures; of these, 129 bills were reported to have been enacted in 39 states.

While the number of bills introduced by a state does not necessarily reflect the full extent of legislative action, it does indicate the unprecedented interest in alcohol legislation. The grass-roots organizations have maintained a close watch on state legislative activity, and the media have publicized such innovative alcohol countermeasures as roadblocks, preliminary breath tests, mandatory sentencing, license suspension, and listing the names of individuals charged with DUI. Many community newspapers give special emphasis to the publication of offenders' names during the year-end holiday period.

TARGETS FOR SAFETY PROGRAMS

The campaign to get drunken drivers off the highway was highlighted further in 1983 by the "Targets of Opportunities" program developed by the National Highway Traffic Safety Administration. This concept targeted ten sites across the country to promote community-based general deterrence alcohol programs. Once again, the multifaceted attack on drunken driving was demonstrated by this approach. These guidelines were in keeping with, and coordinated with, the recommendations of the commission's interim report. The emphasis was on (1) the short-term general deterrence approach, creating a public perception of increased risk of arrest for drunken driving; (2) community focus; (3) system approach; (4) self-funded programs; (5) citizen support; and (6) long-term prevention, changing the societal attitudes toward drinking and driving by developing responsible attitudes toward alcohol use and driving in the predriving population.

As an example, Salt Lake City's Target of Opportunity program opened April 4, 1983. Ten years before, the very same area was involved in ASAP, and an evaluation of the ASAP indicated that Salt Lake City was one of the twelve sites that had achieved significant reduction of traffic fatalities. The ongoing concern for highway safety and the coordinated system approach in Utah have made it a leader in the campaign to reduce the carnage on the nation's highways. For example, 151 of the traffic deaths were alcohol related in 1981; 113 were alcohol related in 1982; arrests for DUI were 8,921 for 1981; in 1982, over 11,000; convictions for DUIs were at 60 percent in 1982, significantly higher than in other jurisdictions.

The sampling for both ASAP and the Target of Opportunity in Utah may be considerably smaller than in heavily traveled, populous sections of the country. However, their records show that a concerted community campaign can and does work to make highways safer. Certainly, funds are needed and guidelines could be provided from the federal government, but the issue must be confronted at the city, county, and state level if it is to be effective and lasting.

Commission Recommendations

In making its final report, the commission again reminded the nation that changes in the laws are not enough. Legal and judicial steps will bring only a short-term solution to the drunken driving problem. What is needed amid a climate of concern and a demand for action is a coordinated, decade-long commitment to the issue. To emphasize one aspect at the expense of all the other elements of safe driving and responsible drinking policies would mislead the American people into thinking a remedy was at hand.

Society has shown itself willing to participate in this crusade for public safety. What must be provided are the long-term leadership and the use of innovative measures for deterrence. The commission, in making thirty-nine recommendations, offered a blueprint designed to sustain an environment that will no longer tolerate the impaired and drunken driver.

In the final distillation of all the recommendations, the major elements were categorized as (1) public awareness, (2) public education, (3) private sector, (4) alcoholic beverage regulation, (5) system support, (6) enforcement, (7) prosecution, (8) adjudication, (9) licensing administration, and (10) education and treatment.

At this point, a detailed treatment of each section is hardly in order. While some overlapping is apparent in a careful study of the report, each one of the thirty-nine recommendations stands on its own. To touch upon some of the major aspects of the report should prove useful. The order in which they are listed is in no way intended to reflect any sense of priority in a timetable for enactment. Some major aspects are:

1. the call for a more extensive nationwide public information and education program;
2. the adoption of twenty-one years as the minimum legal purchasing and public possession age for all alcoholic beverages;
3. the enforcement of mandatory sanctions for first offenders with a license suspension of not less than ninety days plus one hundred hours of community service or a minimum of forty-eight consecutive hours in jail (the sanctions are increased for repeat offenders);
4. the elimination of plea bargaining;
5. a prompt license suspension with a thirty-day jail sentence for one who drives with a suspended or revoked license;
6. self-funding mechanisms at the state and local levels;
7. private sector involvement, especially on the part of the motor vehicle, insurance, and alcoholic beverage industries;
8. annual training sessions for police, prosecutors, lawyers, and judges;
9. the creation of task forces in states where they do not exist; and
10. the encouragement of citizen action groups and the need to expand them.

Despite the dramatic nature of the issue, drunken driving is not the only important social problem that clamors for public attention. Nonetheless, public service announcements, billboards, and well-planned media releases can keep the DUI issue before the public long after initial interest has passed. Likewise, at home and in the work setting, family, friends, and associates should become acquainted with deterrent strategies to keep an intoxicated person from driving. The "brother's keeper" concept should not be ignored.

One technique that has been used to accentuate social disapproval of drunken drivers is to print the names of all persons arrested and/or convicted of DUI in the daily newspapers (as in the St. Louis area). The public needs to be made more aware of the risks of apprehension or accidents when driving while impaired, not just drunk.

Too many people are confused about the amount of alcohol which can cause impairment. A handy "know your limits" card details BAC for different weights and the number of drinks. The myth that one can drive as well after drinking as when cold sober must be dispelled. The macho image portrayed in some alcoholic beverage advertisements is a source of great concern to safety-minded people. The message must come through loud, clear, and coordinated that drinking and driving do not mix—the combination maims, kills, and destroys property.

PERSUASION NOT PROHIBITION

Perhaps the question of alcoholic beverage regulation is the most challenging one. This involves a matter of states' rights guaranteed with the repeal of the Volstead Act in 1933. Prohibition is not a valid response to the issue, either as one person's problem or as it relates to public safety. Appropriate governmental supervision means not only taxes, but also concern for the health and welfare of the citizenry.

The commission recommended that the alcoholic beverage industry, servers, and state control agencies should cooperate in efforts to warn the public of the hazards of drinking and driving. With so much drinking outside the home, the likelihood is that even more impaired drivers will be on the road. The growth of "happy hours" at hotels and bars and weekend partying are prime examples of increasing risks to safety on the highways.

Some twenty states have specific statutes or court decisions which impose dram shop liability. These laws are directed at sellers and servers of alcoholic beverages, whether they are part of a commercial operation or a private party. The failure to prevent intoxicated individuals from driving could prove costly if damages are assessed in dram shop cases. A growing number of cases have resulted in extremely heavy settlements against drinking establishments, communities, and private parties.

In a society that is ready to file a suit for every conceivable reason, the old maxim *caveat emptor* (let the buyer beware) has changed to "let the seller beware." For example, a bar in Texas is part of a $2.5 million judgment in a drunken driving accident; the town of Ware, Massachusetts, was sued for $873,000 because the town police did not recognize the drunkenness of a stopped motorist who subsequently had an accident that killed a man and his infant daughter.

With the hope of reducing the frightening death rate among young people, the commission urged the immediate adoption of twenty-one "as the minimum legal purchasing and public possession age for all alcoholic beverages." Any number of studies have shown that by raising the legal drinking age, nighttime fatal crashes involving drivers ages eighteen to twenty-one decreased by an average of 28 percent.

A patchwork of legal minimum ages exists—eighteen in some states and nineteen, twenty, or twenty-one in others; but as of 1983, nineteen states had set twenty-one as the minimum. A problem arises, however, when bordering states have a lower drinking age. Unless regional uniformity exists, there is no way to counter the dangers inherent in commuting to consume beverages denied youths in their own states. Governors of seven northeastern states have proposed the uniform age of twenty-one. Of that group, New Jersey and Pennsylvania have adopted the proposal. The commission recommended that legislation should be enacted at the state and federal level requiring twenty-one as the minimum legal age for purchasing and possessing all alcoholic beverages. The commission went on to say that "such legislation should provide that the Secretary of the United States Department of Transportation disapprove any project under Section 106 of the Federal Aid Highway Act (Title 23, United States Code) for any state not having and enforcing such a law."

The critics of age twenty-one legislation argue since eighteen-year-olds can marry, vote, serve in the armed forces, and hold property, to deny them the freedom to drink is a violation of rights. The legislation's advocates do not see any magic in this cutoff point, but they point to statistics that show a startling correlation between age and alcohol related accidents. This provision does not seek to punish unduly one particular age group, but it does recognize a threat to public safety. The commission looked at this age issue as essentially that of experience in drinking habits and acquired driving skills.

CHALLENGES TO THE COURTS

One of the early steps taken by the grass-roots organizations was to monitor court cases. Most often they would find DUI cases thrown out of court. The "there but for the grace of God go I" attitude has too long prevailed in the courts—hence, the reluctance to impose jail sentences or to mandate community service. However, the adjudication of DUIs must be swift, certain, and just.

Judges must be allowed discretion, but they should not disdain the need for more severe sanctions for repeat offenders. It is not enough for the judiciary to safeguard the rights of the offenders; the rights of the public and the immediate victims of the DUI offenses cannot be ignored. Justice Learned Hand said, "If we are to keep our democracy, there must be one commandment, 'Thou Shalt Not Ration Justice.' "

Since DUI cases are not viewed with the alarm that is sounded in sensational cases, the victims are frequently the forgotten victims of our legal system. In some judicial quarters the victims, when organized (as with MADD and RID), are regarded as obstructionists. Controversy and protests do occur after judges dismiss with little or no penalties drunken drivers who have killed people. In jurisdictions where judges are subject to election, citizen action groups have been effective in targeting lenient justices during political campaigns.

It is unseemly for judges to complain about the intensification of the public campaign against drinking and driving, as did one district court justice in Maryland. After acquitting a governor's aide of a DUI charge on August 3, 1983, the judge responded to the local aroused citizen group, calling them "sanctimonious nondrinkers who look down their noses at anyone who drinks" (*Baltimore Sun*, August 12). It would be hard to believe such a jurist could ever appreciate victims' impact statements.

Lacking a high priority in the eyes of some prosecutors, DUI cases often are the special object of plea bargaining. This has resulted in reduced charges that reaffirm the social acceptability of drinking and driving. In many cases, the first offender has the charge wiped out and, without an effective tracking system such as a computerized national driver register, the "next arrest" continues to be the "first." There have been cases involving as many as forty dismissed charges.

There are trial difficulties relating to BAC, breath testing, and other evidence of impairment. To offset this problem, the commission recommended enactment of 0.10 percent illegal per se. A person should be regarded as in violation of this law if a blood alcohol test is taken within three hours and shows 0.10 percent or higher. Forty-one states had this law in 1983, while only twelve had it in 1981.

Furthermore, 0.08 percent level should be presumed to be driving under the influence. Medical and driving tests show that most people are impaired at that level. As of January 1, 1983, the state of Maine places the level for teenage drivers at 0.02 percent, which is the result of drinking one beer.

Because they believed that plea bargaining runs counter to the will of the people and minimizes the consequences of drunken driving, the commission said, "Prosecutors and courts should not reduce DUI charges." This spoke directly to the questionable practice of "filing cases" or dismissing charges without a written report. Prosecutors are enjoined to charge accurately without routinely altering DUI charges to non–alcohol related offenses. It is this element in the prosecution stage that has made MADD and similar groups really "mad."

Driving with a suspended or revoked license is not uncommon. Since the risk of apprehension for motor vehicle violations is perceived as very low, many drivers will not hesitate to go on the road without a license. It was recommended that any person convicted of driving with a suspended or revoked license should receive a mandatory jail sentence of at least thirty days. Many may recall the tragic accident that claimed seven lives in 1983 at a Connecticut tollgate. The truck driver had any number of offenses involving license suspensions and revocations.

Once again, all licensing administration and prosecution will be helped immeasurably when a computerized national driver register (NDR) is fully operational. Four states will be selected for a pilot project on the register, and it is planned to have this equipment in all fifty states in the future. Unlike written inquiries that take as long as two weeks for answers from state to state, the NDR will supply information in a matter of minutes. Such a computerized system that lists all violations against all drivers will halt the practice of going from one state to another for licenses.

QUESTIONS OF COST

The limited monies flowing from Washington to the states make self-funding at the local level imperative. The commission recommended dedicated funding emphasizing the need for offender fines and fees for alcohol treatment programs.

In this fashion, New York has been able to return millions of dollars received to local jurisdictions. The smallest offender fee in New York is $250; it increases for multiple convictions. All the fines collected are returned to counties, which then channel funds to the municipalities. The language is broad enough in the Stop DWI (driving while intoxicated) Program to allow the local jurisdictions discretion. However, there is accountability to the state, and there must be state approval of alcohol countermeasure programs. In 1982, the first year of this program, $7 million was returned to the counties to support municipal subdivisions. Over $10 million was distributed to the counties in 1983. Although an infusion of funds is no assurance that new countermeasures will work any better than some previous programs, certainly this aid to local enforcement and prosecution agencies allows an enhancement of effective programs.

Besides the responsibility of the alcoholic beverage industry in the ongoing campaign against drinking and driving, private sector support must be found in all industries, particularly motor vehicle and insurance industries. Employee programs should be part of company sponsored events. Timing these programs with vacation periods and holidays takes advantage of "teachable moments" to illustrate the need for caution, moderation, and responsibility.

Community, social, civic, and other common interest organizations can join in educational efforts to strengthen the support network. Also, these groups can join hands with corporations to deal with employees and members who are experiencing alcohol abuse problems. Prevention is more desirable than punitive measures, and it is in these natural social and work settings that intervention should occur, a necessity if attitudes, not only laws, are to change.

A support system looks to all the components in society to combat the drunken driving scourge. The commission recognized the importance of grass-roots groups and task forces as crucial to effective local and state responses to the drunken driver. These organizations also help to monitor the effectiveness of activities already in place and to call for the implementation of new procedures and policies.

Solutions for Safety

With the completion of its work on December 31, 1983, the Presidential Commission on Drunk Driving, in conjunction with the National Safety Council, established the nongovernmental

National Commission Against Drunk Driving. The overall goal of this new commission is to assist in the realization of a public attitude that holds that "drunkenness and drunken driving are socially unacceptable behavior." The main thrust of this commission at the outset will be to monitor implementation of the recommendations of the PCDD. This body will continue to serve as a bridge between the public and private sectors in much the same manner that the presidential commission served as a catalyst for national attention to the issue and action at every level of government. A number of the presidential commission members are serving as members of this new commission, thereby assuring a sustained campaign to reduce drunken driving.

Drunken driving is not the intractable problem that many see it to be, but finding a solution is a challenge that faces the nation. The commission did not offer a cure-all for a longstanding social ill. Rather, it made recommendations to serve as guidelines of official response to the issue. The prompt adoption of these recommendations will assure a workable and fair criminal justice system. They are designed to deter where possible and to treat and/or punish where necessary. While the publicity surrounding its work may have focused on the areas of enforcement, prosecution, and adjudication, the commission stressed that prevention is the only long-term hope to solve the DUI problem.

Fortunately, the political climate and the public atmosphere have never before been so favorable for undertaking and underwriting educational efforts to prevent drunken driving. In the past, public awareness had to be built; now it is very high. The lonely voices of those crying out to stop the slaughter on our highways have grown into a nationwide chorus of concern. This level of consciousness suggests that the American public is prepared for the next step—educational programs designed to prevent intoxication and drunken driving in their own social surroundings.

To further increase highway safety, drivers should be reminded to "'buckle up" when they get in their vehicles. The responsible use of safety belts and child restraints is the best defense mechanism against the ever-present danger of the drunken driver on the road. Despite the evidence pointing to the value of seat belts, the current usage rate in the United States is very low, about 11 percent. It is estimated that the use of seat belts reduces the chance of a fatality or serious injury in a collision by 50 percent. Since 50 percent of all traffic fatalities are alcohol related, the value of a seat belt is even more important. The commission strongly urged the enactment of safety belt and child restraint usage laws.

RECOGNIZING THE TYPES

It is left to others to examine at length the types of drinkers. A very small percentage of social drinkers cause accidents, but because their number is so great, the percentage translates into the majority of accidents. However, it is known that heavy or problem alcohol abusers account for a disproportionate share of drunken driving incidents compared to the total drinking and driving population.

If education and prevention systems are to be effective, rehabilitation programs and alcohol treatment centers must identify each type of drinker. Return of a suspended or revoked license should be contingent upon the successful completion of an appropriate program. The commission made it abundantly clear that those convicted of DUI should understand that rehabilitation programs are definitely a *supplement* to—not a substitute for—sanctions. In all its deliberations, the commission recognized alcoholism as an illness. The concern for public safety has to be balanced with the need to treat, rather than merely automatically punish, an offender.

Drinking is here to stay, and driving is a prized privilege of the majority of Americans. Yet it is unrealistic to expect every car on the road to be operated by a "dry" driver. It is wise, and perhaps lifesaving, to heed the slogan "friends don't let friends drive drunk."

Encouraging Signs

What America must reconcile is the value of human life, the common good, the license to drive, the freedom to drink, the responsibility for public safety. The open road beckons a very mobile people, and the open container of one's favorite alcoholic beverage can prove refreshing, perhaps even beneficial. If they choose to drink at all, all citizens must learn to drink reasonably and protect their privilege to drive—safety is everyone's responsibility.

Some significant changes did take place in 1983. It was mentioned previously that over 763 bills on alcohol legislation were introduced and 129 enacted in 39 states—almost double the 378 introduced in 1982. In fiscal year 1983, some 38 percent of Section 402 highway funds ($39.6 out of $104.6 million) was allocated to drunken driving programs. In addition to this funding were the incentive grants (Section 408) allocating an amount up to 50 percent of the Section 402 funds for alcohol projects.

It is heartening to report that 5,580 fewer Americans were victims of highway accidents in 1982 compared to 1981—49,301 versus 43,721—which marks the best record in forty years (except for the oil embargo year of 1974). These figures are encouraging, but they indicate that the anti—drunken driving movement cannot be allowed to stall. There is still a long way to go to reduce the present tragic death toll.

Public safety is no accident, and everyone has a stake in it at home, at work, and on the road. America cannot afford to let drunken driving be socially acceptable on what is—apart from the tragic impact of alcohol—the world's best highway system. The social issue becomes a pressing moral imperative when lives are wasted needlessly because someone chose to drive irresponsibly.

In 1983 the PCDD, the grass-roots organizations, and the private and public sectors joined hands in this battle that is not won but only just begun. The issue of safety and sobriety must continue to be a concern of the whole spectrum of American society. The drama of the issue may feature drunken driving, but *all* the threats to public safety at home, work, and play when alcohol is abused must not be overlooked. To save one life would make the sacrifices of any individual worthwhile. What, then, can be said when the stakes are higher, the safety of human beings by the thousands? Drinking will not cease; driving will continue; the challenge for all Americans is to work for a social policy that makes the deadly combination unacceptable.

Ernest P. Noble, Ph.D., M.D.

7

Prevention of Alcohol Abuse and Alcoholism

Historical Perspective

Drastic shifts in attitudes about prevention of alcohol problems have occurred in our nation through its relatively brief history. During the colonial period, drinking alcoholic beverages was seen as a valued, indeed healthful, custom. Taxes derived from alcohol financed the militia and, in some colonies, the education and correction systems. But while drinking was cherished, habitual drunkenness was reviled and punished by whipping, by the stocks, and, in some instances, by exile. The issue at that time was not alcohol itself; rather, the fault was seen as the defective moral

ERNEST P. NOBLE *is the Pike Professor of Alcohol Studies and director of the Alcohol Research Center in the Department of Psychiatry and Biobehavioral Sciences at the University of California at Los Angeles. He was formerly the director of the National Institute on Alcohol Abuse and Alcoholism and later the associate administrator for science in the Alcohol, Drug Abuse, and Mental Health Administration. Upon leaving the federal government, Dr. Noble joined the faculty at the University of California at Irvine. He has been a speaker before distinguished national and international audiences. The author of numerous book chapters, abstracts, and national reports, Dr. Noble is also the coeditor of the two-volume work,* Biochemistry and Pharmacology of Ethanol.

character of those who indulged to the point of inebriation. Nevertheless, problems with alcohol were controlled and relatively minor in nature; society was small and homogeneous, social customs were powerful, and threats from the immediate environment were imminent.

As the country grew, traditions and social controls weakened, and by the 1750s alcohol was becoming "big business." A Baptist preacher made the first Kentucky whiskey in 1789, two years after the Constitution was ratified. By the end of the century, 2,000 distillers produced over 2 million gallons of liquor a year. At that time, Americans were consuming five gallons of whiskey a year for every man, woman, and child. Drunkenness became a common and bothersome problem in the growing cities. Even Thomas Jefferson complained that ardent spirits were a problem for his administration and "more trouble to me."

The temperance movement grew from the seed of that discontent. In 1826 the American Society of Temperance was founded, and it rapidly found followers, especially in the middle class. The central notion of this movement was that alcohol, previously viewed as innocuous and even healthful, is dangerous and addictive. The Civil War interrupted the movement, but it convened shortly thereafter and grew in stature and force, culminating in the Eighteenth Amendment, which was ratified in 1919.

The Eighteenth Amendment, like the Volstead Act that implemented it, did not actually forbid drinking—it merely attempted to make it difficult. Specifically, prohibition banned the manufacture, sale, and transportation of intoxicating beverages and gave the states equal power to enact and enforce prohibitory laws. However, the need of a thirsty public ready to pay higher prices for black-market alcohol, coupled with the unwillingness of authorities to commit essential funds to enforce these laws, created corruption and lawlessness and contributed to a counterprohibition movement.

Our nation, in the deep depression, elected a President who saw that repeal would be a popular movement and a means to rejuvenate an industry, create jobs, and fill government coffers with taxes. Franklin D. Roosevelt campaigned for repeal and shortly after inauguration modified the Volstead Act to permit the sale of beer. Congress followed suit, and in December 1933 the repeal process was ratified in the form of the Twenty-first Amendment.

The perception lingers that prohibition was an abject failure. This, in part, is true but the "Noble Experiment" was not without its benefits to the health of Americans. Certainly, the increased crime associated with bootlegging, the demise of the legal alcoholic beverage industry, and the loss of tax revenues were on the negative side of the prohibition ledger. However, the curtailment of the availability of alcohol had the salutary effect of substantially reducing alcohol related morbidity and mortality. Still, in the hubris of "happy days are here again" the federal government, except for tax collection and some minor regulatory controls, passed its responsibility for alcohol issues to the states in the form of alcohol beverage control (ABC) laws.

A completely different view began to emerge regarding alcohol problems and their prevention in the 1930s when alcoholism was recognized as a disease. Within this concept, alcohol itself was not imputed with universally toxic and addicting characteristics, nor was the drinker considered to be a weak, morally depraved individual. Rather, the problem was seen as the result of a unique biochemical interaction between alcohol and certain drinkers. As such, the problem could never be cured, but recovery was possible through abstinence. This view was advanced by Alcoholics Anonymous, and its advocates were the recovering alcoholics, their families, and their friends.

The Yale School of Alcohol Studies, with its distinguished scholars (notably E. M. Jellinek), brought academic credibility to the view of alcoholism as a disease. The National Council on Alcoholism (NCA), organized and established in 1944 by recovering alcoholics, brought to national visibility the efforts of volunteers on behalf of alcoholic persons. Its efforts aimed at getting the alcoholic person into treatment, destigmatizing the disease, and educating the public about the disease of alcoholism. The movement gained further breadth and legitimacy when the American Medical Association (AMA), the American Psychiatric Association (APA), the World Health Organization (WHO), and other voluntary and professional organizations, in addition to the alcoholic beverage industry, declared alcoholism a disease. The primary emphasis was treatment; the problem was seen to be "in the person and not in the bottle," and prevention efforts were essentially relegated to public information and education.

Primarily through the efforts of recovering alcoholics—Senator

Harold Hughes, Thomas P. Pike, Marty Mann, R. Brinkley Smithers, and other notable figures—a major focus formed in the federal government when Public Law 91–616 was enacted in 1970 establishing the National Institute on Alcohol Abuse and Alcoholism (NIAAA). Most funds appropriated for NIAAA were earmarked, not unexpectedly, for treatment and services to the alcoholics. A much smaller percentage was allotted for research and prevention—a situation in marked contrast to other health institutes within the Public Health Service.

In 1976 Congress mandated the director of the NIAAA to take a hard look at the scope of the national alcohol problem and consider the agency's effectiveness in controlling it. It was readily apparent that NIAAA, with the collaboration of voluntary agencies, was highly successful in increasing the nation's awareness of alcoholism as a problem, fostering the destigmatization of the disease, and helping to stimulate programs for the identification and treatment of the afflicted. However, primary prevention efforts were few and weak and based essentially on educating the public about "responsible drinking." Unfortunately, the prevailing scene showed that alcohol problems were enormous, and practically every indicator since Repeal revealed a worsening of these problems.

In the *Third Special Report to Congress on Alcohol and Health* (Noble, 1978) NIAAA experts estimated that 10 million adults and 3.3 million teenagers suffered from alcohol problems. In 1984 the NIAAA reported that annual deaths totaled between 61,000 and 97,000. The economic burden of alcohol problems reported for the nation in 1978 was $43 billion annually. (In a report submitted in March 1983 by the Congressional Office of Technology Assessment, this rose to $120 billion.) Per capita alcohol consumption in the United States in the 1970s (approximately 2.7 gallons per year) was higher than in the period that preceded Prohibition and the highest level in recorded history. Thus, despite the dedicated and well-intentioned efforts of many, the nation appeared to be losing the battle against the alcohol problem. This called for a serious examination of goals and objectives, particularly in the area of prevention.

As the NIAAA reviewed the extensive biomedical, clinical, and epidemiological literature, an inescapable truth kept constantly recurring—the more an individual, a group, or a society drinks alcohol, the more that entity experiences alcohol problems. The institute assessed the scholarly writings on alcohol problem prevention, paid site visits to various prevention programs both in the United States and abroad, evaluated its own efforts in prevention, and held extensive discussions with experts in the field. It became apparent that—with the exception of programs aimed at teenage drinkers and drunken drivers—the strategies for prevention of alcohol problems were primarily directed at early identification and treatment of alcoholics. Furthermore, much of the work in prevention focused on the host or individual; less attention was paid to environmental variables, and practically no serious efforts were devoted to alcohol itself.

The NIAAA, in its Five-Year National Plan, proposed in 1977 a broad-gauged prevention program, *part* of which intended to stabilize the levels of per capita alcohol consumption. At first a great hue and cry was heard from several alcoholism organizations and the alcoholic beverage industry, labeling the plan as "neoprohibitionistic" since one aspect of the plan dealt with measures to control the availability of alcohol. Over time, however, considerable support was obtained for NIAAA's 1977 prevention approach.

The American Medical Society on Alcoholism was one of the first to support the approach, followed by the Institute of Medicine of the National Academy of Sciences. That prestigious body concluded in at least two reports and several conferences that policies for the control of alcohol availability are a necessary and viable component for effective prevention of alcohol problems. The NCA, the largest and most powerful of the voluntary organizations, originally took no position on NIAAA's prevention plan but came forth in 1982 with a "Prevention Position Statement" that strongly endorses control measures, curbs on advertising, higher taxes, minimum legal drinking ages (MLDAs), and labeling of alcoholic beverages. The Presidential Commission on Drunk Driving, in its final report of December 1983, recommends that all states increase the MLDA to age twenty-one. WHO, in numerous past and recent reports prepared by panels of international experts, provides evidence for the importance and effectiveness of control measures in the prevention of alcohol problems. (See Brunn et al., 1975; Edwards, 1983; Edwards et al., 1977; Mosher, 1982; WHO, 1980.)

The field of alcohol abuse and alcoholism approaches another crossroad. The fifty years after Prohibition witnessed a humane understanding for treatment of the alcoholic. That effort should and must continue. However, the great challenge now—indeed, one the public is demanding—is how to effectively minimize the enormous burden of harm of the third major health problem in America. The knowledge and tools to do so do exist, as crude as they may be. Does America have the energy and the will to begin in earnest? Or is the nation destined by inaction, ineffective efforts, or emotion to repeat the errors of the past?

Etiological Bases of Alcohol Problems

The reasons people drink or experience alcohol problems are poorly understood. A plethora of biological, psychological, and sociocultural theories abounds (Armor et al., 1978), but no simple discipline or theory has adequately explained the progression from abstention to social drinking to alcoholism or other alcohol problems.

Biologists have proposed theories that postulate that alcoholism is due to an inherited metabolic defect for which alcohol acts as a caloric substitute (genetotrophic theory) or that endocrine dysfunctions, particularly pituitary adrenal insufficiency, constitute a stimulus to drink (endocrine theory). Unfortunately, these theories have not been substantiated by empirical findings. More recently, biologists have suggested that alcoholics may have a unique capacity to form and accumulate in their bodies substances with addictive properties (tetrahydroisoquinolines) as a consequence of alcohol ingestion. Others have proposed an inborn deficit in levels of endogenous morphine-like substances (endorphins) in their brain; they drink alcohol to increase the levels of these euphorogenic substances.

There are also notions that the neuronal membrane (structure that surrounds the neuron) in the brains of alcoholics is different in composition and, therefore, in susceptibility to alcohol than in those who are not destined to become alcoholics. This may explain some findings that show that sons of alcoholic fathers display different brain electrical activity and greater tolerance to alcohol than sons of nonalcoholics. Still others suggest that some ethnic groups, such as Orientals, are biologically protected from becoming alcoholics because they lack a specific liver enzyme (an isozyme of aldehyde dehydrogenase) that results in the alcohol flush when they consume alcohol. An opposing idea suggests that alcoholics and their children produce high amounts of a toxic substance (acetaldehyde) when they consume alcohol that not only damages tissues but produces addictive substances.

These and other interesting ideas, while generating further experimentation, remain unproven. At this time there are no biological markers for determining who will or will not become an alcoholic. However, given that hereditary factors play a role in certain forms of alcoholism, it is not unduly optimistic to predict that accurate biological markers for some types of alcoholism and alcohol related problems will become available in the near future.

Since human beings are thinking, feeling, and behaving animals, psychological theories have also been advanced to explain alcohol problems. Psychodynamic formulations have received considerable attention in this regard. These attribute alcohol problems to faulty parent-child relationships that lead to feelings of dependency, powerlessness, and lack of self-esteem, which are compensated by the pharmacological properties of alcohol and the oral gratification it provides. Unfortunately, disruptive experiences of childhood are not uniquely associated with alcohol problems; they may increase the likelihood of other types of psychopathology as well. Furthermore, psychoanalysis has not been shown to be a generally useful treatment for the active alcoholic.

Another psychological theory attributes the development of alcoholism to certain universal personality traits—low stress tolerance, perceptual dependence, negative self-image, feelings of insecurity, isolation, and depression. Unfortunately, most of the research done on personality traits has been undertaken on alcoholics after they have developed their problems. Therefore, cause and effect variables cannot be easily separated. As yet no premorbid "alcoholic" personality has been found. However, with recent advances in neuropsychological theory and testing, especially as they relate to assessing attention, visual-spatial configurations, cognition, and information processing, it soon may be quite feasible to use these tests to identify individuals who carry a high risk for certain types of alcoholism.

In yet another psychological area, behavioral theorists believe drinking to be a learned pattern involving social situations and customs, emotional and cognitive experiences, personal expectations, and reinforcing conditions. Alcoholism and related problems are viewed as maladaptive behavioral responses that can be "unlearned" through appropriate behavioral modifications. Attention is paid to a wide variety of factors that serve to initiate or trigger excessive drinking. Many of these behavioral learning approaches unfortunately do not take into consideration the basic properties of alcohol as a drug, and their application to treating the alcohol dependent person remains highly controversial.

There is also a wide variety of sociocultural theories to explain alcohol problems. While acknowledging the importance of biological and psychological variables, socioculturalists assert that problem drinking can be predicted by demographic variables that include age, sex, religion, ethnic origin, socioeconomic status, and urbanization. One popular theory postulates that cultural norms define acceptable and unacceptable alcohol use. Another attributes an important role to familial patterns in providing role models and social learning experiences for children.

Social instability, crisis, and stress have been proposed also as a model for contributing to alcohol problems. Social factors that have frequently been implicated in excessive drinking include, among others, changing roles experienced in transition to adolescence, marriage, parenthood, separation, divorce, unemployment, and death of a spouse.

In addition to social factors, larger cultural stress factors have been implicated in problem drinking. Among these are overcrowding, threat of war and annihilation, adverse economic conditions, poverty, high crime rates, and other indigenous cultural stress factors.

Research, just as other human endeavors, is influenced by the prevailing *Zeitgeist*. Investigative activities on alcohol problems in the post-Prohibition era, therefore, emphasized unique host vulnerabilities and thus, for a considerable period, underplayed alcohol's role in contributing many biomedical and psychosocial problems. However, as the knowledge base on alcohol and alcohol problems expanded, particularly since the mid-1970s, the evidence began to show strongly that alcohol itself is a drug imbued with potentially toxic and addictive characteristics and that its excessive use can contribute to personal and social perturbation. Thus, while factors within the host's metabolism, psyche, and society may contribute to the development of alcohol problems, alcohol in its own right does alter metabolism, psyche, and society in such a manner as to cause seriously dysfunctional states.

Prevention

A DEFINITION

Prevention of alcohol problems is defined as actions that are designed to bar, to delay, or to diminish the detrimental effects of alcohol. Prevention has been divided into three categories: (1) *primary*—actions that promote health or are undertaken prior to detection of the problem; (2) *secondary*—detection of problems in their early, asymptomatic stages and intervention to arrest their progress; and (3) *tertiary*—intervention after the development and full manifestation of the problem in order to reverse or arrest its progression.

This chapter will focus essentially on primary prevention. Lesser attention will be given to secondary prevention. Since tertiary prevention, or the treatment of alcohol abuse and alcoholism, is discussed in chapter 1, it will be alluded to here only briefly.

MAJOR CATEGORIES

What are the alcohol problems that are the aim of preventive efforts? A broad spectrum of biomedical and psychosocial problems exists. Presented here are six major categories where prevention is needed. Although examples within each category are given, these are by no means exhaustive.

Chronic Illness or Disability and Early Mortality—The results of excessive drinking appear in gastrointestinal disease, certain forms of cancer, cardiovascular dysfunction, malnutrition, endocrine abnormalities, peripheral neuropathies, infectious disease, diabetes, hypoglycemia, metabolic disorders, and fetalembryopathy (more commonly known as the fetal alcohol syndrome).

Acute Health Problems—Damage caused by alcohol includes alcohol overdose, alcohol-drug interactions, hypothermia, aspiration pneumonia, cardiac arrhythmia and failure, and allergic reactions.

Drunken Comportment—These problems include offensive, aggressive, and violent behavior such as robbery, assault, rape, homicide, and family violence. Victimization of drunken persons themselves also falls in this category.

Injuries, Death, and Property Loss—Traffic accidents, falls, fires, and drownings are among the accidents related to drinking.

Social Problems—The chronically excessive drinker's inability to fulfill major social roles appears in the form of loss of productivity and lack of opportunity to learn and earn, as well as the disruption of family life and adaptive social networks.

Mental Problems—Examples of problems associated with drinking include depression, suicide, anxiety, brain damage, alcohol withdrawal delirium, alcohol hallucinosis, and alcohol amnestic disorder.

STRATEGIES FOR PREVENTION

A major—perhaps the most effective—approach in the prevention of alcohol problems is to consider *both* the *supply* and the *demand* for alcohol. The control of supply strategy assumes that a reduction in the availability of alcoholic beverages and, therefore, their consumption will be followed by a reduction in problems related to alcohol, realized, in part, by laws and regulations that bear on alcohol. The control of demand strategy assumes that alcohol problems will be diminished through education, training, and treatment programs.

The demand or the supply strategy alone is not as effective as when the two strategies are combined. Applied together they produce a synergistic outcome in decreasing alcohol problems. Many prevention programs contain, in varying proportions and emphases, elements of both approaches. In other programs these elements are less readily discernible or sometimes not present at all.

Various strategies for the prevention of alcohol problems have been and are being tried. (See Blane and Hewitt, 1977; Cameron, 1979; DeLuca, 1981; Moore and Gerstein, 1981; Noble, 1978; Popham et al., 1978; Robinson, 1982; Staulcup et al., 1979.) Some have promise for future development depending on the advancements in science and technology. Seven major strategies are presented here.

1. *Prohibition*—Enforce legal prohibition on the manufacture, distribution, and sale of alcoholic beverages.
2. *Consumption*—Employ strong and effective controls on the indiscriminate availability of alcohol.
3. *Knowledge*—Provide educational and promotional campaigns to dissuade people from excessive drinking and to make those with alcohol problems aware that they need to seek help.
4. *Alternative*—Assist individuals to engage in healthful and satisfying activities as alternatives to alcohol abuse.
5. *Treatment*—Identify individuals with alcohol problems and aid them in the recovery process.
6. *Deterrence*—Punish, through the use of the criminal justice system, certain problem drinkers who perpetrate harm upon themselves and others.
7. *Altering Contingencies*—Provide biomedical, physical, and social barriers to protect the drinker and others from harm.

The Public Health Model

Prevention strategies can be realized under the public health model (Noble, 1978). The three key elements of this model are (1) the host—the individual and his or her biopsychosocial susceptibilities to alcohol problems as well as the individual's knowledge about alcohol, attitudes that influence drinking patterns, and drinking behavior itself; (2) the agent—alcohol, its content, characteristics, distribution, and availability; and (3) the environment—the setting or context in which drinking occurs and the community mores that shape drinking practices.

All three elements are interactive and interdependent. Thus, in approaching the prevention of alcohol problems, the most effective strategies would be those that deal with all three elements of the public health model. This country learned from past experiences a painful lesson with the alcohol problem when it essentially dealt with only one of these elements.

THE HOST

Of the three elements of the public health model, the host has received by far the greatest attention during the past fifty years. The preponderant approach has been to treat individuals whose drinking has produced the most severe dysfunction (tertiary prevention) and, to a lesser extent, to identify and help those who are just manifesting alcohol problems (secondary prevention). Primary prevention attempts have been aimed mostly at two groups—youth and drinking drivers. More recently, the prevention of fetal alcohol syndrome has received some attention (Streissguth et al., 1980). However, major areas for primary prevention have either received inadequate attention or have remained untried.

Alcohol problems, besides being distributed in the general population (Cahalan and Room, 1974), find fertile ground for development in hosts with certain characteristics. Among these are heavy social drinkers in high-stress occupations such as the military; the recently separated, divorced, retired, and bereaved; families (particularly children) of alcoholics; delinquents; certain minority groups; and women, whose drinking patterns are changing and who are increasingly experiencing alcohol related problems. These high-risk and vulnerable groups are in strong need of host oriented primary prevention approaches.

Modes for changing the drinking practices of the host to healthier patterns of behavior have included education, mass communication, provision of alternatives, and intervention and treatment. The potential to decrease susceptibility to alcohol's harmful effects by biologically manipulating the host is a viable but futuristic approach.

Education—Alcohol education programs are perhaps the most visible of all prevention methods (Noble, 1978). Although some still teach complete abstention, the goals of such programs have gradually shifted toward (1) promoting responsible decision making about drinking, (2) reducing deviant drinking, (3) focusing on values as guides to and influences on behavior (values clarification) with or without specific reference to alcohol, and (4) improving psychological and social skills to cope with difficulties so that resorting to alcohol will be less likely.

Alcohol education has been mandatory in primary and secondary schools in every state since the temperance era, although relatively little attention has been directed to college or adult education programs. Workers in the temperance movement hoped that alcohol education would teach children the evils of alcohol and that an abstinent generation would grow up free of alcohol's problems. With the end of the domination of temperance interests over alcohol education, the goal of alcohol education in the schools became uncertain. Reviewing the alcohol education literature of the recent past, Milgram (1976) found recurring themes and stated: "In the 1940's alcohol education was characterized as weak and chaotic. . . . In the 50's . . . the approach was hit-or-miss. . . . In the 60's alcohol education was described as being ineffective. . . . Alcohol education in the schools in the 70's can be characterized as inadequate, ambivalent, and vague."

Although the effectiveness of alcohol education has not been demonstrated in the evaluative literature (Blane and Hewitt, 1977; Mandell, 1982; Moore and Gerstein, 1981), in general it is still considered important in preventing alcohol related problems. This belief is held because education as a solution to social problems is a longstanding faith in the United States. Consequently, the conventional response to criticism of alcohol education is to call for improvements in program design, program implementation, and evaluation. However, fundamental questions have been raised about the value of alcohol education in public school settings. Some have questioned the propriety of using an essentially academic institution for moral training and the prevention of social problems. Others have questioned whether school-based alcohol education can be effective when the adversary relationship that often exists between students and teachers is considered (Room and Sheffield, 1976).

There are further complications. It is generally illegal in the United States for anyone under the age of eighteen to purchase alcohol or be served a drink in a public establishment. In practice, however, half of all teenagers start drinking by age fifteen. This discrepancy between official community standards and actual behavior tends to promote emphasis on safe and innocuous issues and the vagueness noted in many alcohol education materials. Skeptics also wonder why the alcoholic beverage industry, with its eye on the bottom line, would like to teach moderation.

Thus there are many reasons why alcohol education as a means of prevention has failed in the United States: (1) the material taught is often unstandardized, ambiguous, and portrays ambivalent attitudes; (2) teachers often are not trained or hold idiosyncratic views in this area; (3) what is taught in schools and what is done in society are entirely different matters; (4) laws that relate to drinking vary from state to state and quite frequently are not enforced; and (5) a great deal of "education" is done via alcoholic beverage advertising and programing that glamorize alcohol and make an appeal to youth to drink.

Mass Communication—Modern mass communication campaigns on alcohol problems bear no comparison to the tremendous outpouring of materials by temperance groups in the nineteenth and early twentieth centuries (Room and Sheffield, 1976). The American public was then flooded with a wide assortment of pamphlets, novels, newspapers, sermons, and lectures during the country's longest and largest organized persuasive effort on a social issue. There was optimism on the part of temperance movement leaders that human behavior could be changed. It was believed that if the public knew the moral, social, and biomedical ill effects of alcohol, temperance behavior would ensue.

A similar attitude about alcohol problems pervades modern mass communication; however, these attempts have been more oriented toward alcoholism treatment than toward prevention. As a consequence of the alcoholism movement, a wide variety of autobiographies, novels, movies, television programs, documentaries, and self-improvement and inspirational works concerned with the detection and treatment of alcoholism have appeared in the last fifty years. Cumulatively, these have changed attitudes about alcoholism as a disease and helped to reduce stigma associated with alcoholism. It is no longer unusual for celebrities and other well-known and admired members of society to openly admit to alcoholism problems and receive help.

In early 1972 the NIAAA began to conduct a media campaign to increase the nation's awareness of the symptoms, consequences, and treatability of alcoholism and to teach individuals "responsible drinking." The media used included radio, television, printed advertisements, posters, and pamphlets. While these efforts increased the public's awareness about alcohol problems, there are serious doubts as to whether or not they brought about healthier drinking patterns. Indeed some (including this author) aver that the theme of "responsible drinking" is superficially seductive and operationally quite meaningless. Who, for example, is to be the arbiter of "responsible drinking" behavior? Should it be the alcoholic beverage industry with its understandable focus on net profits? Should it be the dedicated prohibitionists with equally sincere convictions? Should it be educators? Should it perhaps be the federal government acting as a well-meaning but intrusive "big brother"? The term "responsible drinking" was too ambiguous; it means what the person who utters it wants it to mean. This could be anything from total abstinence to not falling over the cat when tiptoing in from a late-night drinking bout. Because of the confusion that the term "responsible drinking" created, it was removed as the mainstay of the NIAAA's prevention efforts.

The thirty-second and sixty-second television public service spots, the usual format for messages warning of alcohol's dangers, did not prove to be a major influence on mores because they were forced to compete with a heavy concentration of advertising and programing that used sophisticated, sexual, and peer pressure themes to promote alcohol consumption. However, this is not to imply that mass media cannot be successfully used to communicate alcohol problem prevention messages, especially in the form of counteradvertising similar to the mass media antismoking campaigns (Moore and Gerstein, 1981; Wallack, 1980). In this respect, the most promising new approach in prevention entails education and training programs that combine carefully designed mass media campaigns with personalized behavioral training provided through schools, volunteer associations, or health maintenance organizations. The most widely known, but by no means the only, example is the Three Community Study (TCS) of the Stanford Health Disease Prevention Project (Farquhar et al., 1977; Farquhar, 1978).

The TCS was intended to determine whether state-of-the-art mass media programing in a community and intensive training of a segment of this community would be effective in modifying behaviors known to contribute to the risk of heart disease. Two towns in central California were selected for public health education, and a third town served as a control. Findings of this study are of particular interest. Smoking cessation was not achieved to any great extent in the town with mass media programing only, but 15 percent of those receiving mass media programing plus intensive instruction had quit smoking after three years (versus 0 to 15 percent of the high-risk controls). Dietary cholesterol levels decreased by more than 30 percent in both experimental communities (versus 10 percent in the control town). Changes in weight were not achieved by either method; in contrast, however, the control sample gained weight.

The TCS project, the project to reduce cardiovascular disease in Finland, and many other projects elsewhere may have valid lessons to be learned and applied to the prevention of alcohol related problems. Prevention projects that use radio, television, and the print media are likely to achieve a greater effectiveness when combined with follow-up such as discussion groups, interpersonal communications, and community involvement. Although directing these campaigns is more arduous, more expensive, and less immediate than simply developing spot announcements, the potential long-range benefits cannot be ignored.

Provision of Alternatives—Many prevention programs use alternative activities as a way of diverting an individual's attention from alcoholic beverages and of increasing self-esteem. Just as alcohol education began during the temperance era, so did the provision of alternatives gain popularity during that period (Room and Sheffield, 1976). The development of coffeehouses, the soft drink industry, YMCAs, YWCAs, parks, libraries, and sports programs was aimed, in part, at diverting individuals from drinking and providing them with positive outlets, sociability, health, and knowledge. However, after prohibition was repealed, alcoholic beverages were used at sports events, soft drinks were promoted as mixers, alcoholic beverages were used in parks and recreational areas, and Ys became less popular with the young.

Still, there is a growing movement to provide alternatives to drinking alcohol. Alcohol-free wines and beers are appearing on the market, and the use of bottled water and other nonalcoholic beverages is gaining popularity, particularly among the middle and upper classes. Alcohol-free bars are opening in various communities, and the ready availability of alcoholic beverages at sporting events is limited in more places. The increasing awareness of alcoholism and alcohol related problems, improvement in life styles, disease prevention, and consumer advocacy movements all contribute toward seeking alternatives to heavy alcohol use.

Early Identification, Intervention, and Treatment—Although the essential focus of this chapter is primary prevention, the total concept of prevention also includes treatment for those who are just beginning to develop alcohol related problems and those with severe manifestations of alcoholism or other alcohol related dysfunctions.

By far the greatest amount of chronically damaging drinking in American society occurs among employed persons and their families; skid row alcoholics represent less than 5 percent of those who suffer from alcoholism and alcohol related problems. Consequently, major themes of the alcoholism movement during the 1970s were the development of mechanisms to reach persons with alcohol problems in all levels of society and the early identification of developing problems. Occupational programs addressing alcohol abuse have been central to these themes (Trice and Roman, 1972).

These occupational programs characteristically focus on the development of systems that enable the maximum number of problem drinking employees to return to health and adequate work performance levels. These systems are based on the assumptions that (1) the most clear-cut mechanism for identifying alcohol related problems is the supervisor's awareness of impaired performance, (2) alcohol abuse should be regarded as a medical problem in the workplace, (3) regular disciplinary procedures for poor performance should be suspended while employees conscientiously seek assistance for their problems, and (4) return to adequate job performance is the sole criterion for judging successful outcome.

Individual companies initiated alcohol abuse programs as early as the 1940s, but the number of companies with formal programs grew slowly through the 1950s and in the 1960s. From 1950 to 1973 the estimated number of operational programs grew from 50 to 500. Due to the national attention focused on the problem, there currently exist more than 5,000 organizations that have some form of occupational alcohol-abuse programs. Evaluations of these programs have shown them to be not only popular but also a useful technique in early identification of problem drinkers and in helping them obtain treatment. There are also good indications that these programs are cost-effective.

Biological Manipulation of the Host—"Euphoric, narcotic, pleasantly hallucinant. . . . What you need is a gramme of Soma. All the advantages of Christianity and alcohol; none of their defects," wrote Aldous Huxley in *Brave New World*. It is said that if alcohol were to be introduced as a new food or drug, the Food and Drug Administration (FDA) would instantly ban it because of its many adverse effects. However, since our present-day legal, but imperfect, "Soma" is consumed by millions of people, are there any means whereby the host's resistance to its harmful effects might be increased? The answer for now is no. But while no single "vaccine" for all alcohol problems is foreseeable, it is highly likely that special methods will be developed to prevent specific alcohol problems.

Active research is currently being conducted on three major alcohol problems—alcohol dependence, cirrhosis, and intoxication (Majchrowicz and Noble, 1979; Mendelson and Mello, 1979). Futuristic application of current theory and research is underway to prevent these three problems.

Depending on which biological theory of alcohol dependence is validated by further laboratory and clinical studies, diet or drugs may be employed to manipulate neural membrane fats in the central nervous system, adjust the level and/or function of central opioid peptides, or use inhibitors that block the formation of morphine-like alkaloids with the aim of preventing the development of dependence upon alcohol. Several histocompatibility (HLA) antigens have been linked to susceptibility to cirrhosis and its accelerated development, possibly by stimulating cytotoxic immune reactions to alcohol damaged liver cells. Developing drugs that abort this autoimmune reaction or inhibit collagen synthesis may prevent cirrhosis development in alcohol users. Intoxication is a major cause of alcohol morbidity and mortality. Over the years, laboratories have studied potential amethystic (sobering) agents in human subjects (Noble, Alkana, and Parker, 1978). Several candidates with significant, but not absolute, efficacy have been found. With further research, more effective agents may be found which, among other applications, could be used for the medical treatment of subjects who have overdosed on alcohol.

The recent explosive advances of knowledge in molecular biology and in the application of genetic engineering techniques to a variety of problems would have fallen under the realm of science fiction thirty years ago. Since there is growing evidence that some aspects of alcoholism and related problems have hereditary components, manipulation of the genome is another approach to minimizing host susceptibility to alcohol harm. Research along this line is being conducted on a number of diseases with simple and predictable hereditary characteristics. For example, researchers studying Huntington's chorea, a disease controlled by a classic dominant Mendelian gene, have found a restriction enzyme marker (a piece of DNA that can be pinpointed with recombinant DNA techniques) that is so near to the Huntington's disease gene that its presence can be used as an indicator for the gene. Moreover, this gene is on chromosome 4 and is somewhere within an area of several million base pairs—an area large enough to hold 100 genes. It is only a matter of time until the Huntington's disease gene (or genes) is isolated. Once this is done, it should be possible to learn what it does biochemically and, perhaps, prevent its expression or prevent at least devastating Huntington's disease symptoms even if expressed.

It is highly doubtful that the inherited forms of alcoholism are as genetically simple as Huntington's disease. Most likely they involve multiple genes dispersed over several chromosomes, each programing certain biochemical reactions that respectively lead to enhanced susceptibility to certain alcohol problems. This approach for alcoholism would be several orders of magnitude more difficult to conduct than for the more simple genetic disorders. However, by the end of this century such research may not be uncommon.

Clearly, research opens up almost limitless vistas in the prevention of alcohol problems. However, the findings will raise as many biomedical and psychological issues as they will moral, political, legal, and economic ones.

THE AGENT

Since the understanding of alcoholism as a disease was established, the prevailing wisdom has been that there are two types of alcohol consumers—social drinkers and alcoholics. As such, it is postulated that in any given population alcohol consumption would exhibit a bimodal distribution—one peak representing social drinkers, who presumably are individuals not harmed by alcohol, and a second, smaller peak consisting of alcoholics, who unfortunately bear the major brunt of alcohol problems. Inherent in this assumption is that, regardless of the level of alcohol consumption, the number of alcoholics in a particular population would remain constant because of the alcoholics' unique and inevitable genetic or metabolic propensity for alcohol problems. What would vary when alcohol consumption is raised or lowered would be the amount of alcohol that social drinkers would consume. Unfortunately, both theoretical and empirical observations have not supported this assumption.

A basic and fundamental fact that has been ignored in the above attractive and somewhat seductive assumption is that alcohol, as a drug, has inherent cytotoxic, psychoactive, and addictive properties. When alcohol is consumed in sufficient amounts and/or over a prolonged period of time, all organisms, including human beings, may suffer its adverse consequences. That there are certain modest health benefits to low consumption levels of alcohol is probably true, but these pale in significance when compared to the overwhelming evidence derived from laboratory, epidemiological, and clinical studies that point to alcohol's broad spectrum of harmful effects. (See DeLuca, 1981; Edwards et al., 1977; Klatsky, Friedman, and Siegelaub, 1978; Majchrowicz and Noble, 1979; Noble, 1978; Schmidt and Popham, 1975.)

There are, as yet, no identifiable genes, metabolic abnormalities, psychological traits, or sociocultural characteristics which will predict with certainty who will and will not become an alcoholic. Alcoholism, like cancer, has multiple forms, categorized by various authors as alpha, beta, delta, gamma, and epsilon; reactive and nonreactive; early onset and late onset; or familial and non-familial alcoholism. For this reason, it is doubtful that a universal marker for alcoholism will ever be found, albeit it is not unlikely that certain types of alcoholism may display unique antecedent characteristics. However, the common and, indeed, the necessary factor in all forms of alcoholism is the agent alcohol. However, while it is axiomatic that there is no alcoholism without alcohol, the dominant view of the past fifty years has paradoxically underplayed the role of alcohol availability and alcohol consumption in the prevention of alcoholism. Assuming that alcoholism is a unitary and inevitable disease uninfluenced by factors that evolve from its agent is a notion that is inconsistent with scientific knowledge and no longer tenable.

Alcohol consumed at less than "alcoholismic" levels—that is, what is commonly called "social drinking"—also may result in a number of negative outcomes (Gross, 1983). Biomedical problems that have been linked to social drinking include gastritis, hypertension, cardiac abnormalities, upper gastrointestinal cancer, fetalembryopathy, adverse drug interactions, and central nervous system dysfunction, as well as a host of others. Social drinkers, moreover, represent a significant number of individuals who experience other alcohol related problems that include drunken driver injuries and fatalities, other accidents, violent crime, and job and family difficulties. It is true that alcoholics, considering their relatively small numbers, contribute to a high proportion of alcohol related problems; however, social drinkers, who represent much larger numbers, contribute significantly to the total problem engendered by alcohol. Thus any prevention effort cannot and should not ignore the social drinking population.

Efforts establishing the relationship between per capita alcohol consumption in the general population and alcohol related problems received their impetus and early empirical support from the pioneering studies and theoretical formulations of Ledermann (1956). Studying nine different population samples consisting of French, Italian, Finnish, Swedish, and American groups, Ledermann found that the distribution of consumption was approximated by a lognormal or unimodal curve highly skewed to the right. That is, there were not two peaks, one for social drinkers and another for alcoholics. Ledermann therefore concluded that reduction in per capita consumption would result in reduction of heavy drinking.

In general, recent population consumption surveys are supportive of Ledermann's unimodal curve, and in any given population a strong relationship exists between average consumption and the prevalence of liver cirrhosis and other alcohol related problems. (See Brunn et al., 1975; Cook, 1981; Edwards et al., 1977; Popham et al., 1978; Schmidt and Popham, 1975.) However, there has been a significant amount of discussion on various aspects of the "Ledermann Curve." While it does not enjoy the status of a universal and inviolate law, Ledermann's formulation remains fundamentally sound, and no convincing data have been presented to refute it. Indeed, the thirty-sixth World Health Assembly, meeting in May 1983, gave high priority to prevention of alcohol problems by reducing availability of the drug.

Of all prevention measures, regulating the supply of alcoholic beverages is the most direct and effective means of dealing with alcohol consumption and its associated harm. However, this will not be easy (Wiener, 1980). Alcohol is the present day "Soma" and will be for many years to come; its use has become a pervasive part of U.S. culture. Alcoholic beverages are a source of revenue for federal, state, and local governments, and their production, distribution, and sale are a $55 billion per year industry. Moreover, the current political structure is not sufficiently motivated to deal effectively with serious prevention efforts, and the alcoholic beverage industry is not without influence upon the nation's superstructure. The treatment of alcoholism is also becoming "big business," and the present alcoholism constituency is divided on how best to prevent the problem.

On the other side of the ledger, contravening factors are developing that may help initiate effective prevention efforts. The nation is becoming sensitized to the tremendous burden of cost that alcohol exacts in both human and financial resources. Experience of the past and new information from prestigious organizations are beginning to identify effective prevention strategies. Parents, youth, and others at the grass-roots level, combined with the forces of consumer advocacy groups, are forming new alcohol problem constituency groups that are making an impact in all levels of society. Finally, the movement toward optimum health and fitness is leading individuals to question those factors in their life styles that are deleterious to their well-being.

Advertising—Alcohol advertising is a major industry in America. Rarely do we watch a televised sporting event without seeing the beer flow. Between 1970 and 1981 the amount spent on advertising almost tripled, far outstripping inflation, so that in 1981 alcohol advertisement budgets surpassed $1 billion for the first time and have continued to grow every day (Jacobson, Hacker, and Atkins, 1983).

Television advertising is, of course, not the only medium for publicizing the virtues of alcohol consumption; other means such as radio, magazines, outdoor billboards, newspapers, and a host of promotional campaigns also exist. The messages are always positive—"drink alcohol, and you will be glamorous, sexually desirable, socially acceptable, successful, and less stress-ridden and bored" (Breed and DeFoe, 1979, 1981A). The appeal is frequently targeted to recruit new drinkers such as youth, women, and blacks into the alcohol market. There are also advertisements that aim at maintaining the market of heavy drinkers, since about 10 percent of all drinkers consume about 50 percent of all alcohol.

The alcoholic beverage industry and its supporters maintain that advertising's major function is to realize an increase in the market share of a particular manufacturer's product rather than stimulate alcohol consumption per se. Moreover, they assert that the industry is a legitimate entity protected by First Amendment rights. They also correctly point out that little empirical evidence exists to show that alcohol advertising directly contributes to alcohol abuse.

Those who disapprove of alcohol advertising argue that in a country where "the medium is the message," the true and total picture about alcohol is seldom, if ever, portrayed accurately in advertising. They maintain that when alcohol is depicted in a false and favorable light, the position of the nondrinker is weakened and, worse, that of the heavy drinker is supported. Unlike other products on the market, alcohol can be a dangerous substance with much potential for harm, and, therefore, it is incumbent upon its manufacturers to warn the public of its darker nature. While their premise is unproven, some see an association between advertising, consumption, and alcohol related problems.

It should be noted that some regulations on alcohol advertising exist and have been established for many years. Government agencies such as the Federal Trade Commission (FTC), the Federal Communications Commission (FCC), and the Bureau of Alcohol, Tobacco, and Firearms (BATF) supervise sets of standards, and self-regulation policies are maintained by the alcohol beverage industry themselves in addition to those of advertisers and media groups. In some selected messages, the alcoholic beverage industry has begun to warn the public of the dangers of drinking and driving. But many still see these governmental and industry attempts as merely ineffective gestures at prevention. In a hearing held in 1976 by former Senator William D. Hathaway of the Subcommittee on Alcoholism and Narcotics, several suggested regulations were offered: warning labels on bottles, bans on alcohol advertising, end of tax deductions for the advertisements, etc. In a 1981 NCA position paper, limitations on alcohol advertising were recommended. In November 1983, the Center for Science in the Public Interest, a consumer advocacy group, filed a petition with the FTC that called for a comprehensive inquiry into alcoholic beverage advertising and marketing practices, as well as tough new restrictions that include a total ban on advertisements aimed at youth and problem drinkers. The petition also urged the FTC to prohibit broadcast commercials for alcoholic beverages or allow them only when balanced by health related "counter-ads" and to require print advertising to carry warning notices.

Many countries, including France, Sweden, Norway, Finland, U.S.S.R., Bulgaria, Netherlands, Canada, Ecuador, New Zealand, and Switzerland, have either banned several kinds of alcohol advertising or placed strict controls on many others. However, in the United States, attempts at instituting stricter regulations have been unsuccessful. Indeed, it is asserted that many of the existing regulations are barely enforced.

Pricing and Taxation—The consumption and price of commodities follow a basic market principle: as prices rise, consumption declines; as prices fall, consumption increases. This principle was most graphically and dramatically illustrated when the flow of oil became limited in the 1970s, and the price of gasoline more than tripled in the United States. Concomitantly, Americans began to consume less gasoline in a variety of ways including less driving, sharing rides, using small and fuel-efficient cars, employing other modes of transportation, and using alternative sources of energy such as gasohol.

Studies on the precise relationship between the price of alcohol and its use are not extensive, but the available data lead to the conclusion that demand for alcoholic beverages, like other commodities, is responsive to price. (See Cook, 1981; Moore and Gerstein, 1981; Ornstein, 1980.) However, some noteworthy differences are found among beer, wine, and distilled spirits. It is particularly significant that over the years the relative price of alcoholic beverages has actually declined. While the consumer price index (CPI) for food rose 113 percent and that for non-alcoholic beverages rose 235 percent from 1970 to 1980, the CPI for alcoholic beverages increased only 65 percent over the same period.

A significant part of the price paid for alcoholic beverages goes to the federal government in the form of federal excise taxes. In

1951, alcohol excise taxes comprised about 5.7 percent of those collections; today the same taxes generate less than 1 percent of federal revenues. Despite rampant inflation that diminished the value of the 1951 dollar by more than 75 percent, federal excise taxes on alcoholic beverages have not been raised since 1951. Considering the enormous deficits projected for the federal budget, there are serious considerations within the government to increasing federal excise taxes to help finance human resource programs. Should these efforts succeed, it is hoped that part of these newly generated revenues would be used to subsidize underfunded national programs for research, prevention, and treatment of alcoholism.

Another salutary effect of increased taxes—a key element in prevention efforts—would be to decrease alcohol related problems by lowering per capita consumption. Several historical instances where large and sustained increases in alcoholic beverage prices occurred and were followed by a decline in alcohol related problems give credence to this statement. Cook (1981) studied tax increases in thirty states over a fifteen-year period, and found that even relatively small changes in prices not only affected the quantity of alcohol consumed but also influenced the most serious health consequences (traffic fatalities and cirrhosis deaths) as well.

Accumulating the evidence on pricing, a 1981 report by the National Academy of Sciences concluded:

> Alcohol consumption and the problem (s) caused by it respond to the price of alcoholic beverages, and we infer that large reductions in the real cost of alcohol to consumers in recent years are likely to have exacerbated drinking problems. The downward trend in alcohol prices could be reversed by indexing Federal excise taxes to inflation or by making the tax proportional to wholesale price rather than volume. A more extreme action would be to restore the Federal tax to, for example, the 1951 level which would mean an increase from $10.50 to roughly $30.00 proof gallon.

The alcoholic beverage industry would undoubtedly vigorously oppose any tax increases on its product. It rightfully contends that its product is already heavily taxed and that further increases in price would cut into its slim margin of profits. However, the alcoholic beverage industry could increase its own prices, help its own profits, and consequently suffer less economic harm. Some also maintain that additional tax and/or price increases would constitute a regressive measure since the burden would fall most heavily on those in low-income brackets. Others disagree and feel that those who consume more heavily should pay more since these consumers are the ones who experience the greatest harm and do the most damage to society. Considering the advantages and disadvantages of raising taxes and/or prices, it is this author's contention that raising the price of alcoholic beverages would constitute one of the most effective measures for reducing alcohol problems and that its benefits will greatly outweigh its costs in the long term.

Alcohol Accessibility—Since prohibition was abolished the states have had the constitutional authority to govern the sales of alcoholic beverages by establishing the minimum legal drinking age and the hours, locations, and number of outlets for sales. The primary underlying basis for state alcohol control codes enforced by ABC boards is the prevention of alcohol abuse and promotion of temperance. However, the direction in the past thirty years has been toward a general relaxation of restrictions on the alcohol market that include lower MLDAs and gradual expansion of outlet numbers, types, and hours (Medicine in the Public Interest, 1979). ABC boards now appear to be more involved with issuing and revoking licenses and in settling disputes among wholesalers and retailers than they are in the possible health or social consequences of alcohol.

The trend toward granting complete rights to the newly enfranchised eighteen- to twenty-year-olds resulted in reducing the MLDA in a number of states during the early 1970s. By the mid–1970s many of these same states decided to raise the MLDA and provided an opportunity for analyzing the impact of this changing law on drinking and driving morbidity and mortality among this age group. The data obtained indicate that MLDA reductions resulted in an increase in automobile collisions and fatalities involving youthful drivers (Douglass, 1979–80; Wagenaar, 1982). This evidence, coupled with other knowledge and grassroots involvement, prompted the Presidential Commission on Drunk Driving in December 1983 to recommend that a national limit of twenty-one years of age be set for the legal purchase of alcoholic beverages.

Studies of the impact of hours, locations, and number of outlets for sales on alcohol consumption and alcohol related problems are limited. The evidence from European, Canadian, and United States studies is, at best, equivocal. Part of the problem is that such studies are difficult to interpret because they do not control a host of variables, and they confuse cause and effect.

Alcoholic Beverage Ingredients and Labeling—Frequently not only is the amount of ethanol unspecified in alcoholic beverages, but other substances added during production remain unknown to the drinker and constitute additional hazards. For example, certain ingredients used in preparing alcoholic beverages are known allergens. Grains, yeast, fruit, spices, egg whites, and fish glue may precipitate allergic reactions. The presence of certain biogenic amines in some alcoholic beverages, when ingested by individuals under the influence of mood elevators, may precipitate headaches and even hypertensive crises. Consumption of alcoholic beverages is also associated with gastrointestinal cancers. The potential carcinogenic potency of asbestos used as filters, coloring agents, other additives, and nitrosamines is enhanced in the presence of alcohol. A tragic example of ignorance regarding the effects of an additive concerned cobalt, a metal used in controlling beer foam. Cobalt cardiomyopathy epidemics occurred in beer drinkers in various parts of the world during the 1960s and frequently resulted in quick deaths. When the cause was identified, brewers stopped adding cobalt to beer, and these epidemics ended. It would be a useful public health service, and not necessarily a betrayal of trade secrets, for the alcoholic beverage industry to describe beverage ingredients.

The alcoholic beverage industry can improve its image—but more importantly its product—in other ways. With some expenditure of funds, it could identify and remove toxic congeners and use additives not damaging to health. Because alcohol consumption depletes a variety of nutrients from the body and malnutrition, certain forms of cardiomyopathy, neuropathies, and anemias frequently found in excessive drinkers respond favorably to vitamins and other nutrients, the alcoholic beverage industry might consider, on a limited and experimental basis, the addition to its products of water-soluble vitamins such as B1, B6, and folic acid, certain amino acids, and trace elements (e.g., zinc) . Some see these strategies as giving quarter to the industry, and others maintain that such measures would encourage drinkers to drink even more. These assertions may be true, but such measures could also diminish the severity of some alcohol related health problems. They would orient the industry toward a healthier psychology by allowing its members the opportunity to compete among themselves in the manufacture of less harmful products than currently exist. Although this is not a panacea, it could be helpful.

Labeling alcoholic beverages with ingredients and warnings has been the subject of several bills introduced in Congress. Notable proponents of labeling have been Senator Strom Thurmond of South Carolina and Congressman George Brown of California. A major congressional hearing was held in 1978 when leading officials of the administration and members of the academic and research community testified in favor of labeling. The alcoholic beverage industry and its supporters disagreed. They argued that labeling would be costly, a cosmetic action that would divert attention from more serious prevention efforts, and ineffective because "drunks don't read labels." Supporters maintained that the cost of labeling is insignificant when compared to the public's right to know what they consume and to be warned if a product is potentially harmful. They saw labeling as part of a broad educational approach in the prevention of alcohol problems.

THE ENVIRONMENT

The preceding two sections dealt with strategies for alcohol problem prevention using two elements of the public health model —the host and the agent. In this section, approaches bearing on the third element of the model—the environment—will be examined as they pertain to the setting in which drinking occurs, the conditions under which a person must function when intoxicated, and the cultural mores and laws that influence drinking behavior. Preventive measures involving the drinkers' environment have not been as extensively investigated as the host or the agent. In addition, many are seen as palliative and unsatisfying because they do not reach the roots of the alcohol problem.

Modification of Drinking Setting—The pharmacological effects of alcohol can be modified by the setting in which drinking takes place. In an atmosphere where drinking is the main focus of activity, as at cocktail parties, bars, and Saturday evening "busts," drunkenness is common. However, where a choice of activities such as music, games, food, nonalcoholic drinking, and friendly conversation exists, the tendency to overindulge in alcohol is controlled. Several prevention programs, particularly those aimed at college-age youth, have used this type of environmental modification with some success.

Insulating Drinking Behavior—As long as people drink, some will become drunk and constitute a hazard to themselves as well as others. Insulating these individuals and their victims is another approach to diminish harm. This strategy can be oriented toward physical, cultural, or temporal separation of the drinking behavior. Physical separation is the most obvious; most states prohibit taverns within a certain distance of schools and churches. Cultural separation includes informal zoning laws where the majority of the community is protected and where behavior not tolerated elsewhere is allowed; skid rows would be an example. Temporal separation refers to measures that allow sufficient time for an individual to regain sobriety between the drinking occasion and potentially harmful situations. Widespread use of ignition interlock devices that require mental alertness to operate could prevent intoxicated people from driving; so, too, would providing beds for intoxicated guests after a party.

Modifying the Consequences of Drinking—The occurrence and outcome of accidents could be changed by a variety of environmental modifications. In this way the consequences of drinking are challenged without changing the drinking behavior itself. For instance, intoxicated individuals are especially likely to benefit from automobile air bag protection systems. A large fraction of the deaths annually due to drunken driving in the United States probably could be prevented by such passive restraint measures. Other worthy measures include fireproof bedding, lower automobile speed limits, better lighted highways, road divider barriers, and the provision of transportation after drinking by hosts or bartenders or community service agencies. Some of these measures are certainly costly, but others need not be, and their benefits may well serve society in other ways as well.

The Criminal Justice System—Alcohol related offenses represent a large part of all arrests each year in the United States. Laws focus primarily on controlling public drunkenness and reducing drunken driving casualties. Their justification is based on the premise that potential offenders would be dissuaded from committing offenses because of fear of an arrest record, fines, jail, loss of license, and public humiliation.

In recent years the alcoholism movement and civil liberties groups have attacked systematically the use of criminal laws as a method of handling public drunkenness. Because these groups consistently have advocated increased treatment rather than imprisonment for intoxicated persons, decriminalization for public drunkenness has been a federal policy since the formation of the NIAAA in 1970. However, the public often remains in favor of criminal sanctions in this area. In recent years, the public has become even more strident and active, demanding and obtaining stricter laws regarding drinking and driving and severe punishment for the offenders.

Several studies have evaluated efforts to increase the preventive effects of the law through stronger penalties or increased enforcement (Cameron, 1979; National Highway Traffic Safety Administration, 1979). Experience from European countries, Canada, and the United States shows an initial—and sometimes dramatic—reduction in alcohol related problems when this approach is used, especially when new laws are accompanied by education campaigns and publicity. When the novelty effects wear off and the campaigns and publicity diminish, however, the criminal justice system becomes overburdened, "business as usual" resumes, and previous levels of drunken driving problems return.

Another type of law gaining considerable attention in the legal community relates to establishing the liability of a host, a bartender, or anyone who serves alcohol to an intoxicated person—the "dram shop act" (Mosher, 1979). In some communities laws already exist to allow a person injured by an intoxicated driver to sue a party for negligently serving an obviously intoxicated person. Difficulty in proving noticeable intoxication, considerations of infringement of civil liberties, and other factors have limited these cases. Nevertheless, in the changing social climate of the 1980s it is likely that more dram shop act laws will be enacted; their impact could help in reducing intoxicated behavior.

Influencing Cultural Mores—Sanctions on drinking within certain religious groups, homogeneous cultures, and isolated communities can exercise great influence over the individual drinker and help establish a norm. The United States, a large industrial-ized nation with a heterogeneous and a highly mobile population, embraces a great diversity of attitudes and beliefs about drinking and drunkenness. Drinking is variously viewed as sinful, fun, healthful, harmful, romantic, or revolting. At the same time, drunkenness is seen as tragic, humorous, dangerous, entertain-ing, frightening, manly, disgusting, or a sign of a weak-willed or sick individual. This diversity of attitudes and beliefs about drinking and drunkenness has its roots in the nation's history, the citizens' upbringings, and the confusing messages with which the public is constantly bombarded. It will not be an easy matter to establish a norm regarding these conflicting behaviors, but con-sensus is developing in certain alcohol problem areas.

One consensus is focusing on the drinking and driving issue. Both formal and informal action is beginning to bear on this problem and showing encouraging results. The hope is that such attempts will become deeply welded into our cultural conscious-ness so that drinking and driving will become one of society's taboos.

Another alcohol problem gaining increasing national attention and impetus from recent scientific findings concerns the adverse effects of prenatal alcohol consumption on the developing organ-ism—the fetal alcohol syndrome (FAS). The federal government and a number of voluntary organizations are warning the public about the dangers of drinking during pregnancy. This concern has struck a responsive chord in the health consciousness of pregnant women. However, a great deal more formal and informal action is needed to address this preventable tragedy.

Drug abuse by youth has been a major national concern for about twenty years. Programmatic, informal, and symbolic efforts have been directed to discourage both cigarette smoking and the use of illegal drugs. There is some recent evidence that these efforts are beginning to pay off. Unfortunately, only minimal or token efforts have been expended in discouraging alcohol use by underage youth—a situation difficult to comprehend since alcohol problems cause more death and disabilities in America's youth than all other abused drugs combined. President Reagan, when governor of California, was asked whether or not he was in favor of drinking by eighteen-year-olds. He said, "Having an

eighteen-year-old, I still feel I should have enough parental control that I don't want her to go into a bar and buy a drink. . . .
I guess we'd all be better off if we didn't have a drink." Similarly
strong statements by admired and respected members of society
(such as the President) that discourage alcohol consumption by
youth, especially those below the MLDA, would have strong
symbolic value in helping to establish desirable norms. These
norms, incidentally, would also be consistent with already established laws, as well as with messages conveyed about other drugs
of abuse.

Changing attitudes, beliefs, and actions about alcohol use and
abstinence toward healthier patterns will not be readily accomp-
lished in America's pluralistic society. However, there is hope
that by incrementally solving specific alcohol problems, a cumula-
tive result will occur that will lead to an atmosphere wherein
drunkenness is no longer socially acceptable and tolerance will
prevail in the acceptance or rejection of a drink. As such, the
mores of future generations will make moderation, temperance,
and sobriety more acceptable—and alcohol problems less severe—
than they currently are.

Recommendations

This first set of recommendations is aimed at increasing the
focus, the monitoring, and the efficient activities of prevention
programs.

Prevention Research—Fundamental to providing basic knowledge and better working models for reducing the incidence and
prevalence of alcohol problems is research. Investigative efforts
for all three elements of the public health model (host, agent, and
environment) should be stimulated. The National Institute on
Alcohol Abuse and Alcoholism, the Office of Management and
Budget, and alcohol-abuse and alcoholism constituencies should
organize their efforts so that at least 15 percent of the NIAAA's
total budget is devoted to prevention research.

Information Repository—Information on alcohol problem prevention is currently scattered and poorly systematized. It is vital
to establish a unit in the Department of Health and Human

Services that would serve as a repository of past and current knowledge on prevention strategies and assess whether data sets are firm, promising, or speculative. This information should be made available to the scientific community, Congress, the administration, and the public.

Channels of Communication—Alcohol and alcohol problem interests are widely dispersed within the federal government, frequently resulting in bureaucratic confusion and inaction. For example, such interests reside in the Departments of Health and Human Services (the NIAAA and the FDA), Treasury (the Bureau of Alcohol, Tobacco, and Firearms and the Internal Revenue Service), Defense, State, Transportation, Agriculture, and Justice and other agencies such as the FTC, the FCC, and the Veterans Administration. It is an urgent need to establish an effective high-level channel through which various government agencies and departments can communicate information, coordinate activities, and share policy decisions regarding the prevention of alcohol problems.

A Constituency for Prevention—While treatment of alcohol problems has a large and powerful constituency and another is rapidly being established for research, prevention does not yet enjoy a viable support structure for the articulation, promotion, and implementation of its objectives. Federal and state governments and the private sector should encourage the development of professional and grass-roots organizations that promulgate programs for the effective prevention of alcohol problems.

Measurement of Prevalence—Per capita alcohol consumption should be used as *one* useful national guide for the prevalence of alcohol problems.

This second set of recommendations is offered to initiate approaches that will help prevent or minimize the development of alcohol problems.

Countering Trends—The federal government should announce a positive commitment to counter the rise in alcohol consumption levels—particularly among the young—and to reduce alcohol related accidents and other disabilities.

Multiple Strategies—The prevention of alcohol problems is not a single-strategy issue. Controlling both the demand and supply of alcohol must be considered in addition to other measures.

Education and Training Programs—Education is a valuable prevention tool, but experience has shown that simply coining catchy phrases, showing a few television spots, presenting a lecture or two, or distributing material about drinking does little to change drinking habits. On the other hand, although more arduous and expensive, a sustained and personalized community alcohol education and training program that incorporates carefully designed mass media campaigns can have a salutary effect on problem drinking behavior.

Occupational Programs—Primary prevention efforts should assume a greater importance in occupational programs than they do at present.

Alcoholic Beverage Control Laws—Alcoholic beverage control laws should be made more uniform and consistent across the nation. At the same time, a greater emphasis must be placed on their relevance to the health and welfare of the community.

Minimum Legal Drinking Age—A national MLDA of twenty-one years should be established for the purchase of all alcoholic beverages.

Advertising—The FTC and the BATF need to enforce both the spirit and the letter of laws that prohibit false, misleading, or deceptive advertising. They also should ban advertising efforts targeted at vulnerable and/or susceptible groups, particularly young people and heavy drinkers.

Labeling—Alcoholic beverage containers should display labels that list ingredients and alcohol content by volume and carry rotating health warning notices.

Taxes—Federal excise taxes on beer, wine, and distilled spirits should be equalized and adjusted for inflation since 1951.

Incentives—The alcoholic beverage industry should be provided with incentives when, through its manufacturing and marketing practices, it promotes significant efforts to decrease the harm engendered by the use of its products.

Public Attitudes—Society, through government leaders and the private sector, should promote moderation, temperance, or sobriety as coequal choices. Heavy drinking and drunkenness should no longer be considered desirable or acceptable forms of behavior.

Epilogue

Over the past thirty years, increasing demands have been placed upon scientists, scholars, and other professionals to enter the arena of public health policy. Experts in their own narrow fields, these individuals often feel discomfited when presented with incomplete data by competing interest groups and asked to render judgments that can bear on the health outcome of the community.

Incontrovertible evidence is properly demanded in basic science. In applied science, however, aggressive application begins before the requirements for absolute certainty are satisfied. In the field of cancer (the second national health problem in America), a number of worldwide epidemiological studies show that incidence of certain cancers differs among countries with different dietary habits. Although not fully consistent, studies of laboratory animals generally indicate that the development of tumors similar to human ones is sensitive to fat consumption, and there is general agreement that high-fat diets are associated with cancer of breast, colon, and prostate. Similarly, in the prevention of cardiovascular disease (the first national health problem), a variety of factors have been identified, such as smoking, overweight, high blood pressure, blood-lipid profile, and certain personality characteristics. Again, the data are less than complete, but the application of this knowledge is beginning to have an effect on this health problem.

Knowledge and awareness of alcoholism and related problems have dramatically increased over the past fifteen years, approximately the same development the cardiovascular field experienced fifteen years ago. While much more information is needed, some fundamental truths have emerged that should be applicable to prevention of alcohol problems. Paradoxically, in areas of environmental pollution, radiation, food additives, medication, and others, where less information is available than in the field of alcohol, both formal and informal controls are part of a palpable and current movement. Yet efforts for the prevention of the third major national health problem in America—alcohol abuse and alcoholism—are essentially insignificant.

Public health policy that relates to alcohol problems, indeed any problem, is important in order to accurately communicate the level of certainty and how to improve it. However, if science is to be used as constructively as possible, the rigid criteria of basic science are often inappropriate. The cry "more research" is used by both detractors and well-intentioned individuals as an excuse for inaction. What is most desired is the best available advice for a complex decision, and the time for that decision has come. Although the current state of knowledge is not fully complete nor protected by the sinews of scientific certainty, it must be soundly evaluated and accurately communicated or emotionally based decisions will be made. Such decisions could lead either to Draconian measures inimicable to America's way of life or serve those manipulating the nation's power structure for their own interests, thereby leading to ineffective prevention programs and even an escalation of the very problem to be prevented.

Sheila B. Blume, M.D.

8

Public Policy Issues:

A Summary

Needed: A National Public Policy on Alcohol

Alcohol related problems have been a subject of concern in the United States since early in our history. The first settlers not only carried with them from Europe their alcohol but also their traditional alcohol problems. In addition, they developed a range of new ones peculiar to North America. The American Indians of the East Coast who first interacted with the colonists were among the few world cultural groups without an indigenous alcoholic beverage for which there were socially prescribed uses. The introduction of European "firewater" led to a series of devastating consequences for this native population.

Thus, examination of our current situation should include both historical and international perspectives. In recent years improved

SHEILA B. BLUME *is a psychiatrist and international consultant on alcohol related problems. Previously director of the New York State Division of Alcoholism and Alcohol Abuse, she was later the medical director of the National Council on Alcoholism. Dr. Blume has received numerous national honors including appointment by President Carter to the National Commission on Alcoholism and Other Alcohol Related Problems. She has contributed chapters to numerous books and written many articles and editorials in various publications.*

communications and world economic forces have produced a convergence of drinking patterns and, along with the spread of other aspects of Western culture, a concurrent worldwide increase in alcohol problems (WHO, 1983; Mosher, 1982).

The World Health Organization (WHO) recently has devoted a great deal of attention to alcohol related public health problems. On May 13, 1983, the Thirty-sixth World Health Assembly adopted a lengthy resolution urging the development of national programs and policies on alcohol consumption and alcohol problems. That resolution reads, in part:

Reiterating its firm conviction that alcohol-related problems rank among the world's major public health concerns and constitute a serious hazard for human welfare, and that it is therefore necessary for the Member States and for WHO to intensify their efforts to reduce these problems;

Seriously concerned by the world-wide trends in alcohol consumption and alcohol-related problems, and by the promotional drives for the increasing consumption of alcohol, especially in countries and in population groups in which its use was not previously widespread;

Believing that increasing alcohol consumption and alcohol-related problems are incompatible with achieving health for all by the year 2000, and hence policies to reduce them must form an integral part of the strategy for health for all;

Recognizing that an effective strategy to tackle the alcohol-related problems necessitates comprehensive national alcohol policies;

Mindful that effective national alcohol policy requires a concerted effort consisting of a wide variety of measures for prevention, appropriate services for management with emphasis on the primary health care approach, and supporting research and evaluation, giving higher priority to prevention by reducing the availability of and demand for alcohol; . . .

1. URGES Member States to identify the actual and anticipated problems associated with alcohol consumption;

2. RECOMMENDS that Member States:

(1) formulate comprehensive national policies, with prevention as a priority, and with attention to populations at special risk, within the framework of the strategy for health for all;

(2) develop mechanisms to coordinate programmes and activities for reducing alcohol-related problems on a planned, continuous and long-term basis;

(3) give serious consideration in their national alcohol policy to all measures suggested in its report by the WHO Expert Committee on Problems Related to Alcohol Consumption;

(4) implement the policy adopted and evaluate its effectiveness with a view to further policy development;

3. REQUESTS the Executive Board to monitor and evaluate the development of WHO's alcohol programme.

Of course, every society has already developed its own set of policies regarding alcohol problems through its traditions, customs, and laws; through public education; and through the symbolic communication of its government's actual behavior. A society's policies reflect its views on appropriate and inappropriate drinking, the nature and causes of alcohol problems, and the proper role of government and other institutions in regulating the behavior of its citizens. Thus the ancient Greeks had multiple and complicated rules for conducting a *symposium* (their word for a drinking party) (McKinlay, 1959), and the Chinese, during the 2000–year period between 700 B.C. and 1312 A.D., are reported to have passed and repealed prohibition laws no less than forty-one times (Moore, 1959). Although each nation may be said to have its own alcohol policy, such policies are less likely to be unified, coordinated, based on an articulated theoretical model, and supported by available research than they are to be haphazard, contradictory, and confused. The United States shares that distinction with much of the world (Moser, 1980). In particular, the tensions between economic interests and public health concerns have contributed to the many paradoxical situations documented in this volume. Additional examples may be given.

1. Many communities in the U.S. have declared drinking and driving their "number one" problem and begun highly publicized police actions. At the same time, they continue to approve applications for establishing bars and taverns located along highways with no access other than by private car.

2. The U.S. government is now probably one of the world's largest alcoholic beverage retailers, selling to a population of 8 million people currently eligible to purchase at military posts. It provides bargain-basement prices. All branches of the military have become concerned about widespread alcohol abuse and have instituted treatment programs, yet any effort to raise prices or control alcohol availability runs into strong local opposition, since profits from beverage sales are used to support recreation activities at each military base, and, therefore, the income is highly valued.

3. The residents of Harlem, a largely minority inner city com-

munity in New York City, complain of an unusually high density of liquor stores in the neighborhood. They feel this constitutes at least a symbolic communication to the black community about the importance of drinking, if not actually encouraging or increasing consumption. This situation is largely attributable to the federal government's Small Business Administration, which, in attempting to aid minority business in setting up new enterprises, underwrote a large number of these outlets.

Moore and Gerstein (1981) have identified three "dominant conceptions" or governing ideas concerning alcohol problems that have prevailed in American history and two "minority conceptions" that have also had an influence. The first of these ideas, the "colonial view," dominated through the revolutionary period. Alcohol was seen as a valuable food and commodity, a "gift of God." Overindulgence was seen as a personal immoral act, and punishment the appropriate response. Our current statutes related to public intoxication, the first of which was passed in 1619 in the Jamestown (Virginia) Colony, are a legacy from the dominant moralistic thinking of the colonial view.

The second governing idea was the "temperance view," which gathered strength from the time of the Revolutionary War and culminated in passage of the Eighteenth Amendment to the Constitution in 1919. This conceptualization saw alcohol as a dangerous drug, intoxicating and addicting in itself and, therefore, hazardous for anyone using alcoholic beverages at all. There was a great deal of debate over whether or not "intoxicating liquors," eventually outlawed during Prohibition, should include only distilled spirits or extend to wine, beer, and cider, which were considered by some the "beverages of moderation." Although the Twenty-first Amendment repealed prohibition in 1933, the temperance view also left a considerable legacy. On one hand, a differential taxation is retained between distilled spirits, which are taxed at a much higher rate in proportion to alcohol content, and beer and wine, which are taxed far less. On the other hand, following the failure of prohibition, there has been pervasive opinion that *any* effort to use control of alcoholic beverage availability as a strategy to reduce alcohol problems is foolish and wasted effort. Thus the major goals of the alcoholic beverage control statutes of the federal and state governments have been to maintain an orderly industry and raise revenues.

The third governing idea, the "alcoholism view," has dominated U.S. thinking since the second quarter of the twentieth century. This view focuses on the disease known as alcoholism as the major problem to be addressed. Alcoholism is understood as a complex disease with biological, psychological, and social features and causes, but neither the substance nor the victim of the illness is seen as evil or to be blamed. (For example, see Jellinek, 1960.) From this governing idea have come the policies promoting alcoholism treatment and programs of education and prevention, the decriminalization of public intoxication, and many of the measures discussed elsewhere in this volume.

The two minority conceptions discussed by Moore and Gerstein are the "control of commerce emphasis" propounded by the Association Against the Prohibition Amendment at about the time of its repeal and the "public health perspective" emphasized by the World Health Organization and gaining increased worldwide attention in the past few years. The former view blamed pre-prohibition commercial practices for the prevalence of alcohol problems. Recommendations made by the association were quite influential in the development of beverage control laws by the states following prohibition's repeal. Eighteen states chose a system of state or county monopoly to control wholesale and/or retail distribution of alcoholic beverages in order to remove a private profit motive from such sales.

The "public health perspective," initially articulated by a collaborative project of the Finnish Foundation for Alcohol Studies, the World Health Organization, and the Addiction Research Foundation of Ontario, focuses on alcoholism (alcohol dependence) as only one of a range of negative health consequences related to alcohol use (Brunn et al., 1975). Alcohol related trauma, cirrhosis of the liver, cancer of the head and neck, and fetal alcohol effects are examples of such consequences. Because alcoholics are not the only ones who suffer such health consequences, prevention policy must be aimed at a far wider target group than alcoholics alone—namely, the entire population. Moore and Gerstein marshal considerable evidence that although clinically diagnosable alcoholics surely have an unusually high rate of alcohol problems, they may account for less than half of the *total* number of Americans who have alcohol related problems and less than half of society's overall problem. For example, while approximately 30 to 50 percent of convicted drunk drivers in the U.S. are thought to be alcoholics, the other 50 to 70 percent are not. Prevention policies should aim at both groups.

Another important recent trend in American thinking has been a rising public consciousness toward health with emphasis on various aspects of *health promotion,* such as diet, exercise, avoidance of smoking, and stress management techniques. This awareness affords a valuable opportunity to improve public education concerning alcohol. Finally, the trend toward promoting the rights of nonusers to be protected from the health-impairing habits of others, which has produced nonsmoking sections on airplanes and in restaurants, is reflected in both anti–drunken driving campaigns and dram shop liability laws. This growing trend in public opinion can also be tapped for support of a rational policy on alcohol.

Toward Developing a Consistent Overall Policy

Although American society encompasses a wide variety of values, customs, and opinions along regional, subcultural, ethnic, philosophical, political, and religious lines, it is still fair to say that a general majority consensus may be reached concerning certain aspects of alcohol and related problems. Such an overall view, although it may engender opposition from economic interests or on other grounds, can and should be the basis of a comprehensive public policy on alcohol. Elements of the conceptualization that are controversial ought to be the specific focus of research on a priority basis. All significant changes in public policy aimed at preventing alcohol problems should be instituted with built-in plans for an adequate evaluation.

If such an overall set of agreed-upon principles can be developed, all proposed changes in the systems of alcohol taxation, regulation, prevention, treatment, and funding can be judged according to the standard. Would such a change promote or deter alcohol problems? Would its potential cost outweigh its potential benefit?

Before attempting a "first try" at constructing and commenting on such a set of principles, it is necessary to point out that making of policy is not exclusively a government exercise. Public policy is also shaped by voluntary organizations (the American Medical Association's 1956 statement on alcoholism), health care institutions (a local hospital's guidelines for handling intoxicated people in its emergency room), the beverage industry (a decision to market heavily on college campuses or to sell sweet, "milk-style" alcoholic beverages), private clubs and community groups (a P.T.A. group's decision whether or not to serve alcoholic beverages at a picnic or a neighborhood baseball club's decision about beer at games). These decisions influence the nation's drinking environment and the lives of the individuals who form public opinion. Such choices might also benefit from a set of principles or guidelines. One example is the set of guidelines for serving alcoholic beverages at an agency dinner or party adopted by the New York State Division of Alcoholism and Alcohol Abuse and made available to other organizations. The guidelines include serving food and nonalcoholic beverages along with alcoholic ones, a preference for a cash bar rather than an open bar, and provision for rides home if needed.

Policy Recommendations

A coordinated national alcohol policy can be based on a series of agreed-upon principles based on present knowledge. Such an outline is presented here with comments and examples of related policy.

ALCOHOLIC BEVERAGE AVAILABILITY

Alcoholic beverages should be commercially available:
1. at a high standard of purity and quality, made known to the consumer;
2. at an appropriate price;
3. marketed in an ethical way in which risks to health are not hidden or denied, claims for nonexistent benefits are not implied, and potential consumers are not urged to drink in patterns that are unhealthy, hazardous, or illegal;
4. in settings for which the location, the environment, the hours of selling, and the range of additional products or services sold are conducive both to public convenience and to health and safety; and
5. only to persons of a suitable age and condition to use the product safely.

Purity and Quality—This principle relates to industry regulation. Current consumer interest efforts have aimed at the development of federal regulations to require alcoholic beverage ingredient labeling, including specifying alcohol content in percentages. At present, labeling of alcohol content in beer varies from state to state, and alcohol content in distilled spirits is expressed as "proof." Development of beverages with low alcohol content and the addition of vitamins to such beverages are additional measures under consideration.

Price—The evidence for using taxation to stabilize or reduce alcohol consumption has been addressed earlier in this volume. Other practical questions present themselves as well. Does American society wish to have a six-pack of beer priced lower than a similar quantity of a soft drink?

Marketing—This area involves both advertising practices and other methods of promotion, such as the sponsorship of college campus rock concerts and sports event. Many countries have banned advertisements of alcoholic beverages on radio and television either entirely or during specified hours (Moser, 1980). Other nations, such as Egypt, Finland, Poland, and Cuba, have banned all public advertising. Still others, such as the Netherlands and the United States, have historically relied to a large extent on voluntary advertising codes. Television advertising is a particularly sensitive issue since it influences children below the age of critical evaluation. Recent criticism has been leveled at alcoholic beverage marketing in the United States, and proposals have been made for reform (Jacobson, Hacker, and Atkins, 1983). In November of 1983, a petition was presented to the Federal Trade Commission by twenty-five national organizations asking for tightening of controls on alcoholic beverage advertising, including abolition of advertising aimed at youths and problem drinkers.

Settings—Regulations requiring that on-premise outlets also serve food are based on the fact that food slows alcohol absorption. Attention to the availability of public transportation in deciding the location and business hours of bars and taverns may influence highway accidents. Does selling beer at gasoline service stations make sense? In this case one must weigh public convenience against symbolic communication.

Sales—Minimum purchase age laws and those that prohibit serving a person who is visibly intoxicated relate to this principle. Most nations have minimum purchase age laws, varying from fourteen (France for beer, wine, cider) to twenty-one for all beverages, but in many countries enforcement is lax. There is convincing evidence that raising the minimum purchase age reduces highway deaths for the age group affected.

DRINKING PRACTICES

The voluntary use of alcoholic beverages in social settings is acceptable:

1. with the exception of certain groups—children outside of religious or controlled family settings, pregnant women, persons suffering from alcohol dependence or other sedative drug dependence, persons taking medication, persons in training for certain athletic events, and those who expect to perform specific activities requiring dexterity and/or judgment for which alcohol could pose a hazard (e.g., a surgeon on call, an airline pilot before a flight, a driver of a car);

2. in a setting which will not offend or interfere with others;

3. in quantities which will not interfere with health and safety; and

4. for purposes which include sociability and/or accompany meals or recreational activities.

Government at all levels and the public in general have an interest in deterring unacceptable drinking practices and in avoiding, through their actions and communications, any policies that would promote such patterns.

High Risk Groups—Public education (in the schools; through health warning labels on alcoholic beverage containers; in public media; through physicians, pharmacists, and nurses; and through health institutions) acts both to inform the public and to shape attitudes. Regulations affecting those who work in the transportation, health care, and other industries are relevant to this principle, as are laws concerning malpractice, negligence, driving while under the influence of alcohol, etc. Programs to identify and treat impaired professionals also relate to this principle.

Setting—Drinking is generally not permitted in schools, churches, places of business, public buildings, etc. Drinking at sports events and concerts which attract large audiences has at times been linked with unruly behavior and violence. This is another instance in which public interests must be balanced.

Quantity—This principle involves two categories of hazard: that which results from acute ingestion and intoxication and that which results from continued ingestion over a long period of time. Although there is a great deal of variation among individuals, standard blood alcohol levels have been generally established as legal definitions of intoxication and impairment. Intoxication not only increases the likelihood of automobile accidents but also of falls, industrial accidents, and similar events. A variety of efforts have been made to define an overall maximum level of long-term safe intake. It should be realized in any such attempt that a lower intake level should be set for women because, compared to men, they weigh less, have proportionately less body water, and reach higher blood alcohol levels under standard conditions. Any measures aimed at deterring overdrinking will relate to this principle, for example the policies followed at officers' clubs and enlisted men's clubs on military bases.

Purposes—Most people will agree that drinking for the purpose of working up the courage to commit a crime is an inappropriate use of alcohol. Alcoholism professionals will also argue that drinking to function better, "drown one's sorrows," or in other ways substitute for developing adequate skills to cope with life's demands is also inappropriate use. Therefore, advertising that promotes alcohol as a way to relax, aid sleep, or handle life problems should be prohibited.

ALCOHOL PROBLEMS

Alcohol use in the United States is associated with problems of a sufficient magnitude of social and personal cost that it is in the national interest to develop a range of strategies to prevent and counteract these problems. Alcohol related problems may be divided in different ways, but they include, at a minimum, alcoholism; other continuing patterns of alcohol abuse; episodic problems in persons who do not manifest ongoing patterns of abuse; fetal alcohol effects; and alcohol use in relation to suicide, violence, accidents, and crime.

1. Alcoholism is a disease which is influenced by both hereditary and environmental factors; predisposes the sufferer to a wide range of other alcohol related illness and injuries; causes greatly increased mortality; adversely affects not only the individual but also members of the family and "significant others"; is amenable to a variety of treatment approaches, as well as self-help group support (all of which in general work best when applied early in the illness); and may be detected through work-based and other intervention programs. Drinking patterns of persons suffering from alcoholism cannot generally be permanently altered by persuasion, punishment, or threat—treatment is required.

Because of the relative newness and unavailability of alcoholism treatment in many parts of the country and because of the effectiveness of such treatment, the public has an interest in removing barriers to alcoholism treatment and assuring a high quality of services. Because of the history of social stigma associated with alcoholism, special confidentiality controls are required for the records of those in treatment.

2. Other ongoing patterns of drinking which are not clinically diagnosable as alcoholism may also damage health and well-being through association with accidents, violence, interpersonal problems, absenteeism, reduced productivity, interference with learning or maturation in youth, or development of alcohol related diseases. Such patterns can be influenced by education, persuasion, treatment, counseling, and social controls.

3. Alcohol use in persons unacquainted with the effects of alcohol or in specific situations of risk is also a cause of morbidity, mortality, and social harm.

4. Alcohol is a teratogen that can cause a variety of types of damage to the developing fetus at all stages of pregnancy.

5. Alcohol alters behavior. Judgment and self-control are affected by drinking alcoholic beverages, both in an acute episode and over the long term. This influences ability to conduct ordinary business and is related to misconduct including suicide, homicide, and other crime.

6. Alcohol is related pharmacologically to other drugs, resulting both in negative consequences of alcohol and drug interaction and in cross-dependency between alcohol and other drugs.

Alcoholism—Acceptance of alcoholism as a disease is the basis for public policies promoting early intervention; treatment; third-party coverage, such as public and private health insurance; services for families of alcoholic persons, with or without the participation of the alcoholic member; prevention services for children of alcoholic parents; and wide-ranging research into the biology, epidemiology, psychology, and sociology of alcoholism. Also related are policies which assure quality, such as program standards and certification by state or voluntary agencies, training programs for health professionals, and examination and accreditation for those who have obtained sufficient training and experience in the field. Public funding of alcoholism services relates to this principle, as does decriminalization of public treatment for punishment. Mandated treatment as a condition of probation or parole for an individual convicted of an offense is an accepted principle in most of the country. However there are differences of opinion concerning mandated treatment for pregnant alcohol abusers because of fetal risk and withholding benefits from alcoholic recipients of public welfare unless they remain in treatment.

Special federal legislation has guaranteed confidentiality of alcohol- and drug-abuse patient records since 1974.

Alcohol Abuse—Prevention policies based on public health education about drinking and alcohol, particularly in the schools, focus on these problems. Programs that center on relationships between parents and children concerning alcohol and drug use, such as those promoted by various parent organizations and by Students Against Driving Drunk, are important influences on policy. Regulations regarding drinking in public parks, rules concerning drinking at school activities, and customs observed in private homes are based on this principle.

Episodic Problems—Although episodic alcohol problems may not be repeated for the individual, the outcome of any one incident may be extreme. Examples would include alcohol induced coma as a result of a fraternity hazing, drowning of an intoxicated person at a beach party, or a fire started by an individual who passes out from alcohol while smoking. Education is directed not only at individual drinkers but at those in their environment, encouraging them to assume responsibility to prevent harm. Also helpful here are efforts to improve environmental safety, such as flame-retardant fabrics, improved automotive and highway design, mandatory seat belt laws, etc.

Effects of Alcohol on the Fetus—Programs of public and professional education, programs to screen for alcohol problems all pregnant women, as well as those planning pregnancy, adequate treatment facilities for such women and their families, and a vigorous program of basic and applied research will be needed to prevent the 1,800 to 2,400 cases of fetal alcohol syndrome annually in the United States (Brandt, 1982). Further research is needed to define safe levels of alcohol use in pregnancy, to delineate the pathological mechanisms involved, and to evaluate treatment and prevention strategies.

Judgment and Self-control—Alcohol ingestion, both acute and chronic, has been a factor in determining the validity of wills and contracts. Criminal responsibility for a variety of antisocial acts may likewise be influenced by alcohol use. The association between alcohol use and suicide, violence (particularly domestic violence), and other crime is established, although mediating factors and causal links are not well understood. Nevertheless, alcohol-abuse intervention programs for people involved in such acts are likely to be effective in preventing recurrence of violence in those with primary alcohol problems. Public policies that promote criminal justice diversion programs, such as suspension of fines or jail terms as long as the participant cooperates in treatment, relate to this principle. Research in these areas is sorely needed.

ALCOHOL PROBLEMS ARE STRONGLY INFLUENCED BY FORCES OPERATIVE ON THE COMMUNITY LEVEL

Reciprocal influences of public, private, voluntary, and self-help groups can worsen or ameliorate a community's alcohol problems.

Community-level cooperation between the various agencies and organizations with an interest in education, health, law enforcement, and public welfare is essential to the success of any effort aimed at decreasing alcohol related problems.

Other Drugs—Policies related to this principle include public education programs about proper use of medicines and a variety of regulations requiring consumer warnings on prescription and nonprescription drugs. Regulation of the manufacture, supply, and medical prescription of psychoactive drugs able to produce dependency are public policies which also have an impact on alcoholism and other alcohol problems.

RESEARCH INTO THE POSSIBLE BENEFITS AND THE
HAZARDS OF ALCOHOL USE IS NEEDED

Basic and applied research is needed to:

1. improve understanding of the role of alcohol in health and disease, delineate safe and hazardous levels of use for specific populations, and clarify the relationship between alcohol use and various social problems;

2. delineate the biological, psychological, and social causes and manifestations of alcoholism, leading to improved biological screening tests, diagnosis, treatment, and prevention;

3. study health care systems to improve recognition and care of alcoholics and alcohol abusers;

4. evaluate prevention programs in criminal law and enforcement, health education, and environmental safety for their effects on rates of alcohol related health and social problems, public attitudes and knowledge, and drinking practices; and

5. understand the role of social custom and social pressure in both promotion and discouragement of hazardous drinking practices. Ways to influence such customs should also be evaluated.

Serious research interest in alcohol problems has been slow to develop in the United States. This is at least partly a result of the political struggles surrounding the temperance movement and the illegality of alcoholic beverages during Prohibition. The late nineteenth and early twentieth century was a fertile period in the growth of medical research that developed scientific methods and technologies, institutions, and training for young researchers. With such a wide variety of infectious and metabolic illness awaiting study, devoting attention to the effects of a stigmatized and illegal substance on human health was not an attractive option to most workers. Even after the repeal of prohibition, the moral stigma clung to alcohol problems. Those few who ventured into the field, such as the original group at the Laboratory of Applied Physiology at Yale University in the 1940s, encountered both individual and institutional resistance. The Yale Center for Alcohol Studies (which moved to Rutgers in 1962) did a great deal to stimulate interest.

The establishment of the National Institute on Alcohol Abuse and Alcoholism (NIAAA) by the U.S. government in 1970 strengthened the federal commitment to support research in alcoholism, but by that time both funding and interest in the field were lagging far behind most other health areas. In 1980, the Institute of Medicine (IOM) of the National Academy of Sciences published a lengthy report entitled *Alcoholism, Alcohol Abuse, and Related Problems: Opportunities for Research.* The document presents a comprehensive review of the status of alcohol research that includes knowledge gained in the past as well as promising leads for the next five years. The review clearly demonstrates that government resources devoted to research in alcohol related problems have been disproportionately low whether calculated in relation to mortality, prevalence, or economic cost. In 1978, for example, health research dollars for alcohol problems, calculated per case, averaged $1.00 compared to $209.00 for cancer. Research support calculated per $1,000.00 of annual societal cost averaged $0.40 for alcohol problems compared to $4.00 for respiratory diseases, $6.00 for heart and vascular diseases, and $30.00 for cancer. The recommendations for research of the IOM report were updated in 1983 by the U.S. Department of Health and Human Services.

The list of needs and opportunities in alcohol research is long. Much of what is now known has been learned in studies of adult white male populations. The need for studies of women and racial groups other than white is of great importance. Heavy drinkers and alcoholics have been shown to be among the greatest users of high-cost medical care. Yet many are treated for complications of alcoholism without being treated for the disease itself. Thus, health care system improvement is an urgent need. Even compared to other alcohol research areas, studies on alcohol and public policies have been particularly scarce. An increasing emphasis on research also requires mechanisms for the recruitment, education, and training of researchers in the appropriate disciplines. This area has also suffered from underfunding.

EVALUATING POLICY MEASURES

To the greatest extent possible, all policy measures undertaken in an effort to prevent alcohol problems should be designed with a strategy for evaluation that uses appropriate scientific method.

Policies are rarely implemented with serious thought to evaluation, making many after-the-fact studies far more difficult and less informative than they might be. Because of the huge stake of societal cost involved, governments should routinely provide sufficient funds to evaluate their prevention efforts.

INTERNATIONAL ASPECTS

International communication, trade, and research performed in other cultural and national settings are important and require continuing cooperation on alcohol related issues with the World Health Organization and with other nations.

The United States has cooperated on a wide variety of international projects of research and policy study relating to mental health, alcoholism, and drug abuse. Influences of international alcoholic beverage marketing on alcohol problems were investigated in a 1981 WHO study that, however, was never released for publication. Powerful economic forces may eventually require international beverage trade regulation. In the field of prevention, other nations can sometimes present opportunities to study the effects of policies that have not been implemented in the United States. Thus international experiences can be directly helpful in developing domestic policy.

Summary

The personal and social costs of worldwide alcohol related problems have prompted renewed interest in the development of coherent national policies relating to alcohol. Both historic and international factors must be considered in understanding the present status of alcohol related policy in the United States.

Bibliography

ARMOR, DAVID J., J. MICHAEL POLICH, AND HARRIET B. STAMBUL, *Alcoholism and Treatment*. Santa Monica, Ca.: Rand Corporation, 1976.

ASHBY, MARY JANE, "Alcohol Consumption, Ischemic Heart Disease and Cerebral Vascular Disease: An Epidemiological Perspective," *Journal of Studies on Alcohol*, 43, no. 9 (1982), 869-887.

BAHNSEN, MOGENS, C. GLUUD, AND S. G. JOHNSEN, "Pituitary-testicular Function in Patients with Alcoholic Cirrhosis of the Liver," *European Journal of Clinical Investigation*, 11 (1981), 473-479.

BANDURA, A., *Principles of Behavior Modification*. New York: Holt, Rinehart and Winston, 1969.

BERRY, RALPH E., JAMES P. BOLAND, C. SMART, AND J. KANAK, *The Economic Costs of Alcohol Abuse and Alcoholism–1975*. Rockville, Md.: National Institute on Alcohol Abuse and Alcoholism, 1977.

BLANE, H., AND K. HEWITT, *Mass Media, Public Education and Alcohol: A State-of-the-art Review*, Report prepared for the National Institute on Alcohol Abuse and Alcoholism, University of Pittsburgh, 1977.

BLUME, SHEILA B., DEE DROPKIN, AND LLOYD SOKOLOW, "The Jewish Alcoholic: A Descriptive Study," *Alcohol Health and Research World*, 4 (Summer 1980), 21-26.

BOHMAN, MICHAEL, "Some Genetic Aspects of Alcoholism and Criminality," *Archives of General Psychiatry*, 35 (1978), 269-276.

BRANDT, EDWARD N., Testimony, *Hearing Before the Subcommittee on Alcohol and Drug Abuse*, U.S. Senate Committee on Labor and Human Resources. Washington, D.C.: U.S. Government Printing Office, 1982.

BREED, WARREN, AND JAMES R. DE FOE, "Themes in Magazine Alcohol Advertisements," *Journal of Drug Issues*, 9, no. 4 (1979), 511-522.

———, "Risk and Alcohol Lifestyle Advertising," *Abstracts and Reviews in Alcohol and Driving*, 2, no. 9 (September 1981A), 5-10.

———, "The Portrayal of the Drinking Process on Prime-time Television," *Journal of Communication*, 31, no. 1 (1981B), 58-67.

———, "Effecting Media Change: The Role of Cooperative Consultation on Alcohol Topics," *Journal of Communication*, 32, no. 2 (1982), 88-99.

BRUHN, JOHN G., AND STEWART WOLF, *The Roseto Story—An Anatomy of Health.* Norman, Ok.: University of Oklahoma Press, 1978.

BRUNN, KETTIL, GRIFFITH EDWARDS, MARTTI LUMIO, KLAUS MAKELA, LYNN PAN, ROBERT POPHAM, ROBIN ROOM, WOLFGANG SCHMIDT, OLE SKOG, PEKKA SULKUNEN, AND ESA OSTERBERT, *Alcohol Control Policies in Public Health Perspective,* Finnish Foundation for Alcohol Studies Volume 25, Helsinki, 1975.

CAHALAN, DON, AND ROBIN ROOM, *Problem Drinking Among American Men.* New Brunswick, N.J.: Rutgers University Center of Alcohol Studies, 1974.

CAMERON, T., "The Impact of Drinking-Driving Countermeasures: A Review and Evaluation," *Contemporary Drug Problems,* 8 (1979), 495-566.

CARRERE, J., "L'environment du Buveur," *Annals of Medical Psychology* (Paris), 2 (1972), 106-114.

COHEN, GERALD, AND MICHAEL COLLINS, "Alkaloids from Catecholamines in Adrenal Tissue: Possible Role in Alcoholism," *Science,* 167 (1970), 1749-1751.

COOK, PHILIP J., "The Effect of Liquor Taxes on Drinking, Cirrhosis, and Auto Fatalities," in *Alcohol and Public Policy: Beyond the Shadow of Prohibition,* eds. Mark H. Moore and Dean R. Gerstein. Washington, D.C.: National Academy Press, 1981.

COOK, PHILIP J., AND GEORGE TAUCHEN, "The Effect of Liquor Taxes on Heavy Drinking," *Bell Journal of Economics,* 13, no. 2 (Autumn 1982), 379-390.

————, "The Effect of Minimum Drinking Age Legislation on Youthful Auto Fatalities, 1970-1977," *Journal of Legal Studies,* January 1984, pp. 169-190.

CUMMING, R. L. C., AND A. GOLDBERG, "Alcohol and the Haemopoietic System," *Clinics in Endocrinology and Metabolism,* 7, no. 2 (1978), 447-465.

DAVIS, VIRGINIA E., AND MICHAEL K. WALSH, "Alcohol Amines and Alkaloids: A Possible Biochemical Basis for Alcohol Addiction," *Science,* 167 (1970), 1005-1007.

DELUCA, JOHN R., ed., *Fourth Special Report to the U.S. Congress on Alcohol and Health,* Department of Health and Human Services. Washington, D.C.: U.S. Government Printing Office, 1981.

DEUTSCH, C., *Broken Bottles, Broken Dreams.* Totowa, N.J.: Teachers College Press, 1982.

DIMAGNO, E. P., J. R. MALAGELADA, AND V. L. W. GO, "Relationship between Alcoholism and Pancreatic Insufficiency," in *Medical Consequences of Alcoholism,* eds. F. A. Seixas, K. Williams, and S. Eggleston. New York: New York Academy of Sciences, 1975.

DORLAND, WILLIAM ALEXANDER, *Dorland's Illustrated Medical Dictionary*. Philadelphia: William A. Dorland, 1981.

DOUGLASS, R. L., "The Legal Drinking Age and Traffic Casualties: A Special Case of Changing Alcohol Availability in a Public Health Context," *Alcohol Health and Research World*, 4 (Winter 1979-1980), 101-117.

DRAPER, R. J., B. FELDMAN, AND H. HAUGHTON, "Undetected Brain Damage in Irish Alcoholics," *Journal of the Irish Medical Association*, 71 (1978), 353-355.

DUBOS, RENE, "Biological and Social Aspects of Tuberculosis," *Bulletin of the New York Academy of Medicine*, 27 (1951), 351.

EAST, W. N., "Alcoholism and Crime in Relation to Manic-Depressive Disorders," *Lancet*, 230 (1936), 161-163.

ECKHARDT, MICHAEL J., THOMAS C. HARFORD, CHARLES T. KAELBER, ELIZABETH S. PARKER, LAURA S. ROSENTHAL, RALPH S. RYBACK, GIAN C. SALMOIRAGHI, ERNESTINE VANDERVEEN, AND KENNETH R. WARREN, "Health Hazards Associated with Alcohol Consumption," *Journal of the American Medical Association*, 246, no. 6 (1981).

EDWARDS, GRIFFITH, Preface for "Alcoholic Beverages: Dimensions of Corporate Power," *The Globe*, 4 (December 1983), 3-8.

EDWARDS, GRIFFITH, M. M. GROSS, M. KELLER, JOY MOSER, AND ROBIN ROOM, eds., *Alcohol-Related Disabilities*, World Health Organization Offset Publication No. 32, Geneva, 1977.

EDWARDS, GRIFFITH, AND JIM W. ORFORD, "A Plain Treatment for Alcoholism," *Proceedings of the Royal Society of Medicine*, 70 (1977), 344-348.

FARQUHAR, J. W., "The Community-based Model of Life Style Intervention Trials," *American Journal of Epidemiology*, 108 (1978), 103-111.

FARQUHAR, J. W., N. MACCOBY, P. WOOD, J. K. ALEXANDER, J. BREITROSE, B. BROWN, W. HASKELL, A. McALISTER, A. MEYER, J. NASH, AND M. STERN, "Community Education for Cardiovascular Health," *Lancet*, 1 (1977), 1192-1195.

FELVER, MICHAEL E., M. RAJ LAKSHMANAN, STEWART WOLF, AND RICHARD L. VEECH, "The Presence of 2,3 Butanediol in the Blood of Chronic Alcoholics Admitted to an Alcohol Treatment Center," in *Alcohol and Aldehyde Metabolizing Systems-IV*, ed. R. G. Thurman. New York: Plenum Publishing, 1980.

FIELD, JAMES B., HIBBARD E. WILLIAMS, AND GLENN E. MORTIMORE, "Studies on the Mechanism of Ethanol-Induced Hypoglycemia," *Journal of Clinical Investigation*, 42, no. 4 (1963).

FOULKS, E. F., AND S. KATZ, "The Mental Health of Alaskan Natives," *Acta Psychiatric Scandinavia*, 49 (1973), 91-96

GERSTEIN, DEAN R., "Alcohol Use and Consequences," in *Alcohol and Public Policy: Beyond the Shadow of Prohibition,* eds. Mark H. Moore and Dean R. Gerstein. Washington, D.C.: National Academy Press, 1981.

GILLIS, L. S., AND G. L. STONE, "A Follow-up Study of Psychiatric Disturbance in a Cape Colored Community," *British Journal of Psychiatry,* 123 (1973), 279-283.

GROSS, L., *How Much Is Too Much? The Risks of Social Drinking.* New York: Random House, 1983.

GUNNAR, R. M., J. DEMAKIS, S. H. RAHIMTOLA, M. Z. SINNO, AND J. R. TOBIN, "Clinical Signs and Natural History of Alcoholic Heart Disease," in *Medical Consequences of Alcoholism,* eds. F. A. Seixas, K. Williams, and S. Eggleston. New York: New York Academy of Sciences, 1975.

GUSFELD, J., "The Prevention of Drinking Problems," in *Alcohol and Alcohol Problems: New Thinking and New Directions,* ed. W. Filstead. Cambridge, Ma.: Ballinger, 1976.

HAGGARD, HOWARD W., "The 'Wets' and 'Drys' Join against Science," *Quarterly Journal Studies on Alcohol,* 6 (1945), 131-134.

HALSTED, C. H., R. C. GRIGGS, AND J. W. HARRIS, "The Effect of Alcoholism on the Absorption of Folate in the Malnourished Alcoholic Patient," *Journal of Laboratory & Clinical Medicine,* 69 (1967), 116-131.

HASELAGER, E. M., AND JAN VREEKEN, "Rebound Thrombocytosis after Alcohol Abuse: A Possible Factor in the Pathogenesis of Thromboembolic Disease," *Lancet,* April 9, 1977.

HED, R., H. LARSSON, AND F. WAHLGREN, "Acute Myoglobinuria: Report of a Case with a Fatal Outcome," *Acta Medica Scandinavia,* 152 (1955), 459-463.

HERBERT, VICTOR, AND G. TISMAN, "Hematologic Effects of Alcohol," in *Medical Consequences of Alcoholism,* eds. F. A. Seixas, K. Williams, and S. Eggleston. New York: New York Academy of Sciences, 1975.

HILLMAN, R. S., "Alcohol and Hematopoiesis," in *Medical Consequences of Alcoholism,* eds. F. A. Seixas, K. Williams, and S. Eggleston. New York: New York Academy of Sciences, 1975.

HINES, J. D., "Hematologic Abnormalities involving Vitamin B6 and Folate Metabolism," in *Medical Consequences of Alcoholism,* eds. F. A. Seixas, K. Williams, and S. Eggleston. New York: New York Academy of Sciences, 1975.

HOLT, S., I. C. STEWART, AND J. M. J. DIXON, "Alcohol and the Emergency Service Patient," *British Medical Journal,* 281 (September 6, 1980).

INSEL, P. M., AND R. H. MOOS, "Psychological Environment—Expanding the Scope of Human Ecology," *American Psychology,* 1974, pp. 179-188.

ISRAEL, Y., H. ORREGO, S. HOLTS, D. W. MACDONALD, AND H. E. MECMA, "Identification of Alcohol Abuse: Thoracic Fractures in Routine X-rays as Indicators of Alcoholism," *Alcoholism: Clinical and Experimental Research,* 4 (1980), 421-422.

Institute of Medicine, *Alcoholism, Alcohol Abuse, and Alcohol-Related Problems: Opportunities for Research.* Washington, D.C.: National Academy of Sciences, 1980.

JACOBSON, MICHAEL, GEORGE HACKER, AND ROBERT ATKINS, *The Booze Merchants: The Inebriating of America.* Washington, D.C.: Center for Science in the Public Interest Books, 1983.

JELLINEK, E. M., *The Disease Concept of Alcoholism.* New Haven, Ct.: Hillhouse Press, 1960.

JOHNSON, W. D., Jr., "Impaired Defense Mechanisms Associated with Acute Alcoholism," in *Medical Consequences of Alcoholism,* eds. F. A. Seixas, K. Williams, and S. Eggleston. New York: New York Academy of Sciences, 1975.

KAPLAN, B. H., J. C. CASSEL, AND S. GORE, "Social Support and Health," *Medical Care,* 15 (1977), 47-58.

KELLER, MARK, ed., *Second Special Report to the U.S. Congress on Alcohol and Health,* National Institute on Alcohol Abuse and Alcoholism. Washington, D.C.: U.S. Government Printing Office, 1974.

KLATSKY, A. J., G. D. FRIEDMAN, AND A. B. SIEGELAUB, "Alcohol Use, Myocardial Infarction, Sudden Cardiac Death, and Hypertension," *Alcoholism: Clinical and Experimental Research,* 3 (1978), 33-39.

KNAPP, T. H., "Revolution, Relevance and Psychosomatic Medicine: Where the Light Is Not," *Psychosomatic Medicine,* 33 (1971), 363-374.

LANGE, L. G., AND B. E. SOBEL, "Mitochondrial Dysfunction Induced by Fatty Acid Ethyl Esters. Myocardial Metabolites of Ethanol," *Journal of Clinical Investigation,* 72 (1983), 724-731.

LEDERMANN, S., *Alcool-Alcoolisme-Alcoolisation. Données scientifiques de caractère physiologique, économique et social,* Institut National d'Etudes Démographiques, Travaux et Documents, Cahier No. 29. Paris: Presses Universitaires de France, 1956.

LEEVY, CAROLL M., T. CHEN, AND R. ZETTERMAN, "Alcoholic Hepatitis, Cirrhosis and Immunologic Reactivity," in *Medical Consequences of Alcoholism,* eds. F. A. Seixas, K. Williams, and S. Eggleston. New York: New York Academy of Sciences, 1975.

LELBACH, WERNER K., "Organic Pathology Related to Volume and Pattern of Alcohol Abuse," in *Research Advances in Alcohol and Drug Problems, Vol. 1,* ed. R. J. Gibbins. New York: John Wiley and Sons, 1974.

LIEBER, CHARLES S., *Advances in Alcohol and Substance Abuse.* New York: Haworth Press, 1982.

LINDENBAUM, J., AND CHARLES S. LIEBER, "Alcohol-induced Malabsorption of Vitamin B12 in Man," *Nature,* 224 (1969), 806.

LUCIA, SALVATORE P., *Wine as Food and Medicine.* New York: Blakiston, 1954.

LUNDQUIST, FRANK, "Interference of Ethanol in Cellular Metabolism," in *Medical Consequences of Alcoholism,* eds. F. A. Seixas, K. Williams, and S. Eggleston. New York: New York Academy of Sciences, 1975.

LYNCH, JAMES J., *The Broken Heart.* New York: Basic Books, 1977.

MAJCHROWICZ, E., AND ERNEST P. NOBLE, eds., *Biochemistry and Pharmacology of Ethanol, Volumes 1 and 2.* New York: Plenum Press, 1979.

MANDELL, W., "Preventing Alcohol-related Problems and Dependencies through Information and Education Programs," in *Encyclopedic Handbook of Alcoholism,* eds. E. M. Pattison and E. Kaufman. New York: Gardner Press, 1982.

MAYFIELD, DEMMIE, "Alcoholism, Alcohol, Intoxication and Assaultive Behavior," *Diseases of the Nervous System,* 37 (1971), 288-291.

MCCOLL, KENNETH E. L., MICHAEL MOORE, GEORGE THOMPSON, AND ABRAHAM GOLDBERG, "Abnormal Haem Biosynthesis in Chronic Alcoholics," *European Journal of Clinical Investigation,* 11 (1981), 461-468.

MCKINLAY, ARTHUR P., "Drinking Practices, Ancient and Modern: The Classical World," in *Drinking and Intoxication,* ed. Raymond G. McCarthy. New Haven, Ct.: College and University Press, 1959.

Medicine in the Public Interest, Inc., *The Effects of Alcoholic-Beverage-Control Laws.* Washington, D.C.: Medicine in the Public Interest, Inc., 1979.

MELCHOIR, C. L., AND R. D. MYERS, "Preference for Alcohol Evoked by Tetrahydropapaveroline (THP) Chronically Infused in the Cerebral Ventricle of the Rat," *Pharmacology, Biochemistry and Behavior,* 7 (1977), 19-35.

MELLINGER, JAMES F., AND GUNNAR B. STICKLER, eds., *Critical Problems in Pediatrics,* Chapters 18 and 19. Philadelphia: J. B. Lippincott, 1983.

MELLO, NANCY K., "Behavioral Studies in Alcoholism," in *The Biology of Alcoholism, Vol. 2,* eds. B. Kissin and K. Begleiter. New York: Plenum Press, 1972.

MENDELSON, J. H., AND NANCY K. MELLO, "Biologic Concomitants of Alcoholism," *New England Journal of Medicine,* 301 (1979), 912-921.

MENGUY, RENÉ B., G. A. HALLENBECK, J. L. BOLLMAN, AND J. H. GRINDLAY, "Intraductal Pressures and Sphincteric Resistances in Canine Pancreatic

Biliary Ducts after Various Stimuli," *Surgical Gynecology and Obstetrics,* 103, no. 3 (1958), 306.

MILGRAM, G., "A Historical Review of Alcohol Education Research and Comments," *Journal of Alcohol and Drug Education,* 2 (1976), 1-16.

MOORE, MARK H., AND DEAN R. GERSTEIN, eds., *Alcohol and Public Policy: Beyond the Shadow of Prohibition.* Washington, D.C.: National Academy Press, 1981.

MOORE, MERRILL, "Drinking Practices, Ancient and Modern: Chinese Wine Drinking," in *Drinking and Intoxication,* ed. Raymond G. McCarthy. New Haven, Ct.: College and University Press, 1959.

MOSER, JOY, *Prevention of Alcohol-Related Problems.* Toronto, Canada: World Health Organization and Addiction Research Foundation, 1980.

MOSHER, JAMES, "Dram Shop Liability and the Prevention of Alcohol-Related Problems," *Journal of Studies on Alcohol,* 40 (1979), 773-778.

————, "International Study of Alcohol Control Experiences: Comments on the Final Report," in *Legislative Approaches to Alcohol-Related Problems,* Institute of Medicine. Washington, D.C.: National Academy Press, 1982.

NATHAN, P., AND S. LISMAN, "Behavioral and Motivational Patterns of Chronic Alcoholics," in *Alcoholism: Interdisciplinary Approaches to an Enduring Problem,* eds. R. Tarter and A. A. Sugarman. Reading, Ma.: Addison-Wesley, 1976.

National Highway Traffic Safety Administration, *Summary of National Alcohol Safety Action Projects,* Publication No. DOT HS 804-322. Washington, D.C.: U.S. Department of Transportation, 1979.

National Institute on Alcohol Abuse and Alcoholism, *Research Monograph 4: Services for Children of Alcoholics,* DHHS Publication No. (ADM) 81-1007. Washington, D.C.: U.S. Government Printing Office, 1981.

NOBLE, ERNEST P., ed., *Third Special Report to the U.S. Congress on Alcohol and Health,* U.S. Department of Health, Education, and Welfare. Washington, D.C.: U.S. Government Printing Office, 1978.

NOBLE, ERNEST P., R. L. ALKANA, AND E. S. PARKER, "Ethanol-Induced CNS Depression and Its Reversal: A Review," in *The Proceedings of the Fourth Annual Alcoholism Conference of the National Institute on Alcohol Abuse and Alcoholism.* Washington, D.C.: U.S. Government Printing Office, 1978.

ORLOFF, MARSHAL J., "Surgical Consequences of Alcoholism," in *Medical Consequences of Alcoholism,* eds. F. A. Seixas, K. Williams, and S. Eggleston. New York: New York Academy of Sciences, 1975.

ORNSTEIN, S. I., "The Control of Alcohol Consumption through Price Increases," *Journal of Studies on Alcohol,* 41 (1980), 807-818.

PAREDES, ALFONSO, DICK GREGORY, O. H. RUNDELL, AND HAROLD L. WILLIAMS,

"Drinking Behavior, Remission, and Relapse: The Rand Report Revisited," *Alcoholism,* 3 (1979), 3-10.

PAREDES, ALFONSO, LOUIS J. WEST, AND CLYDE C. SNOW, "Biosocial Adaptation and Correlates of Acculturation in the Tarahumara Ecosystem," *The International Journal of Social Psychiatry,* 16, no. 3 (1970), 163-174.

PENDERY, MARY L., IRVING M. MALTZMAN, AND LOUIS J. WEST, "Controlled Drinking by Alcoholics? New Findings and a Reevaluation of a Major Affirmative Study," *Science,* 217 (1982), 167-175.

PEQUIGNOT, GUY, "Ascitic Cirrhosis in Relation to Alcohol Consumption," *International Journal of Epidemiology,* 7 (1978), 113-120.

PILISUK, M., AND C. FROLAND, "Kinship, Social Networks, Social Support and Health," *Social Science and Medicine,* 12 (1978), 272-280.

POLICH, J. MICHAEL, DAVID J. ARMOR, AND HARRIET BRAIKER, *The Course of Alcoholism: Four Years After Treatment.* Santa Monica, Ca.: Rand Corporation, 1980.

POPHAM, ROBERT E., WOLFGANG SCHMIDT, AND J. DELINT, "Government Control Measures to Prevent Hazardous Drinking," in *Drinking,* eds. J. A. Ewing and B. A. Rouse. Chicago: Nelson Hall, 1978.

PRINZ, PATRICIA N., TIMOTHY A. ROEHRS, PETER P. VITALIANO, MARKKU LINNOILA, AND ELLIOT D. WEITZMAN, "Effect of Alcohol on Sleep and Nighttime Plasma Growth Hormone and Cortisol Concentrations," *Journal of Clinical Endocrinology and Metabolism,* 51, no. 4 (1980), 759-764.

RIPLEY, A. S., "Suicidal Behavior in Edinboro and Seattle," *American Journal of Psychiatry,* 130 (1973), 995-1001.

ROBINSON, D., "Alcoholism: Perspectives on Prevention Strategies," in *Encyclopedic Handbook of Alcoholism,* eds. E. M. Pattison and E. Kaufman. New York: Gardner Press, 1982.

RON, M. A., W. ACHER, G. K. SHAW, AND W. A. LISHMAN, "Computerized Tomography of the Brain in Chronic Alcoholism," *Brain,* 105 (1983), 497-514.

ROOM, ROBIN, AND S. SHEFFIELD, eds., *The Prevention of Alcohol Problems— Report of a Conference.* Sacramento, Ca.: Office of Alcoholism, 1976.

RUTSTEIN, DAVID D., "2,3 Butanediol, A Marker for Severe Alcoholism in Males," *Lancet,* September 3, 1983.

RUTSTEIN, DAVID D., AND RICHARD VEECH, "Genetics and Addiction to Alcohol," *New England Journal of Medicine,* 298 (1978), 1140-1141.

RYBACK, RALPH S., MICHAEL J. ECKHARDT, AND CHARLES P. PAUTLER, "Biochemical and Hematological Correlates of Alcoholism," *Research Communications in Clinical Pathology and Pharmacology,* 29 (1980), 533-550.

SACHEL, JOSÉ, AND HENRI SARLES, "Modifications of Pure Human Pancreatic

Juice Induced by Chronic Alcohol Consumption," *Digestive Diseases and Science,* 24, no. 12 (1979).

SAXE, LEONARD, DENISE DOUGHERTY, KATHERINE ESTY, AND MICHELLE FINE, *Health Technology Case Study 22: The Effectiveness and Costs of Alcoholism Treatment.* Washington, D.C.: Office of Technology Assessment, 1983.

SCHIFRIN, LEONARD G., "Societal Costs of Alcohol Abuse in the United States: An Updating," in *Economics and Alcohol,* eds. M. Grant, M. A. Plant, and A. Williams. New York: Gardner Press, 1983.

SCHMIDT, WOLFGANG, "The Epidemiology of Cirrhosis of the Liver: A Statistical Analysis of Mortality Data with Special Reference to Canada," in *Alcohol and the Liver,* eds. M. M. Fisher and T. G. Rankin. New York: Plenum Press, 1977.

SCHMIDT, WOLFGANG, AND ROBERT E. POPHAM, "Heavy Alcohol Consumption and Physical Health Problems: A Review of the Epidemiological Evidence," *Drug and Alcohol Dependence,* 1 (1975), 27-50.

SELLING, L. S., *The Role of Alcohol in the Commission of Sex Offenses,* Medical Record of New York, Volume 151, 1940.

SENIOR, JOHN R., "Digestive Diseases Information Center Fact Sheet," *Alcoholic Liver Disease,* 2 (1983).

SHUPE, L. M., "Alcohol and Crime," *Journal of Criminal Law and Criminology,* 44 (1954), 661-664.

SJOQUIST, BIRGITTA, S. BORG, AND J. KUANDE, "Salsolinol and Methylated Salsolinol in Urine and Cerebrospinal Fluid from Health Volunteers," *Substantial Alcoholic Actions,* 2 (1981), 73-77.

SJOQUIST, BIRGITTA, ANDERS ERIKSSON, AND BENGT WINBLAD, "Salsolinol and Catecholamines in Human Brain and Their Relation to Alcoholism," in *Beta-Carbolines and Tetrahydroisoquinolines.* New York: Alan R. Liss, 1982.

SLAVIN, GERARD, FINBARR MARTIN, PETER WARD, JONATHAN LEVI, AND TIMOTHY PETERS, "Chronic Alcohol Excess Is Associated with Selective but Reversible Injury to Type 2B Muscle Fibers," *Journal of Clinical Pathology,* 36 (1983), 772-777.

STAULCUP, H., K. KENWARD, AND D. FRIGO, "A Review of Federal Primary Alcoholism Prevention Projects," *Journal of Studies on Alcohol,* 40 (1979), 943-968.

STREISSGUTH, A. P., S. LANDESMAN-DWYER, J. C. MARTIN, AND D. W. SMITH, "Teratogenic Effects of Alcohol in Humans and Laboratory Animals," *Science,* 209 (1980), 353-361.

TALBOTT, G. D., "Primary Alcoholic Heart Disease," in *Medical Consequences of Alcoholism,* eds. F. A. Seixas, K. Williams, and S. Eggleston. New York: New York Academy of Sciences, 1975.

THOMSEN, ROBERT, *Bill W.* New York: Harper and Row, 1975.

TOMASULO, P. A., R. M. J. KATER, AND FRANK L. IBER, "Impairment of Thiamine Absorption in Alcoholism," *American Journal of Clinical Nutrition,* 21 (1968), 1340-1344.

TRICE, H. M., AND P. M. ROMAN, *Spirits and Demons at Work,* New York State School of Industrial and Labor Relations, Cornell University, 1972.

ULLELAND, C., R. P. WENNBERG, N. J. IGO, AND D. W. SMITH, "Offspring of Alcoholic Mothers," *Pediatric Research,* 4 (1970) 474.

VAILLANT, GEORGE E., *The Natural History of Alcoholism: Causes, Patterns, and Paths to Recovery.* Cambridge, Ma.: Harvard University Press, 1983.

VAN THIEL, DAVID H., "Ethanol: Its Adverse Effects upon the Hypothalamic-Pituitary-Gonadal Axis," *Journal of Laboratory Clinical Medicine,* 101 (1983), 21-122.

WAGENAAR, A., "Raised Legal Drinking Age and Automobile Crashes: A Review of the Literature," *Abstracts and Reviews in Alcohol and Driving,* 3 (1982), 3-8.

WALLACK, L. M., "Assessing Effects of Mass Media Campaigns: An Alternative Perspective," *Alcohol Health and Research World,* 5 (1980), 17-29.

WANBERG, K. W., AND J. L. HORN, "Alcoholism Syndromes Related to Sociological Classifications," *International Journal of Addiction,* 8 (1973), 99-120.

WARBURTON, CLARK, *The Economic Results of Prohibition.* New York: Columbia University Press, 1932.

WEINSTEIN, BARBARA G., "Optimal Liquor Regulation," unpublished dissertation. Ann Arbor: University of Michigan, 1983.

WIENER, C., *The Politics of Alcoholism: Building of an Arena around a Social Problem.* New Brunswick, N.J.: Transaction Books, 1980.

WILLIAMS, K., "Introduction: Part VI. Infectious Disease," in *Medical Consequences of Alcoholism,* eds. F. A. Seixas, K. Williams, and S. Eggleston. New York: New York Academy of Sciences, 1975.

WINOKUR, GEORGE, "The Division of Depressive Illness into Depression Spectrum Disease and Pure Depressive Disease," *International Journal of Pharmacology and Psychiatry,* 9 (1974), 5-13.

WOEBER, K., "The Skin in Diagnosis of Alcoholism," in *Medical Consequences of Alcoholism,* eds. F. A. Seixas, K. Williams, and S. Eggleston. New York: New York Academy of Sciences, 1975.

WOLF, STEWART, *Social Environment and Health.* Seattle: University of Washington Press, 1981.

WOLF, STEWART, MICHAEL E. FELVER, MARK D. ALTSCHULE, NICHOLAS T. WERTHESSEN, ROBERT GERNER, AND RICHARD VEECH, "Abnormal Metabolite in Alcoholic Subjects," *British Journal of Psychiatry,* 142 (1983), 388-390.

WOLFGANG, MARVIN E., AND R. B. STROHM, "The Relationship between Alcohol and Criminal Homicide," *Quarterly Journal of Studies on Alcohol,* 17 (1956), 411-425.

WOODSIDE, MIGS, *Children of Alcoholics,* Report to the Governor, New York State Division of Alcoholism and Alcohol Abuse, 1982.

World Health Organization, *Problems Related to Alcohol Consumption, Report of a WHO Expert Committee,* Technical Report Series 650, Geneva, 1980.

————, "Alcohol Problems: A Growing Threat to Health," *WHO Chronicle,* 36, no. 6 '1983), 222-225.

Index

FINAL REPORT
of the
SIXTY-SIXTH AMERICAN ASSEMBLY

Following three days of intensive deliberation and discussion, participants in the Sixty-sixth American Assembly, on *Public Policy on Alcohol Problems*, at Arden House, Harriman, New York, April 26-29, 1984, reviewed as a group the following statement. While the statement represents general agreement, no one was asked to sign it, and not every participant necessarily subscribed to every conclusion or recommendation.

PREAMBLE

Alcoholism and alcohol abuse cause America many serious problems in terms of health, safety, and the quality of life. Alcohol-related problems have their impact everywhere—homes, schools, workplaces, the military services, on highways, and even on the waters and in the air above our land. The cost is enormous, the damage widespread, the suffering severe, the magnitude growing, and the consequences incalculable.

The background of relevant facts studied by the group in its deliberations included observations that alcohol-related problems (1) cost the United States more than $60 billion a year; (2) are responsible for 20 percent of the national expenditure for hospital care; (3) cause the birth of a great many disabled children every year; (4) are involved in more than a third of our suicides, half of the fatal highway accidents, a large number of rapes and sex crimes, the majority of homicides and other violent crimes, two-thirds of the deaths by drowning, 70 percent of deaths by falls, 83 percent of deaths by fire, and a majority of domestic violence episodes; (5) cause many deaths through alcoholic damage to the stomach, liver, heart, brain, and immune system; and (6) in these and various other ways kill up to 200,000 Americans a year.

Meanwhile, alcoholics are still widely stigmatized, there is insufficient public awareness of the facts about alcoholism as a disease, treatment programs lack adequate funds, and research in the field does not receive appropriate support. Alcohol-related problems affect not only those who drink, but also members of their families, particularly children. Clearly, a bold new initiative is needed for the formulation of improved public policy on alcohol problems in America at all levels of government.

NATIONAL POLICY

A national alcohol policy to promote health and reduce alcohol-related problems need not threaten the rights of individuals to drink or of businesses to produce and sell beverages containing alcohol, subject to appropriate constraints required by public health and welfare considerations. Such a national policy should be based on the proposition that alcohol, as a drug that is potentially dangerous, should be depicted as such and recognized by the public as such.

Responsibility rests with both public and private sectors for assuring reduction of the problems related to drinking and for providing persons with alcoholism and alcohol-related illnesses and their families access to treatment. All levels of government and the private sector (including foundations, corporations, and citizen groups) should be encouraged to contribute financial support to research, prevention, and treatment efforts.

The unique contributions of Alcoholics Anonymous, Al-Anon, and other self-help groups should be recognized as integral components in the alcoholism-care continuum.

Recommendations

1. National policy should promote educated choices about drinking and the rights of nondrinkers, acknowledging that healthy lifestyles require individuals to make healthy lifestyle decisions.

2. National policy should recognize personal and family responsibilities regarding the use of or abstinence from beverage alcohol but should promote abstinence among underage individuals, pregnant women, alcoholics, and other individuals experiencing—or likely to experience—deleterious health effects, with provision of treatment for all those who need it to abstain.

3. National policy should promote a social norm that alcohol use not be glamorized and its abuse not be accepted or condoned.

4. National policy should recognize age, gender, ethnic, and cultural differences in the development of prevention, treatment, and research programs and place special emphasis on providing accessibility to appropriate services to women, and to Black, Hispanic, native American, and other special populations.

5. National policy should emphasize that ethyl alcohol is equally dangerous whether in beer, wine, or distilled spirits and that every individual and every segment of the population is vulnerable—directly or indirectly—to its harmful potentialities.

PREVENTION

All sectors of the community—families, schools, religious institutions, government agencies, legal systems, voluntary organizations, media, business, labor, health care professionals, and the alcoholic-beverage industries—should be involved in the development and implementation of a strategy for prevention of alcoholism and alcohol-related problems.

In formulating a prevention policy there is room for many different approaches. The present diversity of state laws, regulations, and programs can furnish fertile ground for researchers to discover what approaches might be more effective than others. There is no need to choose between alternative approaches such as education versus regulatory controls. However, evaluation of the effectiveness of such programs should be undertaken henceforth, so that, eventually, relative cost effectiveness can be estimated. All policy measures undertaken in an effort to prevent alcohol problems should be designed with a strategy for evaluation that uses appropriate scientific method.

A comprehensive prevention policy must consider such questions as minimum purchase age, advertising, drinking and driving, uniformity and consistency among the several states of various laws, labeling of alcoholic-beverage containers, media programing, alcoholic beverage control (ABC) laws, along with tax and pricing policies in the development of a comprehensive prevention strategy.

There is an important role for education in any sound alcohol-abuse prevention policy. Information regarding the health, social, and economic consequences of alcohol abuse and alcoholism should be disseminated to specific segments within the community (e.g., physicians, educators, lawyers, labor and business leaders, clergy, policy makers), as well as the public as a whole, as an essential part of a prevention strategy.

Prevention strategies should include specially designed messages directed toward high-risk groups, particularly children of alcoholics. Information about prevention of alcoholism and alcohol-related problems should be clear, accurate, unambiguous, and age appropriate. Messages, particularly those directed toward youth, should be clear about the similarities and differences between alcohol and other drugs.

In consideration of the foregoing, and in the light of our general comprehension of the scope of the alcohol problem and the need for development and implementation of a prevention strategy, the following comments and recommendations have been formulated:

Recommendations

1. Education of the entire society should play an important role in any sound alcohol-abuse prevention policy. Special efforts should be made to reach youth at earlier ages and to promote the establishment of student assistance programs.

2. Prevention programs are no better than the research on which they are based. Therefore, the most cost-effective and beneficial methods of implementing successful prevention programs should be studied. Prevention research investigators should be recruited to develop and carefully evaluate new and more effective prevention initiatives. Longitudinal studies are needed. Ample and stable funding will ensure the presence of capable investigators.

3. Uniformity and consistency of laws with respect to the minimum purchase age are important. The federal government should provide incentives and otherwise encourage states to adopt a minimum legal purchase age of twenty-one.

4. Prevention strategies should be developed and coordinated among federal, state, and local governments.

5. Those engaged in the production, marketing, distribution, and sale of alcoholic beverages have a responsibility to inform the public about the potentially adverse consequences of alcohol consumption and the circumstances under which these occur. They should do so pursuant to rules, regulations, and guidelines established by appropriate public agencies.

6. Policies should be formulated and adopted to ensure that consumers are fully informed about the contents of alcoholic-beverage containers and the possible consequences of consuming those contents. Alcoholic-beverage containers should bear labels listing ingredients, giving the proportion of alcohol contained therein, and providing a specific health warning about the risk of birth defects.

7. Recognizing the pervasive influence of advertising in our daily lives, we encourage the development of advertising guidelines and policies designed to promote improved public health and safety with respect to alcohol consumption. Advertising for alcoholic beverages should not market or promote directly or indirectly the sale of alcohol to those under the minimum legal purchase age. Legal or regulatory avenues to require the alcoholic-beverage industry—or their advertising media—to contribute counter advertising (warning about alcohol's dangers) should be explored.

8. The film and other entertainment industries should refrain from glamorizing alcohol use or accepting or condoning alcohol abuse. Drunkenness should be shown only if required by the artistic content of the program.

9. The news media, both electronic and print, should be encouraged to report accurately the adverse consequences of alcohol use.

LEGAL, ECONOMIC, POLITICAL

There is a significant relationship between the legal, economic, and political environment and the incidence, consequences, and extent of alcoholism and alcohol abuse. It is in this arena that the scope and adequacy of the public's response to the problem is defined. Program funding levels are determined, health care resources are allocated, sanctions for unacceptable behavior are established, costs are assessed, and rules are forged determining who gets assistance and under what circumstances. Our ability to reduce the incidence of alcohol abuse will, in large measure, depend upon our ability to harness and target the resources of both government and the private sector.

Recommendations

1. In line with the continuing trend toward decriminalization of public inebriacy, health and welfare programs for alcoholics must be strengthened by increasing public resources for the care of inebriates and significantly extending private insurance coverage for appropriate treatment of alcoholism, thus allowing the public sector to concentrate its limited resources on the needs of the indigent.

2. Recognizing that employee assistance programs (EAPs) are quite effective in early intervention with alcohol abusers and in the treatment of alcoholism, the EAP concept should be strengthened by (a) developing EAP consortia to extend coverage to employees in small organizations; (b) ensuring the availability of EAPs to federal, state, and local government workforces, including all levels of employees and elected officials; (c) fostering the cooperation of business, labor, foundation, and government resources in developing research on the contributions EAPs can make to health-care cost containment and health-care promotion efforts; (d) emphasizing and further developing EAP standards and guidelines on confidentiality and job performance; (e) exploring innovative financing mechanisms; and (f) expanding the role of the National Institute on Alcohol Abuse and Alcoholism (NIAAA) in providing information and technical assistance to the private and public sectors in the development and expansion of EAPs.

3. Excise tax rates on alcoholic beverages should be increased, adjusted for inflation, and made equitable according to alcohol content. The resulting increase in revenue should encourage government at all levels to improve resource allocation for research, prevention, and treatment of problems associated with alcohol use.

4. All recommendations of the President's Commission on Drunk Driving should be adopted rapidly by the states.

5. Appropriate health-care service system components should be developed and funded to provide for the growing number of those requiring rehabilitation following alcohol-related offenses.

RESEARCH

The greatest hope for significant improvement in the alcohol field lies in more and better research. The NIAAA should be strengthened for this purpose. Its function as a centralized source of data through its National Clearinghouse on Alcohol Information (NCALI) should also be strengthened. Only through basic and applied research can we expect to develop essential breakthroughs on prevention, early diagnosis, identification of risk factors, and improved treatment of alcoholism and its complications at every stage of the disease.

Support for research on alcoholism and alcohol abuse should be increased to reflect the size and importance of the problem. A climate more favorable to effective research on the causes, prevention, treatment, net costs, incidence, and prevalence of alcoholism and alcohol-related problems is essential. Public awareness of the personal, social, economic, and health costs to the nation of alcoholism and alcohol abuse must be expanded.

Recommendations

1. Research should be greatly increased and expanded on all aspects of alcoholism, alcohol abuse, and related problems. This will require broadening the base of research support so as to include greater contributions from private industry, foundations, and various governmental sources.

2. The NIAAA research budget should be doubled as soon as possible and steadily increased thereafter.

3. The Veterans Administration; Indian Health Service; Departments of Defense, Education, Transportation, and Justice; and other agencies should be directed to support alcohol-related research relevant to their responsibilities.

4. All of the National Institutes of Health should be directed to give favorable consideration to research proposals of good quality concerning the relationship of alcohol to the diseases with which they are concerned. These proposals should be supported directly by the appropriate institutes and not necessarily shifted to the NIAAA for funding. The leadership role of the NIAAA in the alcohol field should be strengthened and expanded.

DIAGNOSIS AND TREATMENT

The earlier alcoholism can be identified and treatment begun, the greater the chances for success and the less difficult and costly the treatment will be. Physicians and other health professionals need more and better instruction about alcoholism (including biological and psychosocial aspects) throughout their professional educational experience. Their training should cover the comprehensive care of patients with alcohol problems, regardless of diagnoses or how patients enter treatment. It is also important that better training about alcoholism be given to those in other systems (e.g., legal, social welfare, educational, industrial) thereby improving and increasing early case finding and appropriate referral of patients for help.

A variety of settings should be available for the care of alcoholic patients. Alternatives to full hospitalization will help to reduce the high cost of care, which presently poses a serious barrier to treatment. Those public and private agencies that pay for alcoholic-treatment services must recognize the validity and economic desirability of these alternative modes of care and provide appropriate coverage. Within this context, special programs should also be devised for certain populations that can benefit by particular approaches.

The improvement of alcoholism-treatment services will favorably influence the quality of health care in general. However, lack of financial support for such services presently poses a significant barrier to progress. Yet, there is good reason to believe that a greater investment in care of alcoholics—especially if it is early and expert—will more than pay for itself by lowering the burden of costs imposed by advanced alcoholism and by forestalling the innumerable medical and surgical complications likely to develop as the disease progresses.

Health care services for alcoholic patients and their families are in very short supply vis-a-vis the need. Quality of services remains very uneven, and quality-assurance procedures are greatly needed. In the public sector, provision of more and better care for alcoholics must await a far greater commitment of funds. The private sector is also a potential source of volunteers who should be encouraged to assist in treatment, supportive services, follow-up studies, and the like. Furthermore, it is more likely that employers or unions will be able and willing to provide payment (either directly or through insurance carriers) than will individuals, who are most likely to deny that they ever could—or already do—need help for drinking problems.

Recommendations

1. The integration of alcohol-abuse and alcoholism treatment into the mainstream of the health care system is essential. The magnitude of the alcohol problem is such that categorical and specialized approaches can address it only in a limited way. All physicians should learn how to make an early diagnosis of alcoholism and to provide or refer such patients and their families to appropriate care.

2. Public and private policy should foster the development of a

broad range of specialized treatment services that will provide for a continuum of care encompassing inpatient, residential, day treatment, and various outpatient services. Medicare and Medicaid should cover such services. Such policy should also recognize and provide for the involvement of nonphysicians; it is likely that much of the professional service will continue to be delivered by social workers, clergy, nurses, psychologists, and certified alcohol counselors.

3. Alcoholism should be dealt with like any other disease, and insurance coverage should be statutorally mandated and provided without discrimination.

4. New methods for financing health care services, such as prospective reimbursement systems, should encourage the development of cost-effective, but professionally sound, care for alcoholics and members of their families.

5. Treatment should be much more extensively provided to alcoholic individuals within the criminal justice system. This will decrease the likelihood of criminal recidivism and thus reduce danger and cost to society.

LORAN D. ARCHER
Deputy Director
National Institute on Alcohol Abuse
  & Alcoholism
Rockville, Maryland

DAN E. BEAUCHAMP
Professor
Department of Health Policy &
  Administration
School of Public Health
University of North Carolina
  at Chapel Hill
Chapel Hill, North Carolina

THE REV. E.W. BELTER
President & Executive Director
A-Center
Racine, Wisconsin

SHEILA B. BLUME, M.D.
Sayville, New York

JACK BRAUNTUCH
Executive Director
The J.M. Foundation
New York, New York

PETER BROCK
President
Johnson Institute
Minneapolis, Minnesota

KENNETH BURGESS
Director
Employee Assistance Program
Gulf Oil Corporation
Pittsburgh, Pennsylvania

** WILLIAM BUTYNSKI
Executive Director
National Association of State Alcohol &
  Drug Abuse Directors
Washington, D.C.

† MORRIS E. CHAFETZ, M.D.
President
Health Education Foundation
Washington, D.C.

STEPHEN F. CHAPPELL
Captain
United States Navy
Commanding Officer
Naval Alcohol Rehabilitation & Training
  Center
San Diego, California

RAY CHAVIRA
Commissioner
Commission on Alcoholism
County of Los Angeles
Los Angeles, California

ALEECE B. CLABES
Chief Probation Officer
Oklahoma City Department of Court
  Administration
Probation Services Division
Oklahoma City, Oklahoma

JARRETT CLINTON, M.D.
Special Assistant for Medical Policy
Office of the Assistant Secretary of
  Defense (Health Affairs)
Washington, D.C.

PHILIP J. COOK
Professor
Departments of Economics & Public
  Policy Studies
Duke University
Durham, North Carolina

CHARLES W.L. DEALE
Director of Communications &
  Membership Development
Wine & Spirits Wholesalers of America,
  Inc.
Washington, D.C.

THOMAS L. DELBANCO, M.D.
Director
Division of General Medicine & Primary
  Care
Beth Israel Hospital
Boston, Massachusetts

*† JOHN R. DELUCA
Vice President & Director
Medical Department
Equitable Life Assurance Society of the
  United States
New York, New York

† ROGER EGEBERG, M.D.
Senior Scholar in Residence
Institute of Medicine
National Academy of Sciences
Washington, D.C.

JOSEPH T. ENGLISH, M.D.
Director of Psychiatry & Associate Dean
  for New York Medical College
St. Vincent's Hospital & Medical Center
New York, New York

DAVID G. EVANS, ESQ.
Chair
Alcoholism & Drug Law Reform
  Committee
Individual Rights & Responsibilities
  Section
American Bar Association
Washington, D.C.

* Discussion Leader
**Rapporteur
† Participated in Panel Discussion
††Delivered Formal Address

ABOUT THE AMERICAN ASSEMBLY

The American Assembly was established by Dwight D. Eisenhower at Columbia University in 1950. It holds nonpartisan meetings and publishes authoritative books to illuminate issues of United States policy.

An affiliate of Columbia, with offices in the Sherman Fairchild Center, the Assembly is a national, educational institution incorporated in the State of New York.

The Assembly seeks to provide information, stimulate discussion, and evoke independent conclusions on matters of vital public interest.

American Assembly Sessions

At least two national programs are initiated each year. Authorities are retained to write background papers presenting essential data and defining the main issues of each subject.

A group of men and women representing a broad range of experience, competence, and American leadership meet for several days to discuss the Assembly topic and consider alternatives for national policy.

All Assemblies follow the same procedure. The background papers are sent to participants in advance of the Assembly. The Assembly meets in small groups for four or five lengthy periods. All groups use the same agenda. At the close of these informal sessions participants adopt in plenary session a final report of findings and recommendations.

Regional, state, and local Assemblies are held following the national session at Arden House. Assemblies have also been held in England, Switzerland, Malaysia, Canada, the Caribbean, South America, Central America, the Philippines, and Japan. Over one hundred forty institutions have cosponsored one or more Assemblies.

Arden House

Home of The American Assembly and scene of the national sessions is Arden House, which was given to Columbia University in 1950 by W. Averell Harriman. E. Roland Harriman joined his brother in contributing toward adaptation of the property for conference purposes. The buildings and surrounding land, known as the Harriman Campus of Columbia University, are fifty miles north of New York City.

Arden House is a distinguished conference center. It is self-supporting and operates throughout the year for use by organizations with educational objectives. The American Assembly is a tenant of this Columbia University facility only during Assembly sessions.